THE WORLD'S BEST RECIPES

Larousse

Front cover photography by Paul Kemp
Inside photography by
Martin Brigdale: pages 183, 184 and 187
James Jackson: pages 2/3, 8/9, 26/27, 40/41, 58/59, 92/93, 108/109,
120/121, 130/131, 144/145, 154/155, 164/165, 178/179, 190/191, 203,
205, 207, 208 and 211
Paul Kemp: pages 11, 23, 29, 33, 64, 82, 85, 88–90, 106, 137,
148, 153, 217, 219 and 221
John Lee: pages 13–15, 18–22, 30, 31, 43, 44, 46, 47, 52–56,
61–63, 66, 70, 71, 76 (right hand picture), 77, 83, 87, 95, 98,
99, 101, 104, 105, 112, 114, 123, 140, 141, 149, 157,
169 (left hand picture), 192–195, 197, 198, 201
David Levin: pages 25, 101 and 160
Fred Mancini: pages 171, 174 (right hand picture), 175 and 176
Vic Paris: page 36
Paul Williams: pages 16, 34, 35, 38, 45, 49, 50, 65, 67, 68, 72,
86, 102, 111, 113, 115, 134, 135, 139, 142, 147, 150, 151, 158,
159, 162 and 163

The authors and publishers would like to thank the following
for supplying or sponsoring photographs:
International Magazine Service (page 37)
Pasta Information Center (page 118)
Mazola Corn Oil (page 124)
Swiss Cheese Union (page 126)
Farmhouse English Cheeses (page 128)
H. P. Bulmer Limited (Cider Makers), Hereford (page 129)
Gale's Honey Bureau (page 215)

First published in the United States by
Larousse and Co., Inc.
572 Fifth Avenue, New York, N.Y. 10036

ISBN 0-88332-367-2
Library of Congress No 84-40269

Set in Monophoto Apollo by Photocomp Limited, Birmingham, England

Printed in Italy

Contents

Useful Facts and Figures

Measuring accurately

Correct measuring of ingredients is essential to ensure consistent results. All measurements given in this book are level unless otherwise stated.

Choosing measuring cups: When purchasing measuring cups choose one set for dry ingredients and another for liquids.

For dry ingredients: Buy a set of four graduated measuring cups consisting of a ¼-cup, ⅓-cup, ½-cup and 1-cup measure. Always level off with the edge of a spatula or knife.

For liquid ingredients: Buy a 1-cup measuring cup, the rim of which is above the 1-cup line to avoid spillage. 2-cup and 1-quart size measuring cups are also very useful. Set the cup on a level surface. Lower your head so that the measuring line will be at eye level and fill the cup to the correct mark.

Choosing measuring spoons: A good set of measuring spoons will give you accurate small measurements. It should include ⅛-teaspoon, ¼-teaspoon, ½-teaspoon, 1-teaspoon, ½-tablespoon and 1-tablespoon measurements. 16 tablespoons equal 1 cup.

Equivalent measures

Pinch	As much as can be held between the tip of the finger and the thumb
3 teaspoons	1 tablespoon
2 tablespoons	⅛ cup
4 tablespoons	¼ cup
5 tablespoons + 1 teaspoon	⅓ cup
8 tablespoons	½ cup
10 tablespoons + 2 teaspoons	⅔ cup
12 tablespoons	¾ cup
16 tablespoons	1 cup
2 cups	1 pint
2 pints	1 quart
1 quart	4 cups
4 quarts	1 gallon
16 oz (dry measure)	1 lb

Can sizes: We have tried to utilize whole cans of ingredients whenever possible.

Flour: Unless specified, either all-purpose or self-rising flour may be used in the recipes. If using self-rising flour, omit baking powder and salt if called for. For fine-textured cakes, you may substitute 1⅛ cups cake flour for each cup of all-purpose flour. Seasoned flour is flour mixed with salt and freshly ground pepper.

Butter or margarine: One (¼-lb) stick of butter or margarine equals ½ cup or 8 tablespoons. If a recipe calls for melted butter, it doesn't matter if you measure it before or after melting – the result will be the same.

Equivalents

Eggs

5 eggs	about 1 cup
8-10 egg whites	1 cup
12-15 egg yolks	1 cup

Butter or margarine

2 tablespoons	1 oz
½ cup	¼ lb (1 stick)
2 cups	1 lb

Dairy products

1 cup milk	½ cup evaporated milk + ½ cup water
1 cup milk	¼ cup powdered whole milk + 1 cup water
1 cup cream	2 cups whipped cream
1 cup cottage cheese	8 oz
¼ lb Cheddar or American cheese	1 cup shredded

Flour Flour is sifted before measuring

4 cups all-purpose flour	1 lb
1 cup cake flour	1 cup all-purpose flour, minus 2 tablespoons
2 tablespoons flour	1 tablespoon cornstarch for thickening
5 teaspoons flour	2 teaspoons arrowroot for thickening

Sugar Confectioners' sugar is measured before sifting
Brown sugar is measured firmly packed

2 cups sugar	1 lb
3¼-4 cups confectioners' sugar	1 lb
2¼ cups brown sugar	1 lb

Miscellaneous

1 orange	about 8 tablespoons juice
1 lemon or lime	2-3 tablespoons juice
Grated rind of 1 orange	about 1 tablespoon
Grated rind of 1 lemon	1½-2 teaspoons
1 lb nuts in the shell	about 2 cups nut meats
¼ lb chopped nuts	1 scant cup
1 lb seedless raisins	about 3 cups
1 square chocolate, unsweetened or semisweet	1 oz
1 square chocolate (unsweetened)	3 tablespoons cocoa + 1 tablespoon butter
1 cup honey	1¼ cups sugar + ¼ cup liquid

Cook's Glossary

Bake: Cook in heated oven. When applied to meat, the correct term is roast.

Baste: Moisten food during cooking, by spooning on liquid.

Blanch: To cover food with cold water, bring to a boil, remove from the heat and drain.

Blend: To thoroughly combine all ingredients until very smooth.

Caramelize: To melt sugar over moderate heat, stirring constantly until result is a golden-brown syrup.

Cream: To beat sugar and fat until smooth, light and fluffy.

Cube: Cut into cubes ½ inch or larger.

Dice: Cut into cubes ½ inch or smaller.

Dot: Scatter bits of butter or margarine over surface of food.

Dredge: Coat or sprinkle lightly with flour or sugar.

Fold: A combination of two mixing motions; one which cuts vertically through the mixture, the other slides the mixing utensil across the bottom of the bowl and up the side, turning over, repeating until the ingredient folded in is evenly combined with the mixture.

Grease: Rub lightly with butter, margarine or oil.

Julienne: To cut into matchlike sticks.

Knead: Shape dough into a flat ball. Pick up the edge of the dough farthest from you. Fold it over to the edge nearest you. With the heels of the hands, press down, pushing the dough away from you 3 or 4 times. Turn dough 90 degrees. Repeat folding, pushing and turning until dough looks smooth, satiny and not sticky.

Macerate: Soak, in juice or liqueur.

Marinate: Let stand in a mixture of liquid, spices, etc.

Mince: Chop very finely.

Mix: Combine in any way that distributes ingredients evenly.

Pare: Cut off skin of potatoes, apples, etc. with a knife.

Peel: Strip off the outer covering (oranges, tomatoes, bananas etc.).

Preheat: Heat oven to desired temperature before putting in food.

Purée: Pass through a fine sieve, food mill or electric blender.

Sauté: Cook in a small amount of hot fat.

Scald: Heat to just under the boiling point.

Simmer: Cook just below the boiling point. Bubbles form slowly and collapse below the surface of the liquid.

Whip: Beat vigorously to incorporate air into mixture.

Whisk: Beat, using a wire whisk.

Oven temperatures

All oven temperatures in this book are Fahrenheit.

200°-250°	very slow	375°	moderately hot
300°	slow	400°	hot
325°	moderately slow	450°-500°	very hot
350°	moderate	over 500°	extremely hot

Soups and Appetizers

The first course can make or mar the meal, so select a tempting recipe to complement the main dish and arouse the appetite. Serve the appetizers, attractively garnished, with crusty bread, crisp toast or hot fresh rolls.

Stuffed Eggs, Melon Cocktail, Mushroom Cocktail
and Mixed Hors d'Oeuvre

Mixed Hors d'Oeuvre

(ILLUSTRATED ON PREVIOUS PAGE)

Arrange a selection of sliced cooked sausage – salami, various German sausages and liver sausage – on a platter with neat rows of sliced or quartered hard-cooked eggs, coated with a little mayonnaise, sliced tomatoes, cucumbers, peppers and onions. Add, if you like, some cooked peeled shrimp, flaked tuna fish or smoked mackerel. Serve a salad dressing made from $\frac{1}{4}$ cup oil, 2 tablespoons wine vinegar, seasoning, sugar and mustard to taste. Biscuits or thinly sliced bread and butter can be served as an accompaniment.

Melon Cocktail

Bridget Jones

(ILLUSTRATED ON PREVIOUS PAGE)

1 small honeydew melon
$\frac{1}{2}$ or $\frac{1}{4}$ watermelon
a few mint sprigs
a little sugar

Halve the honeydew melon and scoop out the seeds. Use a melon ball cutter to remove the flesh in neat balls. Make the watermelon flesh into balls, again removing the seeds.

Mix all the melon balls in a bowl and add the mint, then sprinkle with a little sugar and chill thoroughly. To serve, spoon the cocktail into glasses and decorate with fresh sprigs of mint. SERVES 4

Mushroom Cocktail

Bridget Jones

(ILLUSTRATED ON PREVIOUS PAGE)

$\frac{1}{2}$ lb small button mushrooms
$\frac{1}{4}$ cup olive oil
2 tablespoons lemon juice
salt and pepper
1 small clove garlic, crushed
2 tablespoons chopped parsley
2 tablespoons diced sweet red pepper
4 scallions, finely chopped

Select small, even-sized mushrooms and trim the ends of the stems. Mix the oil with the lemon juice and pour over the mushrooms. Toss well with seasoning and the remaining ingredients, then allow to marinate in a cool place for at least an hour.

Toss the mushrooms before serving them in small dishes or on a few crisp lettuce leaves. SERVES 4

Stuffed Eggs

Bridget Jones

(ILLUSTRATED ON PREVIOUS PAGE)

4 hard-cooked eggs
$\frac{1}{2}$ (8-oz) package cream cheese
salt and pepper
1 tablespoon chopped fresh herbs
a selection of garnishes, for example stuffed
olives, smoked salmon rolls, bacon rolls,
anchovies, caviar, gherkins and fresh herbs

Shell and halve the eggs, then scoop out and mash the yolks. Beat the cream cheese with the yolks, seasoning to taste and herbs. Pipe this mixture back into the egg whites and garnish neatly with colorful, well-flavored ingredients.

The eggs can be served on a little green salad, or as part of a mixed hors d'oeuvre platter. SERVES 4

Breton Fish Soup

— Audrey Ellis —

$\frac{1}{2}$ lb cod or haddock fillet
$1\frac{1}{4}$ cups water
1 tablespoon lemon juice
1 stalk celery, sliced
1 medium-size carrot, sliced
$\frac{1}{2}$ lb potatoes, sliced
1 medium-size onion, sliced
1 clove garlic, crushed
salt and pepper
2 tablespoons butter
$1\frac{1}{2}$ tablespoons flour
$1\frac{1}{4}$ cups milk
2 tablespoons chopped parsley

Place the fish in a saucepan with the water, lemon juice, celery, carrot, potatoes, onion, garlic and seasoning. Bring to a boil, cover and cook gently for 20 minutes. Lift out the fish with a slotted spoon, remove the skin and roughly flake the flesh. Continue to cook the vegetables for a further 10 minutes, or until they are soft. Strain and reserve the liquid and vegetables separately.

Melt the butter in a large clean saucepan and stir in the flour. Gradually add the milk and reserved liquid, bring to a boil, stirring, and cook for 2 minutes. Stir in the fish and the vegetable mixture and finally add the parsley. Taste and adjust the seasoning if necessary. Serve with freshly baked biscuits. SERVES 4

Country Herbed Bread

— Audrey Ellis —

Slice a large crusty white loaf of bread (preferably a long one), cutting through almost to the bottom. Soften $\frac{3}{4}$ cup butter, mash and season with salt, pepper, a crushed garlic clove and chopped fresh mixed herbs to taste. Spread this herb butter generously into the cuts in the bread. Press the slices together to re-form the loaf and wrap in foil. Place the bread in a preheated 375° oven and bake for 15 minutes. Serve the slices, cut apart, in a napkin-lined basket. SERVES 6

Cream of Fennel Soup

Jill Spencer

2 heads of fennel (about $1\frac{1}{4}$ lb)
juice of $\frac{1}{2}$ lemon
3 tablespoons butter
3 tablespoons flour
$2\frac{1}{2}$ cups chicken broth
$1\frac{1}{4}$ cups milk
$\frac{1}{2}$ teaspoon mace
salt and pepper
a little chopped parsley
fennel sprig for garnish

Trim and wash the fennel, cut it into quarters and cook in boiling salted water with the lemon juice until tender – about 30 minutes.

Drain and roughly slice the fennel. Melt the butter in a large saucepan and sauté the fennel in it for a few minutes. Stir in the flour, then add half the broth and half the milk, the mace, seasoning and parsley. Purée the soup in a blender or food processor, or by pressing it through a food mill.

Pour the soup back into the saucepan, add the remaining broth and milk, and bring to a boil. Simmer gently, stirring occasionally, for 10 to 15 minutes. Serve hot, garnished with a sprig of fennel. SERVES 4

French Onion Soup

Jill Spencer

$\frac{1}{4}$ cup butter
1 tablespoon oil
1 lb onions, finely sliced
a little chopped parsley
1 quart well-flavored beef broth
1 teaspoon imported yeast extract (optional)
salt and pepper
4 slices French bread
1 cup grated cheese

Melt the butter in a saucepan with the oil. Add the onions and stir well, then fry gently over a low heat until browned.

Add the parsley to the fried onions, with the broth, yeast extract and seasoning to taste. Bring to a boil, then reduce the heat and simmer the soup for 20 minutes.

While the soup is simmering, top the bread with plenty of grated cheese. When you are almost ready to serve the soup, broil the cheese until golden brown. Pour the soup into four individual bowls and place a piece of bread on top of each. SERVES 4

Tomato and Carrot Soup

Jill Spencer

$\frac{1}{4}$ cup butter
1 small onion, finely chopped
$1\frac{1}{2}$ cups finely chopped carrots
2 cups peeled and finely chopped tomatoes
$\frac{1}{4}$ cup flour
1 quart mixed herb or chicken broth
1 teaspoon sugar
1 teaspoon dried oregano
$\frac{1}{2}$ teaspoon paprika · $\frac{1}{2}$ teaspoon mace
2 tablespoons tomato paste
salt and pepper
4-6 tablespoons light cream

Melt the butter in a saucepan and lightly cook the chopped vegetables in it. Stir in the flour and add the broth, sugar, oregano, spices, tomato paste and seasoning, stirring continuously. Bring to a boil, reduce the heat and cover the pan, then simmer for 30 minutes.

Purée the soup in a blender or food processor, or by pressing it through a food mill. Return the soup to the rinsed out saucepan and reheat to boiling point. Serve in individual bowls, with a tablespoon of light cream swirled into each portion. SERVES 4 TO 6

Oatmeal and Vegetable Soup

Rosemary Wadey

1 large onion, finely chopped
1 white turnip, finely chopped
2 large carrots, chopped
1 large leek, trimmed, thinly sliced
and washed
$\frac{1}{4}$ cup butter
3 tablespoons medium oatmeal
1 quart chicken broth
salt and pepper · 2 cups milk

Cook all the vegetables in the butter for about 5 minutes without browning. Stir in the oatmeal and continue cooking for a few minutes, stirring frequently. Pour in the broth and add seasoning, then bring to a boil. Cover the pan and simmer the soup for about an hour.

Add the milk, taste and adjust the seasoning, then bring back to a boil and cook for 3 to 4 minutes. SERVES 4 TO 6

Cream of Cauliflower Soup

Rosemary Wadey

$\frac{1}{4}$ cup butter
1 large onion, chopped
1 small cauliflower, trimmed and
roughly chopped
$2\frac{1}{2}$ cups chicken broth
$2\frac{1}{2}$ cups milk
salt and pepper
bay leaf
2 blades mace
$\frac{3}{4}$ cup light cream
chopped parsley for garnish

Melt the butter in a saucepan and fry the onion in it until soft. Reserve a few florets of cauliflower for garnish; add the remaining florets to the onion and continue cooking gently for 5 minutes. Pour in the broth and milk, and bring to a boil. Season to taste, add the bay leaf and mace, then cover the pan and simmer the soup for 30 to 40 minutes or until the cauliflower is tender. Discard the bay leaf and mace at the end of the cooking time.

Process the soup until smooth and return it to the pan. Taste and adjust the seasoning, if necessary, and stir in the cream, then reheat without boiling. Garnish with the reserved cauliflower florets and parsley. Serve with melba toast (below). SERVES 6

Note: To make melba toast, lightly toast medium-thick slices of bread on both sides. Working as quickly as you can, before the toast cools and becomes crisp, cut off the crusts and slice horizontally through the middle of each piece of toast to give very thin slices. Place these under the broiler, untoasted side uppermost, and cook until the toast curls and browns.

Borscht

Rosemary Wadey

1 lb uncooked beets, grated
2 carrots, chopped
1 onion, chopped
bay leaf
1 quart chicken broth
salt and pepper
a little lemon juice
$\frac{3}{4}$ cup sour cream

Put the beets in a saucepan with the carrots, onion, bay leaf, broth and seasoning. Bring to a boil, cover the pan and simmer for about 45 minutes. Strain the soup and pour it back into the saucepan. Taste and adjust the seasoning and sharpen the soup with lemon juice. Bring back to a boil and serve, topping each portion with a spoonful of sour cream. SERVES 6

Spinach Soup

— Rosemary Wadey —

2 tablespoons butter
1 onion, finely chopped
1 clove garlic, crushed
4 slices lean bacon, finely chopped
1 (8-oz) package frozen chopped spinach
2 tablespoons flour
1 quart chicken broth
salt and pepper · a little grated nutmeg
$\frac{1}{4}$ cup grated Cheddar cheese

Melt the butter in a saucepan and gently fry the onion, garlic and bacon in it for 5 minutes. Add the spinach and continue to cook gently, stirring frequently, until it has thawed. Stir in the flour, then gradually whisk in the broth. Bring to a boil and season to taste with salt, pepper and nutmeg. Cover the pan and simmer the soup for 25 to 30 minutes.

Either leave the soup as it is, or process it if a smooth soup is preferred. Pour the soup back into the pan, bring back to a boil and taste and adjust the seasoning. Serve sprinkled with cheese. SERVES 4 TO 6

Minestrone

— Rosemary Wadey —

$\frac{1}{3}$ cup dried navy beans
7 cups chicken broth
3 tablespoons oil
2 tablespoons butter
2 carrots, chopped
1 large onion, chopped
1 clove garlic, crushed
2 leeks, trimmed, thinly sliced and washed
1 (16-oz) can peeled tomatoes
1 tablespoon tomato paste
bouquet garni
salt and pepper
2 oz spaghetti, broken up
grated Parmesan cheese for serving

Soak the beans in $2\frac{1}{2}$ cups of the broth overnight. The following day add a further $2\frac{1}{2}$ cups of broth and simmer the beans gently for 1 hour.

Heat the oil with the butter in a saucepan. Fry the carrots, onion, garlic and leeks in this mixture until soft and just beginning to color – about 5 minutes. Add the tomatoes, tomato paste, bouquet garni and simmered beans with any of their cooking liquid. Season to taste, then pour in the remaining broth and bring to a boil. Cover and simmer gently for 1 hour or until the beans are tender. Add the spaghetti and continue cooking for a further 10 to 15 minutes until tender.

Discard the bouquet garni, taste and adjust the seasoning if necessary and serve, sprinkled with Parmesan cheese. SERVES 4 TO 6

16

Kipper Cocktail

— Carol Bowen —

1 (7-oz) can kipper fillets
$\frac{1}{2}$ cup sour cream · $\frac{1}{2}$ lemon
1 tablespoon tomato ketchup
2 teaspoons Dijon-style mustard
3 tablespoons mayonnaise
salt and pepper
2 large apples
3 stalks celery
$\frac{1}{2}$ cup cashew nuts
parsley sprigs or celery leaves for garnish

Drain the canned kippers and cut them into small bite-sized pieces. Beat the sour cream until smooth and creamy. Grate the rind from the half lemon and add to the sour cream with the tomato ketchup, mustard and mayonnaise. Stir well to blend, then season to taste with salt and freshly ground black pepper.

Core the apples and cut them into small chunks. Put these in a bowl with the kippers and sprinkle with the juice squeezed from the half lemon. Clean and slice the celery and add it to the kipper and apple mixture together with half the nuts.

Pour the sauce over the kipper and apple mixture and toss so that the ingredients are lightly coated. Divide the mixture between six glasses, cover and chill them for at least 1 hour.

Serve the chilled cocktails sprinkled with the remaining nuts and garnished with parsley sprigs or celery leaves. SERVES 6

Taramasalata

— Carol Bowen —

4 slices white bread
about 3 tablespoons water
1 cup tarama (available in specialty food shops)
3 tablespoons lemon juice
1 cup olive oil
1 small onion, finely grated
1 teaspoon chopped fresh dill (optional)
GARNISH
ripe olives · lemon slices

Trim off and discard the crusts from the bread and soak the slices in the 3 tablespoons water for 2 minutes; remove and squeeze dry.

Place the tarama, bread, lemon juice, oil, onion and dill, if used, in a blender and process until smooth.

Alternatively, mash the tarama, bread, onion and dill by hand with a fork. When smooth, blend in the lemon juice and olive oil slowly, stirring continuously, until well blended. Beat with a whisk until pink and creamy.

Chill before serving. Garnish with ripe olives and twists of lemon. SERVES 4 TO 6

Gazpacho

— Carol Bowen —

3 small slices brown bread, cut into
1-in cubes
$2\frac{1}{2}$ cups canned tomato juice
2 cloves garlic, finely chopped
$\frac{1}{2}$ cucumber, peeled and finely chopped
1 green pepper, seeded and finely chopped
1 large onion, finely chopped
1 sweet red pepper, seeded and finely chopped
$1\frac{1}{2}$ lb tomatoes, peeled, seeded and finely chopped
$\frac{1}{4}$ cup olive oil
2 tablespoons red wine vinegar
$\frac{1}{2}$ teaspoon salt
$\frac{1}{4}$ teaspoon freshly ground black pepper
$\frac{1}{4}$ teaspoon dried marjoram
$\frac{1}{4}$ teaspoon dried basil
ice cubes (optional)
GARNISH
croûtons (see below)
chopped ripe or green olives
chopped cucumber
chopped sweet green and red peppers
chopped onion

Place the bread cubes in a mixing bowl and pour in the tomato juice. Leave to soak for 5 minutes, then squeeze the bread to extract all the juice. Transfer the squeezed-out bread to a large mixing bowl and reserve the tomato juice.

Add the garlic, cucumber, green pepper, onion, red pepper and tomatoes to the bread and stir to mix, then purée the mixture in a blender, food processor or food mill. Stir in the reserved tomato juice.

Add the oil, vinegar, salt, pepper, marjoram and basil to the purée and mix well; the soup should be the consistency of light cream, so add more tomato juice if necessary.

Pour the soup into a deep tureen and chill for at least an hour. Just before serving, stir the soup well and float ice cubes on the surface, if you like. Serve with small bowls of croûtons, chopped olives, cucumber, peppers and onion. SERVES 4

Croûtons To make croûtons, fry small, neat cubes of bread in a mixture of oil and butter, turning them frequently, until golden brown all over. Drain on paper towels.

Vichyssoise

Rosemary Wadey

3 leeks
3 tablespoons butter
1 onion, thinly sliced
1 lb potatoes, chopped
1 quart chicken or veal broth
salt and pepper
pinch of grated nutmeg
1 egg yolk
½ cup light cream
chopped chives for garnish

Wash and trim the leeks, removing most of the green part, then finely slice the remainder. Melt the butter in a saucepan and fry the leeks and onion in it for 5 minutes without browning. Add the potatoes, broth, seasoning and nutmeg, and bring to a boil. Cover the pan and simmer the soup for about 30 minutes, or until the vegetables are soft.

Process the soup until smooth, return it to the pan and reheat until it is almost boiling. Blend the egg yolk with the cream, then whisk into the soup and reheat gently without boiling. Adjust the seasoning, cool and chill thoroughly. Serve the soup sprinkled with the chives. SERVES 4 TO 6

Iced Lemon Soup

Rosemary Wadey

3 tablespoons butter
1 onion, chopped
1 clove garlic, crushed (optional)
2 tablespoons flour
1 quart well-flavored chicken broth
grated rind and juice of 1 large lemon
salt and pepper
bay leaf
1¼ cups light cream
GARNISH
thin slices of lemon
mint sprigs

Melt the butter in a saucepan, add the onion and garlic and fry until soft but not browned. Stir in the flour, then gradually add the broth, stirring continuously, and bring to a boil. Add the lemon rind and juice, seasoning and bay leaf. Cover the pan, reduce the heat and simmer for 20 minutes.

Remove the bay leaf, process the soup until smooth and pour it into a serving tureen or individual bowls. Stir in the cream and taste and adjust the seasoning. Cool, then chill thoroughly.

Garnish by floating thin slices of lemon in the soup, and top each portion with a sprig of mint. Serve with breadsticks. SERVES 6

Cucumber Soup

——— Rosemary Wadey ———

1 large cucumber, diced
1 quart chicken broth
2 tablespoons finely chopped onion
2 tablespoons butter
2 tablespoons flour
salt and pepper
a little lemon juice
a little green food coloring (optional)
2 egg yolks
$\frac{1}{4}$ cup light cream
GARNISH
mint sprigs
cucumber slices

Place the cucumber in a saucepan with the broth and onion. Bring to a boil, cover and simmer for about 20 minutes, or until the cucumber is tender. Cool, then process in a blender or food processor.

Melt the butter in a pan, stir in the flour and cook for 1 minute. Gradually add the cucumber purée. Bring to a boil, stirring frequently, simmer for 2 minutes, then season to taste with salt, pepper and lemon juice. Add a little green food coloring, if liked. Blend the egg yolks with the cream, then whisk in a little of the soup. Return this mixture to the pan and reheat gently, whisking continuously, but do not boil the soup. Cool and chill thoroughly. Serve garnished with mint sprigs and cucumber slices. SERVES 6

Chilled Avocado Soup

——— Rosemary Wadey ———

2 tablespoons finely chopped onion
3 tablespoons butter
2 tablespoons flour
3 cups chicken broth
2 ripe avocados
1-2 teaspoons lemon juice
salt and pepper
$\frac{1}{2}$ cup milk
$\frac{1}{2}$ cup light cream

Fry the onion gently in the butter for 3 to 5 minutes without allowing it to brown. Add the flour and cook for 1 minute. Gradually add the broth and bring to a boil, then simmer for 5 minutes. Quarter the avocados, remove the seeds and peel. Cut off and reserve a few slices for garnish; dip these in a little lemon juice. Roughly chop the remaining avocado and add to the soup with the rest of the lemon juice and the seasoning. Simmer for 3 to 4 minutes to prevent the avocado from discoloring.

Process the soup until smooth, stir in the milk and cream and adjust the seasoning. Cool, then chill thoroughly. Serve garnished with the reserved slices of avocado. SERVES 4

Shrimp Soufflés

Diana Jaggar

1½ tablespoons butter
1 teaspoon paprika
½ lb peeled and deveined shrimp
a few drops of hot pepper sauce
salt and pepper
2 cups Béchamel sauce (below)
2 tablespoons light cream
2 tablespoons finely grated cheese
2 tablespoons browned bread crumbs
3 egg yolks
4 egg whites

Melt the butter in a saucepan and add the paprika. Cook for 1 minute, then add the shrimp, pepper sauce, salt and pepper. Stir in the sauce and cream and allow the mixture to cool slightly. Mix the cheese and bread crumbs and set aside.

Beat the egg yolks one at a time into the shrimp mixture, making sure they are thoroughly incorporated. Beat the egg whites until stiff but not dry and stir 1 tablespoon into the mixture, then carefully fold in the remainder. Spoon into six well-greased individual ovenproof soufflé dishes, place them on a baking sheet and sprinkle with the cheese and bread crumb mixture. Bake in a preheated 350° oven for 20 to 25 minutes, until risen and crisp. Serve immediately. SERVES 6

Béchamel Sauce Melt 3 tablespoons butter in a saucepan. Stir in 3 tablespoons flour and cook for 1 minute. Gradually add 2 cups milk which has been infused with a bay leaf, a blade of mace and a slice of onion and then strained. Boil, cook for 2 minutes and season.

Sardine-stuffed Lemons

Rosemary Wadey

4 lemons
2 tablespoons sour cream
1 (4¼-oz) can sardines in oil, drained and mashed
2 tablespoons finely chopped cucumber
1 tablespoon chopped capers
salt and pepper
dash of hot pepper sauce
1 small head of lettuce

Cut the tops off the lemons and cut a sliver from the base of each so that they stand. Scoop out the lemon flesh and squeeze 1 tablespoon of juice from it.

Mix together the sour cream, lemon juice, mashed sardines, cucumber and capers. Season to taste with salt, pepper and pepper sauce. Spoon the mixture into the lemons, chill and serve on lettuce leaves. SERVES 4

Gratin au Fruits de Mer

———— Diana Jaggar ————

$\frac{3}{4}$ lb skinless cod fillet, cut into strips
$\frac{1}{4}$–$\frac{1}{2}$ lb peeled and deveined shrimp
6 sea or ocean scallops, cut into quarters
juice of 1 lemon
salt and pepper
$\frac{1}{4}$ cup butter
1 small onion, finely chopped
$\frac{1}{2}$ cup dry white wine
3 tablespoons flour
2 cups milk, infused with a bay leaf, a blade of mace
and a few peppercorns
$\frac{1}{4}$ cup grated Parmesan cheese
a few parsley sprigs for garnish

Mix the cod strips, shrimp and scallops with the lemon juice and seasoning, then divide between six deep scallop shells or ovenproof dishes.

Melt the butter in a saucepan, add the onion and cook until soft, then add the wine and bring to a boil. Simmer until reduced by half, whisk in the flour and cook until smooth, stirring continuously. Strain in the infused milk, bring back to a boil and simmer for 2 to 3 minutes. Taste and adjust the seasoning and spoon this sauce over the fish to cover it completely. Sprinkle with the cheese and bake in a preheated 375° oven for 20 to 30 minutes, or until golden brown on top. Serve immediately, garnished with sprigs of parsley. SERVES 6

Shrimp Newburg

———— Rosemary Wadey ————

1 small onion, finely chopped
$\frac{1}{4}$ cup butter
$\frac{1}{2}$ lb peeled and deveined shrimp
2 tablespoons lemon juice
$\frac{1}{4}$ cup sherry or Madeira wine
salt and pepper
$\frac{1}{3}$ cup long-grain rice, cooked
2 egg yolks
$\frac{3}{4}$ cup light cream
watercress sprigs for garnish

Fry the onion in the butter until soft. Add the shrimp and cook gently for 5 minutes, shaking the pan frequently. Stir in the lemon juice, sherry or Madeira and seasoning and bring to a boil. Add the cooked rice and mix thoroughly.

Beat the egg yolks into the cream and add to the pan. Heat gently, stirring continuously, but do not allow to boil. Adjust the seasoning and serve in small dishes, garnished with the watercress. SERVES 4

Chicken Liver Pâté

Rosemary Wadey

1 onion, very finely chopped
1 or 2 cloves garlic, crushed
$\frac{1}{4}$ cup butter
1 lb chicken livers
salt and pepper
2 tablespoons heavy cream
2 tablespoons red wine
$\frac{1}{3}$ cup melted butter
GARNISH
bay leaves · capers

Fry the onion and garlic in the butter until soft but not browned. Wash and drain the chicken livers, add to the pan and cook gently for 10 minutes, stirring occasionally to prevent them from sticking. Remove the pan from the heat and stir in the seasoning, cream and wine.

Process the pâté until smooth, adjust the seasoning to taste and pack into six individual dishes. Garnish each with a small bay leaf and a few capers. Cover the tops with a thin layer of melted butter and chill thoroughly. SERVES 6

Farmhouse Pâté

Rosemary Wadey

$\frac{1}{2}$ lb pork liver, cubed
$\frac{1}{2}$ lb beef for stew, cubed
$\frac{1}{2}$ lb fresh pork sides, cubed
1 large onion, roughly chopped
1 or 2 cloves garlic, crushed
$\frac{1}{2}$ cup soft white bread crumbs
1 large egg, beaten
salt and pepper
$\frac{1}{8}$ teaspoon grated nutmeg
3 or 4 tablespoons red or white wine
$\frac{1}{2}$ lb bacon
GARNISH
chopped sweet red pepper
chopped cucumber

Coarsely grind or process the liver, beef, pork and onion. Add the garlic, bread crumbs, egg, seasoning, nutmeg and wine, and mix thoroughly.

Stretch the bacon slices by placing them on a board and running the blunt edge of a knife along them, pressing firmly. Line an $8\frac{1}{2} \times 4\frac{1}{2} \times 2\frac{1}{2}$ in loaf pan with the bacon and spoon the pâté mixture into the pan. Press down evenly and fold the ends of the bacon over the top. Stand the pâté pan in a roasting pan and pour in hot water to a depth of 1 in. Cook in a preheated 350° oven for $1\frac{1}{2}$ to 2 hours. Place a weight on the top of the pâté, allow to cool and chill for several hours.

Serve cut into neat slices, garnished with chopped sweet red pepper and cucumber, with hot toast and butter. SERVES 6 TO 8

Chicken Liver Terrine

— Audrey Ellis —

½ lb bacon
½ lb chicken livers
¼ lb bulk pork sausage meat
1 cup soft white bread crumbs
2 tablespoons lemon juice
grated rind of 1 lemon
¾ cup diced cooked chicken meat
salt and pepper

Stretch the bacon slices with the back of a knife. Use to line a 5 × 3 × 2 in loaf pan.

Finely chop the chicken livers and combine them with the sausage meat. Soak the bread crumbs in the lemon juice for a few minutes, then work evenly into the sausage meat mixture, adding the lemon rind. Press half this mixture into the prepared pan, then cover it with the diced chicken. Season generously and top with the remaining sausage meat mixture. Press the sausage meat down evenly using the back of a metal spoon. Cover the pan with greased foil and stand it in a roasting pan half-filled with warm water. Cook in a preheated 350°oven for 1¾ hours.

Allow to cool, and leave until the terrine shrinks away from the sides of the pan. Unmold and serve with crusty French bread. SERVES 4 TO 6

Pork and Olive Pâté

— Jane Todd —

4 scallions, chopped
1 lb ground pork
½ lb bulk sausage meat
1 tablespoon chopped fresh sage
12 pimiento-stuffed olives, sliced
salt and pepper
¼ cup hard dry cider
GARNISH
tomato slices
chopped parsley

Mix together the scallions, pork, sausage meat, sage and olives, adding plenty of seasoning. Bind the mixture with the cider and pack it into a greased 5 × 3 × 2 in loaf pan. Cook the pâté in a preheated 350° oven for 1¼ hours.

Place a weight on the pâté and leave to cool in the pan. Chill for several hours. Unmold onto a serving dish and garnish with tomato slices and a sprinkling of chopped parsley. Serve with toast or French bread. SERVES 6

Brandied Turkey Mousse

Carol Bowen

2 envelopes unflavored gelatin
2½ cups boiling turkey or chicken broth
1 cup finely diced cooked, boned smoked turkey
1 tablespoon tomato paste
1 teaspoon dried tarragon
2 egg yolks
1 cup heavy cream
½ cup brandy
salt and pepper
a few lettuce leaves
1 head Belgian endive, separated into leaves
orange wedges for garnish

Place the gelatin in a small bowl. Gradually add the broth, whisking well to dissolve the gelatin. Cool.

Place all the ingredients except the lettuce leaves and endive in a blender and process until smooth and creamy. Turn into a 5-cup fluted mold and chill until set.

To serve, line a serving plate with the lettuce leaves. Unmold the mousse onto the plate and arrange the endive leaves around the edge. Garnish with orange wedges and serve. SERVES 4

Asparagus and Parma Ham Rolls

Carol Bowen

1 (10-oz) can asparagus tips
salt and pepper
2 tablespoons mayonnaise
5 thin slices Parma ham or prosciutto
chopped parsley for garnish (optional)

Drain the asparagus tips and trim off the ends of the stalks to give 3-in lengths. Finely chop the trimmings, season well and fold into the mayonnaise.

Sandwich four asparagus tips together using a little of the mayonnaise mixture and roll them up in a slice of Parma ham. Repeat with the remaining slices of ham. Place on a serving dish and garnish with chopped parsley, if used. MAKES 5.

Lamb Meatballs with Cream and Caraway Dip

Jane Todd

1 lb ground lamb
2 teaspoons ground cumin
1 tablespoon chopped fresh mint
2 scallions, chopped
salt and pepper
½ cup soft white bread crumbs
1 egg, lightly beaten
CREAM AND CARAWAY DIP
1 cup sour cream
1 teaspoon caraway seeds

Mix together the lamb, cumin, mint, scallions, seasoning and bread crumbs, then bind the mixture with the lightly beaten egg. Flour your hands and shape the mixture into 1-in meatballs. Place them in a greased baking pan and cook in a preheated 425° oven for 15 minutes or until well browned.

Meanwhile make the dip: mix the sour cream and caraway seeds. Spoon the dip into a serving bowl placed on a large plate or tray. Arrange the meatballs around the bowl. Serve toothpicks to spear the meatballs for dunking into the dip. MAKES ABOUT 30

Edam Dip

Jane Todd

1 whole Dutch Edam cheese
2 lb small-curd cottage cheese (4 cups)
¼ cup sour cream
6 tablespoons chopped parsley or chives
2 teaspoons horseradish sauce
salt
paprika

Cut a slice from the top of the Edam cheese and cut the edge in a zig-zag pattern using a sharp knife. With a melon ball cutter, scoop out as many balls of cheese from the inside as possible. Using a teaspoon, hollow out the remaining cheese, leaving an empty shell. (These odd bits of cheese can be grated and used for other dishes.) Place the cottage cheese in a bowl and beat with a wooden spoon to soften it. Mix in the sour cream, parsley or chives and horseradish sauce. Season well with salt and paprika.

Stand the Edam shell on a large platter and pile in the cottage cheese mixture. Chill for about 30 minutes.

Serve surrounded with the scooped-out cheese balls, crackers and sticks of raw vegetables to dip into the cheese filling. SERVES UP TO 15

Fish and Seafood

Fish can be cooked in a multitude of ways to make light meals
or filling family fare. To extend your repertoire, here is a
selection of recipes ranging from simple fried fish to hearty
casseroles and light seafood moulds.

Lemon Seafood Bake, Fried Fish Fillets, Broiled Fish
and Baked Mackerel

Fried Fish Fillets

(ILLUSTRATED ON PREVIOUS PAGE)

Allow one or two skinless fish fillets per person. Coat the fillets in a little seasoned flour. Dip each fillet in beaten egg, then coat each one in fine dry bread crumbs, making sure that the fish is well covered to protect the flesh during cooking.

Fry the fillets, one or two at a time, in a little oil in a skillet. When the underside is golden, turn the fish and cook the second side. Drain on paper towels and serve immediately, garnished with wedges of lemon and parsley sprigs.

Lemon Seafood Bake

Bridget Jones

(ILLUSTRATED ON PREVIOUS PAGE)

1 lb cooked white fish
$\frac{1}{4}$ lb peeled and deveined shrimp
$\frac{1}{4}$ lb button mushrooms, halved
4 sea or ocean scallops
$1\frac{1}{4}$ cups dry white wine
salt and pepper
2 tablespoons chopped tarragon or parsley
grated rind of 1 lemon
$1\frac{1}{4}$ cups Béchamel Sauce (page 20)
GARNISH
halved lemon slices
parsley sprigs

Cut the fish into chunks, removing any bones and skin. Mix the fish with the shrimp and mushrooms in an ovenproof dish. Poach the scallops in the wine with a little seasoning for 5 minutes, then remove them from the liquid and cut each one in half. Boil the cooking liquid until it is reduced to about a quarter of its original quantity. Place the scallops in the dish with the fish.

Stir the reduced cooking liquid, tarragon or parsley and lemon rind into the béchamel sauce. Pour over the fish mixture. Bake in a preheated 400° oven for 20 to 30 minutes, or until lightly browned. Serve immediately. SERVES 4

Broiled Fish

(ILLUSTRATED ON PREVIOUS PAGE)

Arrange fillets or steaks on a foil-lined broiler pan. Season to taste and add a few bay leaves if you like. Dot with butter or brush with a little oil. Cook under the broiler, about 5 in from the source of heat, for 2-10 minutes, depending on the thickness of the fish. Turn fish steaks over and top with more seasoning and more oil or butter, then cook for the remaining time.

Arrange the fish on a heated serving dish, or on individual plates, and pour the cooking juices on top. Garnish with lemon wedges, parsley or fresh bay leaves and serve immediately.

Baked Mackerel

Bridget Jones

(ILLUSTRATED ON PREVIOUS PAGE)

4 small fresh mackerel, cleaned
8 bay leaves
1 onion, sliced into rings
salt and pepper
$\frac{1}{3}$ cup butter *or* 2 tablespoons oil
lemon wedges for garnish

Leave the heads on the fish if you like. Rinse the body cavities and lay the fish on a large piece of greased cooking foil, on a baking sheet. Place 2 bay leaves, a few onion rings and plenty of seasoning in each body cavity. Sprinkle seasoning over the top of the fish and dot generously with butter or sprinkle with the oil. Fold the foil around the fish and seal the edges together. Bake in a preheated 350° oven for 40 to 50 minutes, or until the fish is cooked through.

To serve, carefully lift the mackerel out of the foil and arrange them on a serving dish. Garnish with lemon wedges and the bay leaves and cooked onion. Serve immediately. SERVES 4

Tuna and Cod Cream

— *Audrey Ellis* —

1 envelope unflavored gelatin
2 tablespoons water
1 (7-oz) can tuna, mashed
6 oz cooked cod, mashed (about 1½ cups)
1¼ cups mayonnaise
salt and pepper
1 (6-oz) can evaporated milk, chilled
1 tablespoon lemon juice
FILLING
2 teaspoons oil
2 teaspoons lemon juice
1 lb tomatoes, peeled and quartered
6 scallions, chopped
GARNISH
radish slices
cucumber slices

Dissolve the gelatin in the water in a cup in a saucepan of hot water. Combine the tuna and oil from the can with the cod and mayonnaise, and season well. Stir in the dissolved gelatin. Beat the evaporated milk with the lemon juice until thick, then fold it into the fish mixture. Pour into a 5-cup ring mold or shallow dish and chill until set.

Mix together the oil and lemon juice for the filling and toss the tomatoes and scallions in this dressing. Fill the center of the unmolded ring with the tomato salad and serve garnished with radish and cucumber slices. If the mixture was set in a shallow dish, then arrange the tomato salad around the edge and place the slices of radish and cucumber on top. SERVES 4

Smoked Trout with Apple and Horseradish Cream

— *Carol Bowen* —

4 small smoked trout
1 lettuce heart, separated into leaves
4 parsley sprigs
1 lemon, cut into wedges
APPLE AND HORSERADISH CREAM
1 large tart apple
1 tablespoon lemon juice
1 tablespoon horseradish sauce
¼ cup heavy cream or sour cream

Fillet the fish, if liked, then place the fillets on a dish lined with the lettuce. Cover the fish eyes with the parsley sprigs and garnish by placing lemon wedges between each fish.

Wash and quarter the apple, removing the core. Grate the apple, including the skin, on the coarse side of a grater. Add the lemon juice immediately to stop the apple flesh from discoloring. Stir in the horseradish sauce and the cream or sour cream, mixing well. Spoon into a sauceboat and serve with the smoked trout. SERVES 4

Cod à la Provençale

Julia Roles

1 lb tomatoes, peeled and chopped
rosemary sprig, chopped
2 thyme sprigs, chopped · salt and pepper
2 tablespoons white wine or water
3 shallots, chopped · 2 cloves garlic, crushed
2 tablespoons olive oil
1½ lb cod fillets
anchovy paste (optional)
chopped parsley for garnish

Place the tomatoes in a saucepan with the herbs, seasoning and wine or water. Bring to a boil, then cover and simmer gently for 15 minutes until soft and pulpy.

Meanwhile, cook the shallots and garlic in the olive oil until softened. Lay the fish in an ovenproof casserole and season lightly. Arrange the shallots on top. Add a little anchovy paste to the tomato sauce, if liked, and pour over the fish. Cover and cook in a preheated 350° oven for 30 minutes. Serve, garnished with parsley. SERVES 4

Finnan Haddie à la Russe

Julia Roles

1½ lb finnan haddie (smoked haddock fillets)
1¼ cups dry white wine
salt and pepper · 2 tablespoons butter
2 tablespoons flour
½ small green pepper, seeded and chopped
¾ cup sour cream
GARNISH
star-shaped pieces of toasted bread
a few parsley sprigs

Place the haddock in a large skillet with the wine and enough water to cover the fish. Season with pepper and bring to a boil, then lower the heat and simmer gently for 5 minutes. Drain the fish, reserving the cooking liquid, and cut it into chunks. Discard any skin and bones. Place in an ovenproof casserole.

Melt the butter in a saucepan and stir in the flour. Cook, stirring, for 1 minute, then remove from the heat and gradually blend in 1¼ cups of the strained cooking liquid from the fish. Return to the heat and bring to a boil, stirring continuously. When the sauce is thick and glossy, add the chopped pepper and season to taste. Pour the sauce over the fish and mix well. Cover and cook in a preheated 350° oven for 20 minutes. Stir in the sour cream and return to the oven to heat through for a few minutes.

Garnish with the bread and parsley. SERVES 4 TO 6

Sole Véronique

Julia Roles

1 small onion, finely chopped
1½ lb sole or flounder fillets
salt and pepper
juice of ½ lemon
¾ cup dry white wine
bay leaf
½ lb seedless green grapes, peeled
2 tablespoons butter
2 tablespoons flour
½ cup heavy cream
watercress sprigs for garnish

Sprinkle the onion over the bottom of a buttered ovenproof casserole. Fold the fish fillets in half and place them on top of the onion. Season to taste and add the lemon juice, wine, bay leaf and enough water to cover the fish. Cover the casserole and cook in a preheated 350° oven for 15 minutes. Reserve a few grapes for garnish and add the remainder to the dish. Return to the oven to heat through. Remove the fish and grapes from the sauce and keep hot. Discard the bay leaf.

Melt the butter in a saucepan, stir in the flour and cook for 1 minute. Remove from the heat and strain in the cooking liquid from the fish, made up to 1¼ cups with extra wine or water. Bring to a boil, stirring, and cook until thick. Take off the heat, add the cream, and heat through but do not boil.

cooking liquid from the fish, made up to 1¼ cups with extra wine or water. Bring to a boil, stirring, and cook until thick. Take off the heat, add the cream, and heat through but do not boil.

Arrange the fish and grapes on a serving dish and pour the sauce on top. Garnish with the reserved grapes and watercress. SERVES 4

Sole Goujons

Moya Maynard

6–8 skinless sole fillets
1 large egg
1 tablespoon water
salt and pepper
soft bread crumbs for coating
oil for deep frying

Cut the fish fillets diagonally into strips about ½ in wide. Beat the egg with the water. Add salt and pepper. Spread the bread crumbs on a sheet of wax paper. Coat the fish strips in the egg, then toss in the bread crumbs.

Heat the oil for deep frying to 350°, add the goujons a few at a time and cook until crisp and golden. Drain on paper towels and serve with tartare sauce. SERVES 4

Moules Farcies Bretonne

Diana Jaggar

1 quart large mussels
$\frac{1}{2}$ lb (1 cup) unsalted butter
1 large onion, finely chopped
3 cloves garlic, crushed
1 tablespoon chopped parsley
freshly ground black pepper
1 cup soft white bread crumbs
$\frac{1}{3}$ cup grated Parmesan cheese
$\frac{1}{2}$ cup dry white wine

Wash and scrub the mussels well under cold running water. Remove the beards and discard any open shells. Place the mussels in a steamer or metal colander over a pan of boiling water. Cover closely with a lid and steam for 2 to 3 minutes, until the shells just open. Do not overcook the mussels. Stir occasionally to ensure that all the shells are steamed. Remove the pan from the heat and lift off the steamer. Break off and discard the empty half of each shell and place the halves with the mussels in on a board. Discard any mussels that do not open at all.

Cream the butter with the onion, garlic, parsley and pepper. Spread a little over each mussel in its shell and arrange close together in four small ovenproof gratin dishes or one large ovenproof dish. Mix the bread crumbs with the cheese and sprinkle over the mussels. Pour in the wine and chill thoroughly.

Place the dish or dishes on a baking sheet and cover with foil. Cook for 15 to 20 minutes in a preheated 350° oven. Remove the foil and continue cooking for a further 5 minutes to brown. Serve immediately with French bread. SERVES 4

Mixed Fish Chowder

Rosemary Wadey

2 slices lean bacon, chopped
1 onion, finely sliced
2 tablespoons butter
1 (16-oz) can peeled tomatoes
3 cups fish broth
bay leaf · salt and pepper
$\frac{1}{3}$ cup long-grain rice
$\frac{1}{2}$ lb cooked haddock or cod, flaked
$\frac{1}{4}$ lb peeled and deveined shrimp
1 tablespoon chopped parsley
2 tablespoons light cream
a few cooked shrimp in shell for garnish

Fry the bacon and onion in the butter until beginning to color. Add the tomatoes, broth, bay leaf, seasoning and rice. Bring to a boil, cover and simmer for 20 minutes, or until the rice is cooked, stirring occasionally. Add the fish and shrimp and continue cooking for 10 minutes. Remove

the bay leaf. Adjust the seasoning, stir in the parsley and cream, then serve, garnished with shrimp in shell. SERVES 4 TO 6

Mediterranean Fish Casserole

Diana Jaggar

1 quart mussels
1 lb cod steaks, skinned and cut into cubes
1 lb halibut, skinned and cut into cubes
a little seasoned flour
6 tablespoons oil
$\frac{3}{4}$ lb onions, halved and sliced
3 cloves garlic, crushed
$\frac{3}{4}$ lb tomatoes, peeled and quartered
1 teaspoon tomato paste
$\frac{1}{2}$ bottle dry white wine
juice of 1 lemon
pinch of dried thyme
$\frac{1}{2}$ teaspoon chopped fennel or dill
1 tablespoon chopped parsley
2 lb cooked shrimp in shell
chopped parsley for garnish

Wash and scrub the mussels well under cold water. Remove the beards and discard any open shells. Toss the cod and halibut in a little seasoned flour. Heat 3 to 4 tablespoons of the oil in a skillet and fry the fish until browned. Remove from the pan and add the remaining oil. Cook the onions and garlic until the onion is soft but not browned. Add the tomatoes, tomato paste, white wine, lemon juice and herbs and bring to a boil.

Return the fish to the pan and simmer gently, covered, for 10 to 15 minutes until just cooked. Add the mussels, cover and leave for 3 to 4 minutes until they open. Discard any that do not open. Add the shrimp and sprinkle with parsley before serving. SERVES 6

Deviled Mackerel

Audrey Ellis

2 tablespoons soft white bread crumbs
2 tablespoons grated onion
pinch of cayenne
1 tablespoon dry mustard
4 fresh mackerel, filleted
$\frac{1}{4}$ cup flour
$\frac{1}{4}$ cup butter
1 medium-size onion, sliced into rings

To make the stuffing, combine the bread crumbs, grated onion, cayenne and half the mustard. Spread each mackerel fillet with a little of this stuffing and roll up. Secure each roll with a wooden toothpick. Mix the flour with the remaining mustard and use to coat the rolls.

Melt the butter in a large skillet, add the fish rolls and fry over moderate heat for about 12 minutes, turning occasionally, until cooked through. Remove the toothpicks from the mackerel rolls and serve hot, topped with the onion rings. SERVES 4

Mackerel with Cider and Rosemary Marinade

Carol Bowen

4 medium-size fresh mackerel, cleaned
$\frac{3}{4}$ cup hard dry cider
2 tablespoons finely chopped fresh rosemary
salt and pepper
a few lettuce leaves
watercress sprigs for garnish

Cut about four deep diagonal slashes into each side of the mackerel. Place the fish in a shallow dish and pour over the cider. Sprinkle with the rosemary and seasoning to taste. Leave to marinate for 2 to 3 hours, turning from time to time.

Remove the fish from the marinade and cook under the broiler, or over medium coals on a barbecue, for about 6 minutes each side, basting frequently with the marinade during cooking. Serve on a bed of lettuce leaves, garnish with watercress and accompany with any remaining marinade. SERVES 4

Smoked Mackerel Gougère

—— *Carol Bowen* ——

$\frac{3}{4}$ lb smoked mackerel fillets, skinned
1 medium-size onion, sliced
$\frac{2}{3}$ cup butter
1 cup plus 2 tablespoons flour
1$\frac{1}{4}$ cups milk
3 tablespoons cider
2 tablespoons plain yogurt
salt and pepper
1$\frac{1}{4}$ cups water · 4 eggs, beaten
$\frac{3}{4}$ cup grated Cheddar cheese
1 tablespoon dry bread crumbs
chopped chives or parsley for garnish

Flake the mackerel. Fry the onion in 2 tablespoons of the butter until golden. Stir in 2 tablespoons of the flour, gradually add the milk and bring to a boil, stirring. Boil for 1 minute, then remove from the heat and mix in the cider, yogurt, flaked fish and seasoning.

Melt the remining butter in a saucepan with the water. Bring to a boil, take off the heat and beat in the remaining flour until just smooth. Gradually beat in the eggs, then the cheese.

Spoon the paste around the edge of a greased 5-cup ovenproof dish. Spoon the fish sauce into the center, sprinkle with the bread crumbs and bake in a preheated 400° oven for 40 to 45 minutes. Serve garnished with chives or parsley. SERVES 4

Russian Salmon Pie

—— *Carol Bowen* ——

$\frac{1}{3}$ cup butter
1 small onion, finely chopped
$\frac{1}{4}$ lb button mushrooms, sliced
3 tablespoons flour
1$\frac{1}{4}$ cups milk · salt and pepper
$\frac{3}{4}$ lb cooked salmon (fresh or canned), flaked
1 hard-cooked egg, chopped
1 (12-oz) package frozen puff pastry, thawed
beaten egg for glazing

Melt the butter in a saucepan and fry the onion in it for 5 minutes, until soft. Add the mushrooms and fry them for 2 to 3 minutes. Stir in the flour and cook for 1 minute, then gradually add the milk, bring to a boil and cook for 2 to 3 minutes, stirring. Season, mix in the fish and chopped egg and leave to cool.

Roll out the pastry thinly to give a 12-in square. Pile the filling in the center and brush the edges with beaten egg. Bring the two opposite corners of pastry to the center of the filling and secure by pinching them together. Bring up the other two points and press these together to form an envelope shape. Press and secure the pastry edges together and flute the seams. Decorate the top with pastry leaves made from any pastry trimmings and glaze with the beaten egg.

Place on a dampened baking sheet and cook in a preheated 425° oven for 30 to 40 minutes, until crisp and golden. Serve hot or cold. SERVES 4

Fish Crumble

—— Carol Bowen ——

1½ lb skinless white fish fillet, cut into
bite-sized pieces
3 tablespoons oil
1 tablespoon vinegar
1 large onion, chopped
salt and pepper
1 cup flour
¼ cup butter or margarine
½ cup grated Cheddar cheese
1 (16-oz) can peeled tomatoes, drained

Place the fish in a 5-cup ovenproof dish. Mix the oil,
vinegar, onion and seasoning to taste, and pour over the
fish. Leave to marinate for 30 minutes.

Meanwhile sift the flour into a bowl, add a pinch of salt
and rub in the butter or margarine. Stir in the cheese.
Place the tomatoes on top of the fish and sprinkle with
the cheese crumble. Bake in a preheated 375° oven for 30
minutes or until golden. Serve immediately. SERVES 4

Fish Boulangère

—— Carol Bowen ——

¼ cup butter
1 clove garlic, crushed
1½ lb skinless white fish fillets (cod, haddock or
flounder for example), cut into bite-sized pieces
salt and pepper
1 large onion, sliced into rings
2 tablespoons chopped parsley
1 lb potatoes, par-cooked and thinly sliced

Mix half the butter with the garlic and spread on the
bottom of a 5-cup ovenproof dish. Cover with the pieces
of fish. Season lightly, top with the onion and sprinkle
with the parsley. Place the potato slices on top, in an
overlapping pattern. Dot with the remaining butter and
bake in a preheated 350° oven for 45 minutes, or until the
potato topping is crisp and golden and the fish is cooked.
SERVES 4

Stuffed Fish Florentine

Diana Jaggar

1½–2 lb fresh spinach, cooked and
thoroughly drained
1 small onion, finely chopped
¼ cup butter
2 egg yolks
a little grated nutmeg
salt and pepper
4 large skinless flounder fillets, trimmed
½ cup dry white wine
juice of 1 lemon
3 tablespoons flour
1¼ cups milk
½ teaspoon Dijon-style mustard
¾ cup grated Cheddar cheese
pinch of cayenne
2 tablespoons light cream

Finely chop the spinach. Cook the onion in half the butter in a small saucepan, then add the spinach and cook, stirring occasionally, for 5 minutes. Remove the pan from the heat and add the egg yolks, nutmeg and salt and pepper to taste. Cool.

Divide the spinach mixture between the fish fillets and roll them up from tail to head. Place in a greased ovenproof dish, pour in the wine and lemon juice, and cover the dish. Bake in a preheated 350° oven for 20 minutes.

Meanwhile, melt the remaining butter in a small saucepan, add the flour and stir for 1 minute. Pour in the milk and bring to a boil, stirring continuously. Stir in the mustard, most of the cheese, the cooking juices from the fish, cayenne, salt, pepper and cream; heat gently without boiling. Coat the fish rolls with this sauce and sprinkle with the remaining cheese, then brown under a hot broiler. SERVES 4

Broiled Salmon Steaks

Elizabeth Pomeroy

4 fresh salmon steaks
salt and pepper
lemon juice to taste
¼ cup butter, softened
GARNISH
lemon wedges
fresh dill leaves

Rinse the salmon steaks to remove any blood. Dry them on paper towels. Season with the salt, pepper and lemon juice. Place on the broiler rack and dot with butter. Preheat the broiler and cook the steaks, about 6 in from the source of heat, for 5 to 10 minutes according to thickness. Turn the steaks over and season the second side. Dot with butter and broil until the flesh shrinks from the backbone.

Place the salmon steaks on a warmed serving plate and garnish with lemon wedges and dill. Serve with Dill Cream Sauce. SERVES 4

Dill Cream Sauce

Elizabeth Pomeroy

3 tablespoons butter
1 tablespoon finely chopped onion
3 tablespoons flour
1¼ cups fish broth or milk
2 tablespoons chopped fresh dill *or*
1–2 teaspoons dill seeds
⅓ cup sour cream
salt and pepper

Melt the butter and fry the onion until transparent. Remove the pan from the heat and stir in the flour. Blend in the broth or milk and bring to a boil. Add the dill and simmer for 3 to 4 minutes, stirring steadily. Stir in the sour cream and seasoning and serve.

Glazed Sea Trout

Carol Bowen

$\frac{1}{3}$ cup butter
1 (5-lb) sea trout, cleaned
2 bay leaves
$2\frac{1}{2}$ cups liquid aspic jelly
a little cucumber skin, cut into matchstick
strips
a few small radishes, trimmed and thinly
sliced
1 teaspoon unflavored gelatin
2 tablespoons boiling water
2 cups mayonnaise
GARNISH (OPTIONAL)
watercress sprigs
cucumber slices
lemon slices

Line a large roasting pan with cooking foil and grease it with 2 tablespoons of the butter.

Wash the fish well and tuck the bay leaves inside the body cavity. Arrange the fish in the pan on its stomach (rather than laying the fish on its side) and curling from opposite corners of the pan to give a curved shape. Dot the remaining butter over the fish. Bring the edges of the foil together, folding them over without letting the foil touch the fish. Cook in a preheated 350° oven for $1\frac{1}{2}$ hours. Baste the fish with the juices in the pan during cooking. Remove from the oven, open out the foil and allow the fish to cool.

When cool, place the fish on a board and remove the skin, leaving the head and tail intact. Transfer to a serving dish and brush the fish with the liquid aspic. Arrange pieces of cucumber skin and radish slices along the side of the fish, dipping each piece into aspic before placing on the fish. Chill to set quickly.

Remove and discard any aspic jelly that has collected around the base of the fish. Spoon the remaining jelly over the fish and "flood" the serving dish with a thin layer. Leave to set.

Dissolve the gelatin in the boiling water. Stir this mixture into the mayonnaise and chill for about 15 minutes until thickened.

Place the mayonnaise in a pastry bag fitted with a large star-shaped nozzle and pipe a decorative design along the backbone of the fish. Garnish with watercress sprigs, cucumber and lemon slices, if liked. Serve chilled, with a cucumber salad and new potatoes. SERVES 8 TO 10

Scallops au Gratin

Carol Bowen

12 sea or ocean scallops, cut into $\frac{3}{4}$-in pieces
$\frac{3}{4}$ cup dry white wine
$1\frac{1}{4}$ cups water
salt and pepper
$\frac{1}{4}$ cup butter
1 medium-size onion, finely chopped
3 tablespoons flour
4 teaspoons chopped parsley
$\frac{1}{2}$ cup light cream
$1\frac{1}{2}$ lb potatoes, boiled and mashed
1 cup soft white bread crumbs
$\frac{3}{4}$ cup grated Cheddar cheese

Place the scallops in a saucepan with the wine, water and seasoning to taste. Bring to a boil, then simmer for about 10 minutes or until tender. Strain and reserve $1\frac{3}{4}$ cups of the cooking liquid.

Melt the butter in a clean saucepan. Add the onion and cook for about 5 minutes, or until soft. Stir in the flour and cook for 1 minute. Gradually add the reserved liquid, stirring continuously, to make a smooth sauce. Bring to a boil and simmer for 2 minutes. Add the scallops, chopped parsley and cream. Adjust the seasoning and reheat gently but do not allow to boil.

Meanwhile, pipe or spoon the potato around the edges of four flameproof dishes. Brown under the broiler until golden. Spoon the scallop mixture into the centers. Mix the bread crumbs and cheese together and sprinkle over the scallops. Lightly brown under the broiler and serve.
SERVES 4

Poultry and Game

From inexpensive supper ideas to extravagant dinner party
dishes – they are all here. For example, there is an economical
Country Chicken and Mushroom Pie to delight your family
on a cold day, or an impressive Pheasant Vallée d'Auge
for more formal occasions.

Stir-fried Chicken, Duck with Black Cherry Sauce,
Deep-fried Chicken and Smoked Chicken in Lemon Mayonnaise

Deep-fried Chicken

(ILLUSTRATED ON PREVIOUS PAGE)

Select small chicken pieces or drumsticks for deep frying. Remove the skin and trim off the wing ends. Coat the pieces in well-seasoned flour and dip them in beaten egg. Cover the surface of the chicken completely with fine dry bread crumbs, repeat the whole process and chill lightly before cooking.

Heat oil for deep frying to 350°. Add the chicken pieces and cook until deep golden – if the chicken browns too quickly the flesh will not be cooked through, so do not allow the oil to become too hot. Drain on paper towels and arrange on a serving dish or napkin-lined basket. Garnish with wedges or slices of lemon and large deep-fried parsley sprigs (cook the sprigs until crisp and drain them on paper towels). Serve with a mixed salad.

Stir-fried Chicken

Bridget Jones

(ILLUSTRATED ON PREVIOUS PAGE)

2 carrots
2 stalks celery
1 tablespoon shredded lemon rind
2 tablespoons oil
$\frac{3}{4}$ lb uncooked boneless chicken meat,
cut into fine strips (about $1\frac{1}{2}$–2 cups)
salt and pepper
$\frac{1}{4}$ lb button mushrooms, thinly sliced
$\frac{1}{4}$ cup flaked almonds
1 bunch scallions, shredded lengthwise

Halve the carrots, slice them lengthwise, and cut the slices into fine strips. Cut the celery into thin strips of a similar length. Mix the carrots and celery with the lemon rind.

Heat the oil in a large skillet and add the chicken and seasoning to taste. Stir-fry until the meat is lightly browned, then add the vegetable mixture and continue to cook for a few minutes. Stir in the mushrooms and cook for a few seconds. The cooked vegetables should be crisp. Transfer the stir-fry to serving bowls.

Quickly toss the almonds in the fat remaining in the pan until they are lightly browned, then stir in the scallions. Spoon this mixture over the top of the chicken and serve immediately. SERVES 4

Duck with Black Cherry Sauce

Bridget Jones

(ILLUSTRATED ON PREVIOUS PAGE)

1 duck (with giblets)
1 small onion, chopped
salt and pepper
1 tablespoon light brown sugar
1 (16-oz) can seedless black cherries
1 tablespoon arrowroot
a little lemon juice
watercress for garnish

Place the duck giblets in a small saucepan and add cold water to cover. Add the onion and a little seasoning and bring to a boil. Cover and simmer gently while the duck is cooking. Check that the stock does not reduce below the level of the giblets during cooking.

Place the duck on a roasting rack and stand it in a roasting pan. Prick the skin all over with a fork and sprinkle with seasoning and the sugar. Roast in a preheated 425° oven for 20 minutes, then reduce the oven temperature to 350° and cook for a further $1\frac{1}{4}$ hours. Baste the duck occasionally during cooking and cover the top with a piece of cooking foil if the skin browns too quickly.

Strain and reserve the giblet stock, boiling it down, if necessary, to give about $1\frac{1}{4}$ cups. Cut the duck into four pieces, arrange them on a serving dish and keep hot. Pour off all the fat from the roasting pan, reserving just the juices. Pour the stock into the pan with the syrup from the cherries and heat to boiling point. Blend the arrowroot with a little cold water and stir the mixture into the sauce. Bring back to a boil, stirring continuously, and simmer for 2 minutes. Taste and adjust the seasoning and sharpen with lemon juice to taste. Stir in the cherries and pour the sauce over the duck. Serve immediately, garnished with watercress. SERVES 4

Poule au Pot

Julia Roles

1 (3½-lb) stewing chicken with giblets
2½ cups water
salt and pepper
3 onions, peeled
¼ cup butter
6 carrots, thickly sliced
3 stalks celery, chopped
2 white turnips, quartered
2 bay leaves
2 tablespoons flour

Place the chicken giblets in a saucepan with the water and 1 teaspoon salt. Bring to a boil, then cover the pan, reduce the heat and simmer for 30 minutes.

Meanwhile, place an onion inside the chicken and truss as for a roasting chicken. Melt half the butter in a large flameproof casserole and brown the chicken all over; pour off the fat. Quarter the remaining onions and arrange around the chicken with the vegetables and bay leaves. Strain in the giblet stock and season with pepper. Cover and cook in a preheated 325° oven for 2 to 2½ hours.

Arrange the cooked chicken and vegetables on a large serving platter and keep hot. Skim any fat off the sauce. Blend together the remaining butter and the flour to form a paste. Add to the sauce, a little at a time and stir over a gentle heat until thickened. Season the sauce and serve separately. SERVES 4 TO 6

Chicken Parisienne

Diana Jaggar

1 (3½-lb) roaster chicken, boned
¼ cup butter, softened
¾ cup chicken broth
3 tablespoons sherry wine
STUFFING
1 onion, finely chopped
2 tablespoons butter
½ lb each of veal and cooked ham, ground
3 tablespoons soft white bread crumbs
2 teaspoons chopped parsley
1 teaspoon chopped tarragon
grated rind and juice of ½ lemon
1 egg, beaten

Open out the chicken and season well.

For the stuffing, fry the onion in the butter until soft. Cool, then mix with the meats, bread crumbs, herbs and lemon rind. Bind with the lemon juice and egg, and add seasoning. Spread this stuffing in the bird and sew up.

Spread the ¼ cup butter over the chicken, place in a roasting pan and pour in the broth and sherry. Cook in a preheated 375° oven for 1½ hours, basting well. Serve the chicken sliced. SERVES 4 TO 6

Poulet au Citron

— *Diana Jaggar* —

2 tablespoons oil · $\frac{1}{4}$ cup butter
1 (3$\frac{1}{2}$-lb) roaster chicken, cut up
1 onion, finely chopped
1 clove garlic, crushed
$\frac{1}{4}$ teaspoon powdered saffron
1 cup dry white wine
1$\frac{1}{4}$ cups chicken broth
pared rind and juice of 1 lemon
salt and pepper
6 oz button mushrooms, quartered
2 tablespoons flour
2 egg yolks
$\frac{3}{4}$ cup light cream

Heat the oil in a large skillet. Add half the butter and the chicken pieces and cook until browned all over. Transfer to a flameproof casserole. Add the onion and garlic to the fat remaining in the pan and cook until softened, then add the saffron, wine and broth. Bring to a boil, adding the lemon juice, salt and pepper, and pour over the chicken. Cover and simmer for 45 to 60 minutes. Cut the lemon rind into fine strips, blanch for a few minutes in boiling water and add most of the strips to the chicken at the end of the cooking time. Strain the cooking juices and keep the chicken hot.

For the sauce, melt the remaining butter in a saucepan, add the mushrooms and cook them for a few minutes. Sprinkle in the flour and cook for 1 minute. Pour in the chicken juices and cook, stirring, until the sauce thickens. Pour some of this onto the yolks and cream, mix well and return to the pan. Reheat gently without boiling, then spoon this sauce over the chicken and sprinkle with the reserved strips of lemon rind. SERVES 4

Chicken Cacciatore

— *Moya Maynard* —

4 chicken quarters · 6 tablespoons butter
1 large onion, chopped
1 medium-size green pepper, seeded and chopped
1 clove garlic, crushed
1 (16-oz) can peeled tomatoes
$\frac{3}{4}$ cup chicken broth
salt and pepper
watercress for garnish

Fry the chicken for 25 to 30 minutes in $\frac{1}{4}$ cup of the butter, or until cooked through. Meanwhile, cook the onion, green pepper and garlic in the remaining butter for about 10 minutes. Stir in the tomatoes, broth and seasoning. Cover and simmer for 15 minutes.

Spoon the sauce over the chicken on a heated serving dish. Garnish with watercress and serve with rice sprinkled with chopped parsley. SERVES 4

Chicken Provençal

—— Carol Bowen ——

$\frac{1}{4}$ cup oil
4 chicken pieces
2 onions, chopped
2 cloves garlic, crushed
2 green peppers, seeded and finely diced
1$\frac{1}{4}$ cups dry white wine or broth
2–3 tomatoes, peeled and chopped
1 tablespoon tomato paste
bay leaf
1 teaspoon dried oregano
salt and pepper

Heat the oil in a flameproof casserole, add the chicken and fry it on all sides until golden. Remove with a slotted spoon and add the onions, garlic and peppers. Cook for about 5 minutes to soften, then drain away any excess oil.

Return the chicken to the casserole. Add the wine, tomatoes, tomato paste, bay leaf and oregano. Season generously, then cover the casserole and simmer it for 1$\frac{1}{4}$ hours.

Remove the bay leaf and taste and adjust the seasoning if necessary before serving with saffron rice. SERVES 4

Salami-stuffed Chicken

—— Carol Bowen ——

1 (3-lb) roaster chicken, boned
$\frac{3}{4}$ cup smooth liver pâté
1 cup soft brown bread crumbs
$\frac{1}{4}$ cup chopped mixed nuts
2 tablespoons chopped parsley
2 tablespoons chopped chives
pinch of grated nutmeg
salt and pepper
1–2 tablespoons milk
$\frac{1}{4}$ lb salami, sliced
2 knackwurst
2 tablespoons butter
parsley sprigs for garnish

Place the chicken, skin side down, on a large board. Thoroughly mix the pâté, bread crumbs, nuts, parsley, chives, nutmeg and seasoning, softening with the milk if necessary. Spread one third of this pâté mixture over the chicken and arrange the salami on top. Spread another third of the pâté on top and cover with the knackwurst, end to end. Top with the final third of pâté.

Sew up the chicken with fine thread to give a good shape, enclosing the stuffing. Season and dot with the butter. Place in a roasting pan and cook in a preheated 375° oven for 1$\frac{1}{2}$–2 hours or until cooked through, basting from time to time.

When cooked allow to cool, remove the thread and chill. Serve sliced, garnished with parsley, with new potatoes and a mixed salad. SERVES 6 TO 8

Poulet aux Amandes

Diana Jaggar

½ cup butter
1 (3½-lb) roaster chicken
tarragon sprig
¾ cup dry white wine or chicken broth
½ cup blanched and shredded almonds
½ lb sweet red peppers, seeded and sliced
1 onion, chopped
1½ tablespoons flour
1¼ cups chicken broth
pinch of mace
salt and pepper
½ cup light cream

Put 1 tablespoon of the butter inside the bird with the tarragon; spread 3 tablespoons of the butter over the top. Place in a roasting pan with the wine or broth. Roast in a preheated 400° oven for 1–1¼ hours.

Fry the almonds in the remaining butter until brown. Add the vegetables and cook until soft. Remove, then add the flour. Cook for 1 minute, then stir in the broth, mace, seasoning, almond and pepper mixture, and strained chicken juices. Boil, reduce the heat and add the cream, then heat gently. Cut up the chicken and arrange it on a dish with the sauce. SERVES 4 TO 6

Coq au Vin

Julia Roles

1 (4½-lb) chicken with giblets, cut up
salt and pepper
¼ lb bacon, chopped
20 pearl onions, peeled
6 tablespoons butter
¼ cup brandy
2 cups red wine
½ lb mushrooms, sliced
2 cloves garlic, crushed
2 teaspoons brown sugar
bouquet garni
pinch of grated nutmeg
3 tablespoons flour
chopped parsley for garnish

Simmer the giblets for 30 minutes in salted water to cover. Cook the bacon and onions in half the butter, in a flameproof casserole, until golden. Remove and brown the chicken in the fat. Add the brandy and ignite. Return the bacon and onions and add the wine, ¾ cup of the strained giblet stock, the mushrooms, garlic, sugar, bouquet garni, nutmeg and pepper. Boil, then cover and cook in a preheated 350° oven for 1 hour.

Remove the chicken and keep hot. Blend the remaining butter and flour, and gradually whisk into the sauce. Heat until thickened. Replace the chicken and sprinkle with parsley. SERVES 4

Poussin à l'Estragon

Diana Jaggar

1 lemon
handful of fresh tarragon
3 (1½–2 lb) Rock Cornish game hens
¾ cup butter
1 cup dry white wine
½ lb onions, finely chopped
½ lb button mushrooms, sliced
3 tablespoons flour
1¼ cups chicken broth
1 tablespoon chopped parsley
salt and pepper

Squeeze and reserve the juice from the lemon. Remove, chop and reserve the leaves from the fresh tarragon. Cut up the lemon skin and put a piece inside each bird with the tarragon stalks and a pat of butter. Keep ¼ cup of the butter and spread the remainder over the birds. Put them in a roasting pan, pour over the wine and cook in a preheated 350° oven for 40 to 50 minutes.

Melt the reserved butter in a small saucepan. Add the onions and cook until soft, then add the mushrooms and cook for a few minutes. Sprinkle the flour into the pan and cook for 1 minute. Gradually stir in the broth, bring to a boil and add the lemon juice, tarragon, parsley and seasoning. Bring to a boil and simmer for 15 minutes.

When the hens are cooked, strain the juices from the roasting pan into the sauce and cook until thickened to a coating consistency. Just before serving, cut each bird in half (poultry shears are best for this) and arrange on a heated serving dish. Spoon over the sauce and serve with fried button mushrooms. SERVES 6

Chicken with Pineapple

Julia Roles

4 chicken pieces
¼ cup olive oil
1 green pepper, seeded and chopped
2 stalks celery, chopped
1 onion, chopped
1 (8-oz) can pineapple rings
1 tablespoon each of soy sauce, lemon juice
and tomato paste
salt and pepper

Fry the chicken in the oil until golden. Transfer to a casserole. Add the vegetables to the pan and cook until softened. Transfer to the casserole with the pineapple syrup, soy sauce, lemon juice, tomato paste and seasoning. Cover and cook in a preheated 350° oven for 45 minutes. Arrange the halved pineapple rings on top of the chicken and return, uncovered, to the oven for a final 15 minutes. Serve with rice and mushrooms. SERVES 4

Roast Tarragon Chicken

————— Elizabeth Pomeroy —————

1 (3½-lb) roaster chicken
¼ cup butter
2 tablespoons chopped fresh tarragon *or*
2 teaspoons dried tarragon
1 small clove garlic
salt and pepper
1¼ cups giblet stock (see below)
2 tablespoons brandy or sherry
¼ cup heavy cream

Truss the chicken neatly. Cream together the butter and tarragon. Crush the garlic and blend it into the butter. Season to taste with salt and pepper. Spread some of the tarragon butter over the bird and put the rest inside.

Place the bird on its side on a rack in a roasting pan. Pour in the stock and cook in a preheated 400° oven for 20 minutes. Turn the bird onto the other side, baste and roast for another 20 minutes. Turn the chicken breast upwards and baste again. Continue roasting for a further 20 minutes or until the juice runs amber-colored when the thigh is pierced with a skewer.

Place the chicken on a heated serving dish and keep warm. Remove the rack from the roasting pan. Pour off the fat, retaining the juices. Add the brandy or sherry, boil, then stir in the cream. Season and pour into a warmed sauceboat. SERVES 4

Pot-roasted Chicken

————— Elizabeth Pomeroy —————

1 (2½-lb) chicken
3 tablespoons butter, softened
1 tablespoon chopped fresh tarragon
1 small clove garlic, crushed
salt and pepper
olive oil for basting
6 or 8 pearl onions, peeled
1 stalk celery, chopped
½ cup dry white wine
3–4 tablespoons sour cream
GIBLET STOCK
chicken giblets
bouquet garni
6 black peppercorns
GARNISH
fresh tarragon leaves

Truss the chicken neatly. Cream together the butter, chopped tarragon, garlic and seasoning. Put this herb butter inside the chicken and brush the chicken liberally with olive oil. Heat a tablespoon of oil in a deep flameproof casserole and brown the chicken over a brisk heat. Add the onions and celery, season with salt and pepper, then add the wine. Simmer for a minute, lower the heat, cover and cook very gently for 45 minutes, turning the chicken from time to time.

Meanwhile, clean the giblets, place in a saucepan with cold water to cover and add the bouquet garni, salt and peppercorns. Cover and simmer gently until required.

Pierce the leg of the chicken. If the juice runs amber colored, the chicken is cooked; if it runs red, continue cooking gently until done. Add a little giblet stock to the casserole if the liquid has evaporated.

When the chicken is cooked, remove from the casserole, tipping it so that the juices inside run out into the pot. Add ½ cup of the giblet stock; boil briskly to reduce. Mix the sour cream with 3 to 4 tablespoons of the chicken gravy, pour this into the casserole and heat through. Adjust the seasoning.

Replace the chicken in the casserole and garnish with fresh tarragon leaves, or serve the chicken on a platter and pass the sauce separately. SERVES 4

Chicken and Ham Pie à la Russe

————— Elizabeth Pomeroy —————

½ cup chopped cooked chicken
¼ cup diced cooked ham
1½ cups diced Cheddar cheese
½ cup chopped mushrooms
1 tablespoon chopped parsley
salt and pepper
1 egg, beaten
½ lb frozen puff pastry, thawed
beaten egg for glazing

Mix together the chicken, ham, cheese, mushrooms and parsley. Season to taste, then stir the egg into the mixture. Roll the pastry thinly into a rectangle 15 × 10 in and pile the filling in the center. Fold the corners of the square to the center and seal the edges with beaten egg. Glaze the pie evenly all over with egg. Use any remaining pastry to make decorations and a tassel, glaze with egg and arrange on the pie. Open the outer corners of the envelope slightly to allow steam to escape during cooking.

Bake in a preheated 425° oven for 25 minutes until well risen and golden brown. Serve hot with tomato quarters and fresh watercress. SERVES 4 TO 6

Chicken and Ham Turnovers

Carol Bowen

3 tablespoons butter or margarine
1 medium-size onion, chopped
$\frac{1}{2}$ cup coarsely chopped mushrooms
3 tablespoons flour
$1\frac{1}{4}$ cups milk
1 teaspoon Dijon-style mustard
salt and pepper
$\frac{3}{4}$ cup coarsely chopped cooked chicken meat
$\frac{1}{2}$ cup cubed cooked ham
1 (12-oz) package frozen puff pastry, thawed
beaten egg for glazing

Melt the butter or margarine in a small saucepan. Add the onion and mushrooms and cook gently for 2 minutes until beginning to soften. Stir in the flour and cook for 1minute. Gradually add the milk to make a sauce. Bring to a boil, stirring, then reduce the heat and cook for 2 minutes. Remove from the heat, add the mustard, seasoning to taste, chicken and ham. Leave to cool.

Roll out the pastry on a lightly floured surface to a 12 × 18-in rectangle and cut into six 6-in squares. Divide the chicken mixture into six portions. Pile onto the pastry squares, brush the edge with beaten egg and press together over the filling, sealing the edges well, to form triangles. Cut two slits in the top of the turnovers to allow any steam to escape. Use any pastry trimmings to decorate the turnovers. Glaze with beaten egg, place on a dampened baking sheet and bake in a preheated 450°

oven for 25 to 35 minutes until golden brown and cooked through. Serve with a crisp salad. MAKES 6

Deviled Chicken Legs

Carol Bowen

about $\frac{1}{2}$ cup dry sherry wine
1 tablespoon tarragon vinegar
2 teaspoons Worcestershire sauce
2 teaspoons prepared English mustard
salt and pepper
4 chicken leg-plus-thighs *or* 8 chicken drumsticks
oil for basting

Mix the sherry, vinegar, Worcestershire sauce, mustard and seasoning to taste in a small bowl. Make a few neat cuts in the chicken flesh and place in a shallow dish. Pour the sherry mixture on top and leave the chicken to marinate for at least 1 hour, turning from time to time in the mixture.

Cook the chicken under a preheated broiler or on a barbecue over medium coals for 10 to 15 minutes on each side, depending on size, basting alternately with the sherry mixture and oil. Serve hot, with salad ingredients and relishes. SERVES 4

Country Chicken and Mushroom Pie

— Elizabeth Pomeroy —

1 small stewing chicken
1 medium-size onion, chopped
1 stalk celery, chopped
1–2 carrots, sliced
bay leaf
1 parsley sprig
thyme or rosemary sprig
salt and pepper
2 oz slab bacon
$\frac{3}{4}$ cup sliced mushrooms
1 (12-oz) package frozen puff pastry, thawed
beaten egg for glazing
SAUCE
$\frac{1}{4}$ cup butter or margarine
3 tablespoons flour
$\frac{3}{4}$ cup milk
1 teaspoon lemon juice
2 tablespoons chopped parsley

Cook the bird in enough water to cover with the onion, celery, carrots, bay leaf, parsley, thyme or rosemary and seasoning. This will take about $1\frac{1}{2}$ hours. When the bird is cooked, lift it from the pan, remove the meat and cut it into neat pieces. Strain the stock and skim off the fat.

Dice the bacon and mix it with the chicken meat. Then make the sauce: melt the butter or margarine in a saucepan, stir in the flour and remove the pan from the heat. Gradually add the milk, stirring continuously. Still stirring, bring to simmering point, then stir in $\frac{3}{4}$ cup of the reserved broth. Season with lemon juice, salt and pepper, and stir in the parsley. Mix in the chicken and bacon and pour into a deep oval pie dish with a pie funnel in the center. Cover with the sliced mushrooms. Allow to become quite cold.

Roll out the pastry to $\frac{1}{4}$ in thick, dampen the rim of the dish and cover with a strip of pastry cut from the outside of the whole piece. Brush the pastry strip with water and cover with the remaining pastry. Press the edges together and trim off the surplus. Flute the edges. Cut two slits for the steam to escape and make a hole into the pie funnel with a skewer. Brush the top with beaten egg and decorate with any pastry trimmings made into leaves. Glaze the decorations and bake the pie in a preheated 450° oven for 20 minutes. Reduce the heat to 375° and bake for a further 20 minutes or until the pastry is completely cooked. SERVES 4

Chicken Kiev

— Elizabeth Pomeroy —

4 skinless, boneless chicken breast halves
with wing bones attached
$\frac{1}{4}$ cup unsalted butter, softened
grated rind and juice of 1 lemon
4 teaspoons chopped parsley
1 teaspoon chopped tarragon or rosemary
pinch of grated nutmeg or mace
salt and pepper
a little seasoned flour · 1 egg, beaten
fine soft bread crumbs for coating
oil for deep frying

Beat the boneless chicken breasts flat.

Cream together the butter, lemon rind and herbs, and flavor to taste with lemon juice, spice and seasoning. Shape into a rectangle and chill until hard. Cut the block of butter into four pieces, lay one on each chicken breast, then fold up neatly, pressing together well. Secure with wooden toothpicks. Roll in seasoned flour and pat off any surplus. Coat with beaten egg and the bread crumbs. Coat a second time with egg and crumbs for a perfect finish. Chill thoroughly before frying.

Heat the fat for deep frying to 375–380°. Put the chicken into the oil and cook until golden brown. Drain on paper towels, remove the toothpicks and put a chop frill on each wing bone. Serve immediately. SERVES 4

Smoked Chicken in Lemon Mayonnaise

— Carol Bowen —

1 (4-lb) smoked chicken
1 small fresh pineapple
juice of 1 lemon
$1\frac{1}{4}$ cups mayonnaise
salt and pepper
$\frac{1}{4}$ cup chopped walnuts
GARNISH
watercress sprigs

Remove the meat from the chicken. Slice the white meat and cut the dark wing and leg meat into bite-sized pieces.

Slice the pineapple, removing the skin and center core. Halve three slices and reserve them for the garnish. Chop the remaining pineapple into bite-sized pieces.

Stir the lemon juice into the mayonnaise and season to taste. Mix about 4 tablespoons of the mayonnaise with the dark meat and arrange on a serving dish. Cover with the chopped pineapple. Lay the slices of white meat on top and coat with the remaining mayonnaise. Sprinkle with the chopped walnuts and garnish the dish with watercress and the reserved halved slices of pineapple. SERVES 4 TO 6

Chicken Croquettes with Almonds

Audrey Ellis

1 whole chicken breast
1¼ cups chicken broth
⅓ cup flaked almonds
¼ cup butter
1 tablespoon flour
¼ cup milk
2 eggs · ¼ teaspoon mace
salt and pepper
seasoned flour
toasted bread crumbs
oil for frying
½ cup whole almonds, blanched

Place the chicken in a saucepan with the broth. Cover and cook gently for 40 minutes, until tender, then leave to cool in the broth. Remove the chicken, reserving the broth. Strip all the meat from the bones and grind it with the flaked almonds.

Melt 1 tablespoon of the butter in a saucepan and stir in the flour. Gradually stir in the milk and 3 or 4 tablespoons of the broth, then bring to a boil. Off the heat, blend in 1 egg yolk, the mace and seasoning. Add the ground chicken and mix well. Chill.

Shape the chicken mixture into twelve croquettes. Beat the remaining egg white with the egg. Coat the croquettes in seasoned flour, then in the beaten egg and egg white, and finally toss them in the bread crumbs. Fry the croquettes, four at a time, in deep hot oil for about 5 minutes, until crisp and golden brown. Drain well on paper towels. Fry the almonds in the remaining butter and serve with a mixed salad. SERVES 4

Moroccan Jellied Chicken

Audrey Ellis

1 (3½-lb) chicken
2 tablespoons corn oil
2 tablespoons lemon juice
½ teaspoon turmeric
½ teaspoon ground cardamom
1 teaspoon salt
¼ teaspoon pepper
½ cup water

Skin the chicken. Combine the oil, lemon juice, turmeric, cardamom, salt and pepper in a flameproof casserole. Pour in the water and stir well. Bring to a boil, then place the chicken in the casserole, cover tightly and simmer for about 1 hour, or until the chicken is tender. Remove the lid to turn the chicken every 25 minutes, and add a little more water if necessary.

Remove the chicken from the pan, spoon over the sauce and allow to cool. The sauce will set to give a golden jelly. Serve with an orange salad. SERVES 4 TO 6

Polish Paprika Chicken

Audrey Ellis

1 clove garlic, finely crushed
$\frac{1}{4}$ teaspoon dried basil
pinch of ground cloves
1 tablespoon paprika
$\frac{1}{4}$ teaspoon mace
$\frac{1}{4}$ cup seasoned flour
4 chicken pieces
1 tablespoon oil
2 tablespoons butter
1 ($2\frac{3}{4}$-oz) can pimientos
$\frac{1}{4}$ cup dry sherry wine
1 tablespoon tomato paste
1 teaspoon sugar
1 tablespoon chopped parsley
$\frac{1}{2}$ cup sour cream

Add the garlic, basil and spices to the seasoned flour. Use to coat the chicken pieces. Heat the oil and butter in a flameproof casserole and brown the chicken on all sides. Drain the pimientos, reserving the juice, finely chop and add to the casserole. Combine the liquid from the can with the sherry, tomato paste and sugar and pour over the chicken. Cover and cook in a preheated 350° oven for about 1 hour, or until tender. Mix the parsley with the sour cream, spoon over the chicken and return to the oven for a further 10 minutes. SERVES 4

Sunshine Chicken

Audrey Ellis

2 tablespoons oil
4 chicken pieces
1 large onion, sliced
2 slices bacon, chopped
$\frac{1}{2}$ cup sliced mushrooms
finely grated rind and juice of 1 orange
1 ($11\frac{1}{2}$-oz) can corn kernels with peppers
salt and pepper

Heat the oil, add the chicken pieces and cook until brown on all sides. Remove and drain well.

Add the onion and bacon to the pan and fry gently until golden brown. Add the mushrooms and fry for a further 2 minutes. Stir in the orange rind and juice and the corn with the liquid from the can. Season well and bring to a boil.

Spoon the corn mixture into an ovenproof dish and place the chicken pieces on top. Cover with foil or a lid and cook in preheated 375° oven for about 1 hour, or until the chicken is tender. SERVES 4

Stir-fried Turkey with Celery

Audrey Ellis

1 lb boneless uncooked turkey
5 stalks celery
2 tablespoons oil
$\frac{3}{4}$ cup sliced mushrooms
1 tablespoon soy sauce
salt and pepper
1 tablespoon cornstarch
$\frac{1}{4}$ cup chicken broth
chopped parsley for garnish

Cut the turkey into slices. String the celery and cut it into short lengths.

Heat the oil in a large skillet and fry the turkey slices briskly for about 5 minutes, stirring all the time. Add the celery, mushrooms and soy sauce and season with a little salt and pepper. Cook the mixture for a further 5 minutes, stirring frequently.

Blend the cornstarch with the broth, add to the mixture in the skillet and bring to a boil, stirring continuously. Simmer for 2 minutes before serving sprinkled with chopped parsley. SERVES 4

Turkey with Red Dawn Sauce

Audrey Ellis

2 teaspoons oil
10 tablespoons water
2 tablespoons vinegar
2 teaspoons brown sugar
salt
2 teaspoons cornstarch
2 cups diced cooked turkey
2 teaspoons tomato paste
2 teaspoons soy sauce
$1\frac{1}{2}$ cups grated carrot

Heat the oil and half the water, then carefully add the vinegar, sugar and salt to taste. Bring to a boil.

Mix the cornstarch with the rest of the water and blend into the sauce. Bring back to a boil, stirring constantly, and cook for 2 to 3 minutes.

Add the cooked turkey, tomato paste, soy sauce and grated carrot and reheat carefully to boiling point. Simmer for 5 minutes. SERVES 4

Pheasant Vallée d'Auge

Diana Jaggar

1 tablespoon oil
$\frac{1}{4}$ cup butter
1 plump ready-to-cook pheasant
$\frac{1}{2}$ cup Calvados or applejack
1 onion, thinly sliced
2 stalks celery, thinly sliced
$\frac{1}{2}$ lb tart apples, peeled and sliced
$1\frac{1}{2}$ tablespoons flour
$\frac{1}{2}$ cup dry white wine
$1\frac{1}{4}$ cups chicken broth
salt and pepper
$\frac{1}{2}$ cup heavy cream

Heat the oil and 2 tablespoons of the butter in a skillet and cook the bird, turning occasionally, until browned. Add and ignite the Calvados. Transfer the pheasant to a flameproof casserole. Cook the onion in the remaining butter for 5 minutes. Add the celery and apple, cook for 5 minutes, then stir in the flour, wine and broth. Bring to a boil, stirring, season and pour over the pheasant. Cover and simmer for 45 to 50 minutes.

Lift the pheasant onto a serving dish and keep it hot. Process the sauce, skimmed of fat, until smooth, bring to a boil, whisk in the cream and heat without boiling. Season and serve with the pheasant. SERVES 4 TO 6

Pheasant Casserole with Chestnuts

Diana Jaggar

1 tablespoon oil
2 tablespoons butter
1 plump ready-to-cook pheasant
$\frac{1}{2}$ lb pearl onions, peeled
$\frac{1}{2}$ lb fresh chestnuts, peeled
2 tablespoons flour
2 cups chicken broth
$\frac{1}{2}$ cup red wine
grated rind and juice of 1 orange
2 teaspoons currant jelly
bay leaf
salt and pepper

Heat the oil and butter in a skillet and brown the bird. Cut it into portions and place in an ovenproof casserole. Cook the onions and chestnuts in the skillet until golden, then transfer to the casserole. Put the flour in the skillet and cook for 1 minute before whisking in the broth, wine, orange rind and juice, and the currant jelly. Bring to a boil, stirring, and add the bay leaf and seasoning. Pour the sauce over the pheasant, cover and cook in a preheated 325° oven for $1\frac{1}{2}$–2 hours. Remove the bay leaf, skim off any fat and adjust the seasoning before serving. SERVES 4 TO 6

Partridge Bourguignonne

—— Diana Jaggar ——

2 ready-to-cook partridges
$\frac{1}{4}$ cup butter
$\frac{1}{2}$ lb lean bacon, cut into strips
$\frac{3}{4}$ cup red wine
1 cup chicken broth
1 teaspoon tomato paste
bouquet garni
salt and pepper
$\frac{3}{4}$ lb pearl onions, peeled
1 clove garlic, crushed
$\frac{1}{2}$ lb button mushrooms
1 tablespoon chopped parsley

Brown the birds in 2 tablespoons of the butter. Transfer to an ovenproof casserole. Brown the bacon, add the wine, broth and tomato paste; boil. Pour into the casserole, adding the bouquet garni and seasoning. Cover and cook in a preheated 350° oven for 30 minutes.

Brown the onions and garlic in the remaining butter. Stir in the mushrooms, add the mixture to the casserole with the parsley and cook for a further 30 minutes.

Cut each bird in half, remove the backbone and trim the bones; place in a serving dish. Season the sauce and spoon over the birds. SERVES 4

Casseroled Grouse

—— Julia Roles ——

4 grouse, trussed
salt and pepper
2 tablespoons butter
2 tablespoons olive oil
6 shallots, roughly chopped
2 stalks celery, chopped
2 cloves garlic, crushed
1–2 tablespoons flour
$1\frac{1}{4}$ cups beef broth
$1\frac{1}{4}$ cups red wine
8 juniper berries, crushed
2 teaspoons chopped fresh marjoram *or*
1 teaspoon dried marjoram
$\frac{1}{2}$ lb button mushrooms

Season the grouse and brown them in the butter and oil in a flameproof casserole. Remove the birds from the casserole. Cook the shallots, celery and garlic in the remaining fat, then add the flour. Brown lightly, then blend in the broth and wine, and boil, stirring constantly.

Replace the grouse and stir in the juniper berries and marjoram. Season, cover and cook in a preheated 350° oven for 1 hour. Add the mushrooms and cook for 30 minutes longer. SERVES 4

Guinea Fowl with Cream, Rosemary and Brandy Sauce

Elizabeth Pomeroy

1 guinea fowl
rosemary sprig
bay leaf
2½ cups water
1 chicken bouillon cube
5 tablespoons butter
1 medium-size onion, chopped
¼ lb button mushrooms
¼ cup brandy
2 teaspoons flour
¾ cup light cream
1 teaspoon finely chopped fresh rosemary *or*
½ teaspoon dried rosemary
GARNISH
lemon slices
rosemary sprigs

Cut the guinea fowl in half down the backbone. Put the giblets in a saucepan with the rosemary sprig, bay leaf and water. Crumble in the bouillon cube, cover and simmer until required.

Melt ¼ cup of the butter in a flameproof casserole, add the onion and mushrooms and fry gently until softened. Put the bird in the casserole and fry briskly until golden brown all over. Warm and ignite half the brandy, pour over the bird and shake the casserole. Add the strained giblet stock, bring to a boil, cover and simmer gently on top of the stove or in a preheated 325° oven for 45 to 60 minutes or until tender. Remove the guinea fowl.

Cream the remaining butter and flour together. Divide into little pieces and whisk them into the cooking liquid. Cook gently, stirring, until thickened to a sauce. Mix the cream, remaining brandy and a little of the sauce and blend this back into the casserole. Season and add the chopped rosemary. Replace the bird, heat without boiling and serve, garnished with lemon slices and rosemary sprigs. SERVES 2

Meat Dishes

These meat recipes, ranging from simple Curried Minced Lamb to expensive Beef Wellington, are intended to inspire you to experiment with the cheaper cuts of meat as well as to attempt an elaborate dinner party dish.

Pasta and Pepper Casserole, Orange-glazed Cutlets and
Pork and Apricot Kabobs

Pork and Apricot Kabobs

— Bridget Jones —

(ILLUSTRATED ON PREVIOUS PAGE)

1 lb lean boneless pork
1 (16-oz) can apricot halves
2 green peppers, seeded
16 bay leaves
salt and pepper
1 tablespoon chopped rosemary
2 tablespoons oil
1 teaspoon prepared mustard

Cut the pork into neat cubes. Drain the apricot halves and reserve the juice. Cut the peppers into eighths. Thread the meat, apricots, peppers and bay leaves onto eight metal skewers.

Mix the syrup from the fruit with seasoning to taste, the rosemary, oil and mustard and brush the kabobs generously with this mixture. Cook under a hot broiler, turning the skewers frequently, until the meat is well browned and cooked through. Brush frequently with the liquid mixture during cooking.

Heat the remaining liquid in a small saucepan and boil rapidly to reduce to a small amount of glaze. Pour this over the kabobs and serve them on a salad or on a bed of cooked rice. SERVES 4

Beef and Walnut Cobbler

— Jill Spencer —

1½ lb chuck steak, cubed
2¼ cups flour
salt and pepper
½ cup margarine
2 onions, sliced
1 green pepper, seeded and sliced
1 clove garlic, crushed
2 cups beef broth
2 tablespoons tomato paste
½ teaspoon baking soda
1 teaspoon cream of tartar
1 egg, beaten
½ cup milk
¼ cup chopped walnuts

Toss the meat in ¼ cup of the flour and plenty of seasoning. Melt half the margarine in a flameproof casserole and cook the vegetables and garlic in it for 5 minutes. Remove and reserve the vegetables, then add the meat and cook until browned. Replace the vegetables, add seasoning, broth and the tomato paste. Cover and cook in a preheated 375° oven for 1½ hours.

Place the remaining flour and margarine, a pinch of salt, the baking soda, cream of tartar, egg and milk in the bowl of a food mixer and switch on to a slow speed to make a soft dough. Knead lightly, roll out and cut out 2 in circles. Place these, overlapping, on top of the meat, glaze with a little egg or milk and sprinkle with the walnuts. Return to a 425° oven and bake for 20 to 25 minutes. Garnish with parsley before serving. SERVES 4 TO 6

Orange-glazed Chops

— Bridget Jones —

(ILLUSTRATED ON PREVIOUS PAGE)

8 lamb rib chops
grated rind and juice of 1 large orange
2 tablespoons oil
1 clove garlic, crushed
salt and pepper
dash of Worcestershire sauce
1 tablespoon light brown sugar
GARNISH
orange slices
watercress

Trim any excess fat off the chops and place them in a foil-lined broiler pan. Mix the orange rind and juice with the oil, garlic, seasoning, Worcestershire sauce and sugar. Brush the lamb generously with this mixture and cook under a hot broiler, brushing frequently with the glaze, until browned on top. Turn the chops, glaze them and cook until the second side is browned and the meat is cooked to taste.

Arrange the chops on a heated serving dish and serve immediately, garnished with whole or halved orange slices and watercress. SERVES 4

Beef Wellington

Diana Jaggar

2½ lb whole beef fillet, trimmed
2 tablespoons brandy
1 clove garlic, cut in half
salt and pepper
¼ cup butter
½ lb onions, finely chopped
½ lb mushrooms, finely chopped
3 slices cooked ham, cut in half
1 (12-oz) package frozen puff pastry,
thawed
beaten egg for glazing

Marinate the fillet in the brandy for a few hours. Rub the meat with the garlic and season with pepper. Brown the fillet all over in the butter, cover with the brandy marinade and ignite. Remove the beef and cool. Add the onions and mushrooms to the fat and fry until soft. Season and cool. Cut the fillet two-thirds through into six portions. Sandwich the folded ham into the cuts.

Roll out the pastry to a large rectangle. Spread with the mushroom mixture and lay the fillet on top, cut side down. Make into a neat parcel and seal the edges.

Place a piece of greased parchment paper on a baking sheet. Lift the beef onto the paper with the folds underneath. Glaze and score the pastry. Use any pastry trimmings to make leaves. Bake in a preheated 450° oven for 30 to 40 minutes until browned. SERVES 6

Sweet and Sour Meatballs

Moya Maynard

½ lb ground beef
½ lb bulk sausage meat
½ cup grated onion
½ teaspoon dried mixed herbs
salt and pepper
2 tablespoons oil
1 carrot, peeled and cut into small strips
2 cups beef broth
¼ cup malt vinegar
½ cup firmly packed light brown sugar
4 teaspoons cornstarch
1 teaspoon soy sauce

Mix the first five ingredients, then form into 18 to 20 balls. Fry in the oil for 15 to 20 minutes and drain. Cook the carrot, broth, vinegar and sugar in a saucepan for 5 minutes. Blend the cornstarch with the soy sauce and a little water, stir in some of the hot liquid, return to the pan and boil, stirring. Serve the meatballs on noodles and pour the sauce on top. SERVES 4

Hungarian Goulash

Julia Roles

3 tablespoons oil
1½–2 lb chuck steak, cubed
3 onions, sliced
1 sweet red pepper, seeded and chopped
2 tablespoons flour
2 tablespoons paprika
1 lb tomatoes, peeled and chopped
2½ cups beef broth
bouquet garni
1 teaspoon dried thyme
salt
½ cup sour cream
parsley sprigs for garnish

Heat the oil in a flameproof casserole, add the meat and cook until browned all over, then remove from the pan.

Lower the heat and cook the onions and red pepper in the fat remaining in the casserole. When they are softened sprinkle in the flour and paprika, then cook, stirring, for 1 minute. Add the tomatoes and broth and bring to simmering point, stirring continuously. Return the meat to the casserole, add the bouquet garni and thyme and season with salt. Cover the casserole and place in a preheated 325° oven to cook for 2½ to 3 hours.

Remove the bouquet garni from the goulash before serving. Spoon a little of the sour cream on top of the goulash and garnish with the parsley. Serve the remaining sour cream separately. SERVES 4

Beef Brazilian Style

Julia Roles

2 lb chuck steak, cut in strips
3 tablespoons oil
3 onions, sliced into rings
1 clove garlic, crushed
2 tablespoons flour
¾ cup black coffee
¾ cup beef broth or red wine
1 (16-oz) can peeled tomatoes
salt and pepper
pinch of grated nutmeg
2 teaspoons brown sugar

Fry the meat in the oil, lower the heat, add the onions and garlic and cook until soft. Stir in the flour and cook for 1 minute. Gradually mix in the coffee and broth or wine, then add the tomatoes. Season, add the nutmeg and brown sugar, bring to simmering point and transfer to an ovenproof casserole. Cook, covered, in a preheated 325° oven for 2 hours. SERVES 4

Boeuf à la Provençale

Julia Roles

2 lb lean chuck steak
3 tablespoons olive oil
$\frac{1}{2}$ lb slab bacon, chopped
$\frac{1}{2}$ lb pearl onions, peeled
$\frac{1}{2}$ lb carrots, sliced
2 tablespoons tomato paste
3 cloves garlic, crushed
$1\frac{1}{4}$ cups red wine
$1\frac{1}{4}$ cups beef broth
bouquet garni
pinch of dried thyme
salt and pepper
1 lb tomatoes, peeled and chopped
$\frac{2}{3}$ cup ripe olives, pitted
2 tablespoons butter
2 tablespoons flour
GARNISH
chopped parsley
triangles of fried bread

Cut the beef into 1-in cubes. Heat the oil in a flameproof casserole and add the beef, then fry until brown and remove from the pan. Add the bacon, onions and carrots and cook for 5 minutes. Stir in the tomato paste, garlic, wine, broth, bouquet garni, thyme and seasoning, then bring to a boil.

Return the meat to the casserole, cover and cook in a preheated 300° oven for $1\frac{1}{2}$ hours. Add the tomatoes and olives and cook for a further hour. Blend the butter into the flour and gradually whisk into the casserole, a little at a time. Heat through but do not boil. Garnish with chopped parsley and triangles of fried bread before serving. SERVES 4 TO 6

Beef Loaf

Moya Maynard

$\frac{1}{2}$ cup beef broth
$1\frac{1}{2}$ cups soft brown bread crumbs
1 lb lean ground beef
$\frac{1}{2}$ cup finely chopped onion
$\frac{1}{4}$ teaspoon dried thyme
$\frac{1}{4}$ cup dried milk powder
1 egg, well beaten
2 teaspoons tomato paste
1 tablespoon chopped parsley
1 teaspoon Worcestershire sauce

Mix all the ingredients and shape the mixture into a loaf in the center of a large piece of foil. Thoroughly seal the edges of the foil over the loaf. Put the parcel in a pan half filled with water and cook in a preheated 400° oven for 1 to $1\frac{1}{4}$ hours. Open the foil and drain off any liquid, then leave to cool in the foil. Serve with salad ingredients. SERVES 6 TO 8

Beef and Bacon Suet Roll

Audrey Ellis

2 cups self-rising flour
salt and pepper
$\frac{1}{4}$ lb ($\frac{1}{2}$ cup) shredded beef suet
about 1 cup water
$\frac{1}{2}$ lb chuck steak, chopped
$\frac{1}{4}$ lb slab bacon, chopped
1 tablespoon chopped parsley

Sift the flour and 1 teaspoon salt into a bowl, stir in the suet and add sufficient water to make a soft dough. Turn out onto a floured surface and knead lightly until smooth. Then roll out to a rectangle about 10 × 12 in.

Mix the beef with the bacon and parsley, and sprinkle with pepper. Spread this filling over the pastry, leaving a narrow rim all around the edge. Dampen the edges and roll up like a jelly roll, pressing the pastry together to seal the filling in.

Wrap the roll in greased foil, allowing room for the pastry to expand and sealing the edges of the foil to make a watertight parcel. Place in a large saucepan and add boiling water to come halfway up the sides of the roll. Cover the pan and boil gently for 2 hours, adding more boiling water to the pan during this time if necessary.

Lift the package out of the saucepan and carefully remove the foil. Serve immediately. SERVES 4

Beef and Parsnip Pie

Jane Todd

1 tablespoon oil
1 onion, chopped
2 carrots, chopped
1 lb ground beef
2 tomatoes, peeled and sliced
salt and pepper
$\frac{1}{2}$ cup beef broth
2 lb parsnips
$\frac{1}{4}$ cup butter
2 tablespoons milk
TOPPING
3 tablespoons soft white bread crumbs
$\frac{1}{4}$ cup grated cheese

Heat the oil in a pan and cook the onion in it until softened. Stir in the carrots and beef and cook, stirring, until the beef is lightly browned. Add the tomatoes, seasoning and broth, bring to a boil and simmer gently for 15 minutes.

Meanwhile, peel the parsnips and cook in boiling salted water for 20 to 25 minutes, until tender. Drain, then mash until smooth. Beat in the butter, milk and a generous amount of black pepper.

Spread half the parsnips in the bottom and up the sides of a greased ovenproof dish. Spoon in the beef mixture and spread the remaining parsnips over the top. Sprinkle the surface with a mixture of the bread crumbs and cheese and bake in a preheated 375° oven for 30 to 35 minutes. SERVES 4

Pasta and Pepper Casserole

— Carol Bowen —

2 lb beef for stew
$\frac{1}{4}$ cup lard or shortening
2 medium-size onions, chopped
2 teaspoons ground ginger
2 teaspoons soy sauce
5 cups beef broth
$\frac{1}{4}$ cup chopped parsley
salt and pepper
grated rind of 1 large lemon
$\frac{3}{4}$ lb pasta bows or rigatoni
1(16-oz) can pimientos, drained and sliced
chopped parsley for garnish

Cut the beef into bite-sized pieces. Melt the lard in a large skillet, add the onions and beef and fry until browned on all sides. Transfer to a large flameproof casserole. Add the ginger, soy sauce, beef broth and parsley, then season generously and bring to a boil. Reduce the heat and simmer gently for about $1\frac{1}{2}$ hours or until the meat is tender.

Add the lemon rind, pasta and pimientos, then cook gently for a further 15 minutes until the pasta is tender and the excess liquid has been absorbed. Adjust the seasoning, if necessary, before serving sprinkled with chopped parsley. SERVES 6

Shepherd's Pie with Cheesy Potato Topping

— Carol Bowen —

1 tablespoon butter
2 tablespoons oil
1 medium-size onion, finely chopped
1 lb roast beef, ground
$\frac{3}{4}$ cup rich beef gravy
2 teaspoons Worcestershire sauce
1 tablespoon chopped parsley
$\frac{1}{4}$ teaspoon dried mixed herbs
salt and pepper
TOPPING
6 tablespoons heavy cream
3 tablespoons butter, melted
2 eggs, lightly beaten
2 lb potatoes, boiled and mashed
$\frac{3}{4}$ cup grated Cheddar cheese

Grease a deep 7-cup ovenproof dish with the butter. Heat the oil in a saucepan, add the onion and cook for 5 minutes. Stir in the beef, gravy, Worcestershire sauce, parsley, herbs and seasoning to taste. Transfer to the ovenproof dish.

For the topping, beat the cream, 2 tablespoons of the butter and the eggs into the hot mashed potato. Add the cheese, mix to blend and season to taste. Pipe or spoon the mashed potato on top of the meat mixture and brush with the remaining melted butter.

Bake in a preheated 400° oven for 20 to 25 minutes until golden brown. SERVES 4 TO 6

Veal and Orange Casserole

Julia Roles

2 lb veal for stew, trimmed and cubed
salt and pepper
flour for coating
2 tablespoons butter
1 tablespoon oil
2 onions, sliced
3 carrots, sliced (optional)
2 cloves garlic, crushed
$1\frac{1}{4}$ cups chicken broth
juice of 4 oranges
1 teaspoon lemon juice
1–2 teaspoons arrowroot (optional)
GARNISH
1 tablespoon grated orange rind
chopped parsley

Coat the meat in seasoned flour. Heat the butter and oil in a flameproof casserole and add the veal, onions, carrots, if used, and garlic, then cook gently for 5 minutes. Drain off any excess fat and pour in the broth mixed with the orange and lemon juice. Bring to a boil, cover and cook in a preheated 350° oven for $1\frac{1}{2}$ hours.

The liquid can be thickened with the arrowroot mixed to a paste with a little water. Add the blended arrowroot to the casserole and stir over a gentle heat until the sauce thickens. Garnish with grated orange rind and chopped parsley before serving. SERVES 4 TO 6

Veal with Capers

Moya Maynard

4 veal cutlets
a little seasoned flour
$\frac{1}{4}$ cup butter
juice of $\frac{1}{2}$ lemon
2 tablespoons capers
GARNISH
anchovy fillets, curled
chopped parsley
lemon butterflies

Place the veal between sheets of wax paper and beat it flat. Coat each piece of veal with seasoned flour.

Melt the butter in a skillet and cook the veal on both sides for about 10 minutes. Remove and keep hot. Add the lemon juice and capers to the pan, heat through and spoon over the veal. Garnish with curled anchovy fillets, chopped parsley and lemon butterflies. SERVES 4

Apricot-stuffed Lamb

———— Carol Bowen ————

1 (4-lb) shoulder of lamb, boned
salt and pepper
2 tablespoons drippings or lard
1 onion, sliced
1 carrot, sliced
bay leaf
$1\frac{1}{4}$ cups chicken broth
STUFFING
1 cup soft white bread crumbs
pinch of dried thyme
$\frac{1}{4}$ cup chopped walnuts
1 tablespoon oil
1 small onion, chopped
1 (8-oz) can apricots
1 egg, beaten

Season the lamb generously and set aside while preparing the stuffing.

To make the stuffing, place the bread crumbs, thyme and walnuts in a bowl. Heat the oil in a small saucepan, then add the onion and cook for about 5 minutes, until soft but not brown. Add to the bread crumb mixture. Drain and coarsely chop the apricots and stir into the stuffing mixture. Season to taste and bind with sufficient beaten egg to make a moist stuffing. Spoon the stuffing along the shoulder and tie it into a long neat shape.

Melt the dripping or lard in a flameproof casserole, add the meat and brown it on all sides. Add the sliced onion, carrot and bay leaf. Pour in the broth and bring to a boil. Cover and cook in a preheated 350° oven for $1\frac{1}{2}$ hours, or until cooked.

Carve the meat and serve with the sieved cooking juices poured over the slices. SERVES 6

Lamb Bourguignonne

———— Carol Bowen ————

$2\frac{1}{2}$ lb boneless lean lamb
$\frac{3}{4}$ lb pearl onions, peeled
3 tablespoons oil
$\frac{1}{4}$ cup butter or margarine
$\frac{1}{2}$ lb button mushrooms
1 cup dry red wine
$1\frac{1}{4}$ cups beef broth
$\frac{1}{2}$ teaspoon salt
pepper
1 tablespoon arrowroot
1 tablespoon water
GARNISH
chopped parsley
croûtons (see page 17)

Cut the meat into bite-sized pieces. Blanch the onions in boiling water for 2 minutes, then drain.

Heat the oil in a large deep skillet. Add the butter or margarine and, when foaming, add the meat and brown quickly on all sides. Remove with a slotted spoon and set aside. Add the onions to the pan and brown evenly. Remove with a slotted spoon and mix with the lamb. Finally fry the mushrooms in the pan juices. Return the lamb and onions to the pan. Stir in the wine, broth and seasoning. Bring to a boil, then transfer to a flameproof casserole. Cover and cook in a preheated 325° oven for about $1\frac{1}{2}$ hours or until the meat is cooked. Remove the casserole from the oven.

Dissolve the arrowroot in the water, add slowly to the casserole and cook for a further 5 minutes over a gentle heat, or until the liquid is clear and thickened. Adjust the seasoning and serve garnished with chopped parsley and fried bread croûtons. SERVES 6

Curried Ground Lamb

— Jane Todd —

1 tablespoon oil
2 onions, sliced
2 cloves garlic, crushed
1 tablespoon curry powder
1½ lb ground lamb
½ teaspoon turmeric
pinch each of ground ginger, paprika and cayenne
salt and pepper
1¼ cups plain yogurt

Heat the oil in a flameproof casserole and cook the onions and garlic in it until softened. Stir in the curry powder and cook, stirring, for 2 to 3 minutes. Add the lamb and cook, again stirring, until evenly browned. Add the spices and seasoning and stir in the yogurt, then cover the casserole and simmer for about 1 hour, until cooked.

Serve with rice and a selection of traditional curry side dishes – tomato and onion slices, salted peanuts, chutney and banana slices sprinkled with lemon juice. SERVES 6

Lamb Patties

— Jane Todd —

6 slices white bread
3 tablespoons milk
3 tablespoons oil
1 onion, chopped
1 clove garlic, crushed
1¼ lb ground lamb
2 tablespoons chopped parsley
pinch of dried rosemary
salt and pepper
1 egg, lightly beaten
12 slices bacon
¼ cup butter

Use a 2-in cutter to cut out twelve rounds from the slices of bread. Discard the crusts, break up the bread trimmings and place them in a bowl. Pour in the milk and leave to soak. Keep the bread rounds to one side.

Heat 1 tablespoon· of the oil in a skillet and cook the onion and garlic in it for about 10 minutes, until softened and golden brown. Mix the lamb, parsley, rosemary and cooked onion, season well and bind the ingredients with the beaten egg and soaked bread.

Stretch the bacon slices with the blade of a knife until they are long and thin. Using floured hands, divide the lamb mixture into twelve equal portions. Shape each portion into a ball, then flatten and shape the meat into patties measuring 2 in. in diameter. Wrap a stretched bacon slice around each patty and secure with a piece of thread or a wooden toothpick. Heat the remaining oil in a large skillet and fry the patties over a low heat for about 15 minutes on each side. Meanwhile melt the butter in a

separate skillet and fry the bread rounds for 2 to 3 minutes on each side, until crisp and brown.

To serve, arrange the bread croûtes on a serving dish. Remove the thread or toothpicks from the patties and place each one on a croûte. Serve immediately. SERVES 6

Lamb Pasties

— Jane Todd —

½ lb ground lamb
4 scallions, chopped
1 carrot, grated
pinch of dried rosemary
salt and pepper
PIE PASTRY
2 cups flour
¼ teaspoon salt
½ cup lard *or* ¼ cup lard and ¼ cup margarine
about ⅓ cup water
beaten egg for glazing

Mix the lamb, scallions, carrot and rosemary with plenty of seasoning.

To make the pastry, sift the flour and salt into a bowl. Rub in the lard or lard and margarine until the mixture resembles fine bread crumbs, then add the water and mix to make a firm dough. Wrap the dough in plastic wrap and chill for 30 minutes.

Roll out the dough on a lightly floured surface and cut out four 7-in rounds. Divide the filling between the rounds, placing it in the center of each. Dampen the edges and bring them together at the top to form a pasty. Press the edges together well and crimp them between your fingers. Place the pasties on a greased baking sheet and brush with beaten egg. Bake in a preheated 425° oven for 15 minutes, then lower the temperature to 350° and bake for a further 15 to 20 minutes, until well browned. Serve hot or cold. SERVES 4

Porc Rôti à l'Orange

Diana Jaggar

2 small (6 bone) loins of pork, skinned
2 tablespoons butter · 1 onion, finely chopped
2 stalks celery, finely chopped
2 cups soft white bread crumbs
grated rind of 1 orange
$\frac{1}{3}$ cup raisins
2 teaspoons chopped parsley
salt and pepper
juice of 2 oranges and $\frac{1}{2}$ lemon
$\frac{1}{3}$ cup firmly packed brown sugar
1 tablespoon Worcestershire sauce
$\frac{1}{2}$ cup each white wine and chicken broth
2 oranges, sliced and fried in butter for
garnish

Ask the meatmean to trim the loins and make them into a guard of honor. Melt the butter in a saucepan, add the onion and celery and cook until the onion is soft. Remove the pan from the heat and stir in the bread crumbs, orange rind, raisins, parsley, salt and pepper, and mix well. Bind the ingredients together with the orange juice. Stand the guard of honor in a roasting pan and spoon the stuffing into the middle.

Bring the sugar, any remaining orange juice, lemon juice and Worcestershire sauce to a boil. Spoon over the meat and roast in a preheated 375° oven for about 2 hours, basting regularly.

Transfer the cooked pork to a serving dish, place chop frills on the bone ends and keep hot. Skim any fat from the juices in the pan, then add the wine and broth. Bring to a boil, season and serve this sauce with the pork. Arrange the halved fried orange slices around the meat. SERVES 6

Broiled Ham with Marmalade Sauce

Moya Maynard

4 medium-size ham steaks, trimmed
a little oil
1 small onion, chopped
$\frac{1}{4}$ cup marmalade
2 teaspoons white wine vinegar
2 teaspoons light brown sugar

Brush the ham steaks with oil and place them under a preheated broiler. Cook gently for 10 to 15 minutes, turning once.

Place the onion in a small saucepan with 1 teaspoon oil, then cook without browning for 5 minutes. Stir in the remaining ingredients, heat gently to dissolve, then boil to reduce. Pour over the ham and serve. SERVES 4

Pork Ragoût

Julia Roles

2 lb pork for stew
2 onions, sliced · $\frac{1}{2}$ lb baby carrots
bay leaf
2 teaspoons chopped fresh sage *or* 1 teaspoon
dried sage
1 tablespoon flour
$\frac{3}{4}$ cup chicken broth
1 (16-oz) can peeled tomatoes
salt and pepper
1 lb fresh peas, shelled
6 medium-size potatoes, peeled and quartered
1 teaspoon sugar

Cut the meat into strips, removing any excess fat. Fry the strips in a dry heavy-based skillet over medium heat until brown. Transfer to a large ovenproof casserole.

Cook the onions in the pork fat until soft, then add to the casserole, together with the carrots and herbs. Sprinkle the flour into the fat remaining in the pan and cook for 1 minute, stirring all the time. Gradually blend in the broth and tomatoes and bring to a boil, stirring. Season then pour over the meat. Cover and cook in a preheated 325° oven for $1\frac{1}{4}$ hours.

Add the peas, potatoes and sugar. Re-cover the casserole and return it to the oven to cook for a further 45 minutes or until the peas and potatoes are tender. Remove the bay leaf before serving. SERVES 6

Pork au Porto

Julia Roles

$1\frac{1}{2}$ lb pork tenderloin
salt and pepper · $\frac{1}{4}$ cup flour
2 tablespoons butter · 2 onions, chopped
1 tablespoon Worcestershire sauce
1 tablespoon mushroom ketchup
2 tablespoons currant jelly
2 tablespoons tomato paste
$\frac{1}{4}$ cup port wine
$\frac{1}{4}$ cup heavy cream
chopped parsley for garnish

Remove the outer skin from the pork and cut it into 1-in slices, then coat the meat with seasoned flour. Melt the butter in a skillet, add the pork and cook in the butter until golden. Transfer the meat to an ovenproof casserole. Cook the onions in the butter remaining in the skillet until soft, then transfer them to the casserole with the meat.

Mix all the remaining ingredients, except the cream, and pour over the pork and onions. Cover and cook in a preheated 350° oven for 30 to 40 minutes or until the meat is tender. Serve, topped with the cream and chopped parsley. SERVES 4

Pork Chops Pizzaiola

— Carol Bowen —

1 teaspoon salt
1 teaspoon freshly ground black pepper
6 pork loin chops, cut $\frac{3}{4}$ in thick
3 tablespoons oil
2 cloves garlic, crushed
1 teaspoon dried basil
1 teaspoon dried thyme
bay leaf
$\frac{1}{3}$ cup dry red wine or beef broth
1 (16-oz) can peeled tomatoes, drained
and finely chopped
2 tablespoons tomato paste
3 tablespoons butter
3 medium-size green peppers, seeded and
finely chopped
1 medium-size onion, sliced in rings
$\frac{1}{2}$ lb button mushrooms (optional)
$4\frac{1}{2}$ teaspoons cornstarch

Rub the salt and pepper into both sides of the pork chops. Set aside.

Heat the oil in a large skillet with a lid, add the chops and brown for 3 minutes on each side. Remove and set aside.

Add the garlic, basil, thyme and bay leaf to the pan. Pour in the wine or broth and bring to a boil, then stir in the tomatoes and tomato paste. Return the chops to the pan and baste them thoroughly with the sauce. Cover the pan and simmer for 40 minutes, basting the chops from time to time.

Meanwhile, melt the butter in a separate skillet and add the peppers and onion. Cook, stirring occasionally, for 5 to 10 minutes. Add the mushrooms, if used, and cook for a further 2 to 3 minutes. Add these vegetables to the pork chop mixture and continue to cook, uncovered, for a further 15 minutes.

To serve, remove the pork chops from the pan and place them in a warmed serving dish. Thicken the sauce with the cornstarch, blended with a little water, and pour over the pork chops. Serve with boiled noodles. SERVES 6

Roast Pork with Apple and Nut Stuffing

— Carol Bowen —

2 tablespoons butter
1 small onion, chopped
$\frac{1}{2}$ cup coarsely chopped cashew nuts
$1\frac{1}{2}$ cups diced crustless white bread
1 tart apple, peeled, cored and diced
1 stalk celery, chopped
2 teaspoons chopped parsley
salt and pepper
2 teaspoons lemon juice
1 ($3\frac{1}{2}$-lb) loin of pork, boned
2–3 tablespoons oil
$\frac{3}{4}$ cup hard cider

Melt the butter in a small pan and fry the onion and nuts until they are lightly browned, about 5 minutes. Add the bread, apple, celery and parsley. Continue to cook for about 5 minutes or until the apple softens, then season to taste and stir in the lemon juice.

Place the stuffing in the pork loin. Roll up and secure with string. Place the meat in a greased roasting pan, brush with the oil and sprinkle with salt. Roast in a preheated 400° oven for 20 to 30 minutes, then reduce the oven temperature to 350° and cook for a further $1\frac{1}{2}$ hours.

Transfer the pork to a warmed serving dish and keep hot. Skim any fat from the meat juices in the roasting pan, add the cider and bring to a boil. Simmer for 5 minutes, stirring well to incorporate any meat residue. Season to taste and serve with the pork. SERVES 6

Wholewheat Sausage Pie

Carol Bowen

WHOLEWHEAT PASTRY
2 cups wholewheat flour
pinch of salt
$\frac{1}{4}$ cup butter or margarine
$\frac{1}{4}$ cup lard or shortening
5–6 tablespoons cold water
beaten egg or milk for glazing
FILLING
$\frac{3}{4}$ lb bulk pork sausage meat
1 small onion, finely chopped
3 tablespoons soft white bread crumbs
1 teaspoon dried mixed herbs
2 tomatoes, peeled and chopped
2 hard-cooked eggs, shelled

To make the pasty, mix the flour with the salt in a bowl. Rub the butter or margarine and lard into the flour until the mixture resembles fine bread crumbs. Add the water and mix to a firm but workable dough. Roll out two thirds of the pastry on a lightly floured surface and use to line a 5 × 3-in loaf pan.

Prepare the filling by mixing the sausage meat, onion, bread crumbs, herbs and tomatoes together. Place half this mixture in the pan. Arrange the two hard-cooked eggs along the center and cover with the remaining sausage meat mixture.

Roll out the remaining pastry to form a lid. Dampen the edge of the pastry with water and cover the pie with the pastry lid. Trim and flute the edges. Use any pastry trimmings to make leaves to decorate the top of the pie. Make a small hole in the center to allow any steam to escape. Brush with beaten egg or milk.

Bake in a preheated 375° oven for 1 hour or until cooked. Serve cold with salad. SERVES 6

Baked Pork Chops with Apple and Sage Stuffing

Elizabeth Pomeroy

4 loin pork chops
$\frac{1}{4}$ cup lard or butter
$\frac{1}{2}$ cup hard cider or dry white wine
STUFFING
2 slices bread
1 medium-size tart apple
$\frac{1}{4}$ cup butter or margarine
1 tablespoon finely chopped onion
1 tablespoon finely chopped celery
2 tablespoons chopped salted peanuts
2 teaspoons finely chopped fresh sage *or*
1 teaspoon dried sage
freshly ground pepper
lemon juice to taste
GARNISH
fresh sage sprigs
watercress sprigs

Trim most of the fat off the chops. Cut a large gash from the rind of each chop down to the bone to make a pocket.

For the stuffing, remove the crusts from the bread and cut the slices into dice. Peel, core and dice the apple. Melt the butter or margarine in a small saucepan and add the onion, celery and apple, then fry these until softened. Add the nuts and the bread and continue cooking, stirring, until the apple is softened. Mix in the chopped sage and season with pepper and lemon juice.

Pack the stuffing into the pockets in the chops and secure with small skewers or wooden toothpicks. Melt the lard or butter in a shallow flameproof casserole or skillet and add the chops. Seal them on both sides, then when they are nicely browned, arrange them in an ovenproof gratin dish. Add the cider or wine and bake in a preheated 350° oven for 45 to 50 minutes or until tender. Remove the skewers or toothpicks and garnish with sprigs of fresh sage and watercress. Serve with baked potatoes. SERVES 4

Note: Veal chops can be stuffed and cooked in the same way as the pork chops in this recipe.

Glazed Ham

— Audrey Ellis —

1 (4-lb) piece boneless country ham
5 cups water
1 large onion, quartered
bay leaf
6 peppercorns
GLAZE
$\frac{1}{2}$ cup firmly packed brown sugar
2 teaspoons dry mustard
cloves

Soak the ham overnight in cold water to cover. Next day, drain and discard the water and place the ham in a saucepan with the 5 cups water, the quartered onion, bay leaf and peppercorns. Cover the pan and bring to a boil, then reduce the heat and simmer for $1\frac{1}{2}$ hours.

Remove the ham from the cooking liquid and cut off the skin. Mark the fat into diamond shapes with a sharp knife and place in a roasting pan. Mix the sugar and the mustard together and press onto the fat. Stick a clove in the center of each diamond.

Bake the ham in a preheated 425° oven for about 15 minutes or until the fat is crisp and golden. Serve with beans and carrots, if liked. SERVES 8

Ham and Split Pea Stew

— Audrey Ellis —

1 cup dried split peas
small unsmoked ham hock
$\frac{1}{4}$ cup butter
2 onions, chopped
2 carrots, chopped
5 cups chicken broth
chopped parsley
pepper
3 frankfurters, halved

Soak the peas and the ham hock separately overnight in cold water to cover. Drain both thoroughly.

Melt the butter in a saucepan, add the chopped onions and carrots and fry gently for 5 minutes. Add the split peas, ham hock, chicken broth, parsley and pepper to taste. Bring to a boil, then reduce the heat and simmer for $1\frac{1}{2}$ hours.

Remove the ham hock, take off and chop any meat. Put this back into the stew with the halved frankfurters. Ladle the stew into individual bowls and serve immediately. SERVES 4

Sausage in Mustard Sauce

Audrey Ellis

4 link pork sausages
4 thick slices lean bacon
2 tablespoons oil
1 onion, sliced
1 tablespoon fine soft bread crumbs
2½ cups Béchamel Sauce (see page 20)
1 tablespoon Dijon-style mustard
juice of ½ lemon
1 tablespoon sugar
¼ lb button mushrooms, sliced
salt and pepper
GARNISH
1 small tomato, sliced
parsley sprigs

Wrap each sausage in a slice of bacon and secure with a wooden toothpick. Broil for 5 minutes on each side.

Heat the oil in a skillet and use to fry the onion gently for 3 minutes. Stir in the bread crumbs. Add the sauce, mustard, lemon juice, sugar, mushrooms and seasoning. Bring to a boil, stirring all the time, and add the bacon and sausage rolls.

Cover and simmer for 20 minutes. Remove the toothpicks from the sausages and serve immediately, garnished with tomato slices and parsley sprigs. SERVES 4

Sausage and Beer Pie

Audrey Ellis

¼ cup butter
1 lb large link pork sausages
¼ lb pearl onions, peeled
3 tablespoons flour
2 cups dark beer
salt and pepper
¼ lb button mushrooms
½ lb puff pastry
beaten egg for glazing
parsley sprig for garnish

Melt the butter in a skillet, add the sausages and fry gently for about 8 minutes, until pale golden. Transfer the sausages to a large baking dish. Add the onions to the fat remaining in the pan and fry until golden, then spoon them over the sausages.

Stir the flour into the remaining pan fat and cook it for 3 minutes. Gradually stir in the beer and season to taste, then bring to a boil, stirring constantly. Add the mushrooms and pour over the sausages.

Roll out the pastry to cover the baking dish. Dampen the rim of the dish and place the pastry lid on top, pressing around the rim to seal. Decorate with pastry trimmings and mark a criss-cross pattern on top with a knife.

Brush with a little beaten egg and bake in a preheated 400° oven for about 30 to 40 minutes until golden and well puffed. Serve immediately, garnished with parsley. SERVES 6

Vegetarian Dishes

Vegetarian main dishes are certainly more interesting than a basic nut roast and here are some recipes to prove it. Try, for example, Italian-style Eggplants, Gougère or Coriander Mushrooms for a deliciously different main course.

Vegetable Curry, Gloucester Pie and
Chick Peas with Peppers

Vegetable Curry

— Bridget Jones —

(ILLUSTRATED ON PREVIOUS PAGE)

2 lb fresh and frozen vegetables, for
example 1 small cauliflower, carrots,
potatoes, eggplant, peppers, zucchini and corn
$\frac{1}{2}$ lb onions
2 tablespoons oil
4 cardamoms
1 cinnamon stick
bay leaf
3 cloves garlic, crushed
2 tablespoons garam masala
$\frac{1}{2}$ teaspoon chili powder
salt and pepper
$1\frac{1}{4}$ cups vegetable stock
2 tablespoons chopped fresh coriander
coriander sprigs for garnish

Prepare your selection of vegetables according to their
type. Finely chop the onions. Heat the oil in a large pan,
add the remaining ingredients, except the stock and
coriander, and cook, stirring continuously, for a few
minutes.

Add the onions to the pan and continue to cook until
they are soft but not browned. Pour in the stock and
bring to a boil, then add the vegetables and cook
gently, covered, until they are tender – about 15 to 20
minutes. Stir in the chopped coriander 5 minutes before
the end of the cooking time, taste and adjust the
seasoning if necessary. Serve garnished with coriander
sprigs. SERVES 4

Chick Peas with Peppers

— Bridget Jones —

(ILLUSTRATED ON PREVIOUS PAGE)

2 tablespoons oil
1 large onion, chopped
1 sweet red pepper, seeded and chopped
1 green pepper, seeded and chopped
1 clove garlic, crushed
salt and pepper
2 (16-oz) cans chick peas, drained
2 tablespoons chopped fresh herbs
a little grated nutmeg

Heat the oil in a saucepan. Add the onion, peppers and
garlic, then sprinkle in seasoning to taste and cook until
the vegetables are softened but not browned.

Stir in the chick peas and cook, covered, over a low
heat until they are heated through. Stir in the herbs and
nutmeg to taste before serving. SERVES 4

Walnut Cheese Dolmas

— Marguerite Patten —

6–8 large, tender cabbage leaves
$\frac{3}{4}$ cup water
salt and pepper
STUFFING
$\frac{1}{3}$ cup cooked long-grain rice or 1 cup soft
wholewheat bread crumbs
$\frac{1}{2}$ cup finely grated Cheddar cheese
$\frac{1}{2}$ cup finely chopped walnuts
1 tablespoon chopped parsley
1 tablespoon chopped chives
2–4 tablespoons margarine, melted
1 egg
CHEESE SAUCE
2 tablespoons butter or margarine
2 tablespoons flour
$1\frac{1}{4}$ cups milk
$\frac{1}{2}$–1 cup grated Cheddar cheese

Wash and drain the cabbage leaves. Bring the water to
a boil and add a little salt and pepper. Put in the
cabbage leaves, boil for $1\frac{1}{2}$ to 2 minutes (just long enough
to soften the leaves) and lift from the liquid. Reserve the
cooking liquid. Cool the leaves slightly and spread each
one flat.

Mix the ingredients for the stuffing, adding salt and
pepper to taste. Divide the stuffing between the leaves,
then fold them to enclose the filling. Put the stuffed
cabbage leaves into an ovenproof casserole with the
cabbage stock, cover tightly and cook in a preheated 325°
oven for 35 to 40 minutes.

Meanwhile make the sauce. Melt the butter or
margarine in a small saucepan, add the flour and cook,
stirring, for a minute. Gradually pour in the milk and
bring to a boil, stirring continuously. Remove the pan
from the heat and stir in the cheese until it melts. Add
seasoning to taste.

Lift the dolmas from the liquid and place them in a
heated serving dish. Top with the cheese sauce and serve
immediately. SERVES 3 TO 4

Italian-style Eggplant

Janet Hunt

2 large eggplants
salt
2 tablespoons oil · 1 egg, beaten
$\frac{1}{4}$ lb mozzarella cheese
TOMATO SAUCE
2 tablespoons oil
2 cloves garlic, crushed
1 lb tomatoes, peeled and chopped *or*
1 (16-oz) can tomatoes
1 teaspoon dried oregano
pinch of brown sugar
salt and pepper
TOPPING
$\frac{1}{2}$ cup grated Parmesan cheese

Wash, trim and slice the eggplants. Lay the slices on a plate and sprinkle them with salt. Leave for 30 minutes, then rinse them thoroughly with fresh water and pat dry.

To make the tomato sauce, heat the oil in a saucepan and add the garlic. Cook for a few minutes, then stir in the remaining ingredients and bring to a boil. Cover and simmer for 15 minutes; process in a food processor or blender until smooth. Set aside.

Heat the oil in a skillet. Dip the eggplant slices in beaten egg and fry them until lightly colored on each side. Slice the mozzarella. Arrange the eggplant, tomato sauce and mozzarella in layers in a small greased ovenproof dish until all the ingredients have been used. Sprinkle the Parmesan cheese over the top and bake for 20 minutes or until the top begins to brown. Serve with a salad made of endive, chicory and lettuce for a fresh, crisp contrast to a rather rich dish. SERVES 4

Variations

This dish can also be prepared using other vegetables instead of the eggplants. Try substituting 2 large bulbs fennel (as illustrated) and make the dish in the same way but omitting the salting process. This is only necessary with eggplant as it removes excess water, making the eggplant easier to cook and more able to retain its shape.

Spanish Rice au Gratin

Audrey Ellis

$\frac{1}{2}$ cup brown rice
$1\frac{1}{4}$ cups water
1 teaspoon salt
1 tablespoon butter
$\frac{1}{2}$ cup chopped onion
1 small green pepper, seeded and chopped
$\frac{1}{2}$ cup chopped celery
1 (8-oz) can peeled tomatoes
1 teaspoon brown sugar
1 teaspoon chili powder (or to taste)
1 cup grated cheese
GARNISH
about 4 ripe olives, pitted
parsley sprigs

Place the rice in a saucepan with the water and salt. Bring to a boil, cover and simmer for 30 minutes.

Meanwhile, melt the butter in a saucepan, add the onion, pepper and celery and cook until soft. Stir in the tomatoes and their liquid, the brown sugar and chili powder. Add the cooked rice and simmer until thick — about 10 minutes.

Transfer the mixture to a greased ovenproof dish and sprinkle the cheese over the top. Bake in a preheated 375° oven for about 30 minutes to melt and lightly brown the cheese. Serve immediately, garnished with the olives and parsley. SERVES 4

Vegetarian Bean Hotpot

Audrey Ellis

$\frac{3}{4}$ cup dried red kidney beans
2 large leeks
2 large carrots, sliced
$\frac{1}{2}$ lb potatoes, sliced
1 onion, chopped
salt and pepper
$1\frac{1}{2}$ cups grated cheese
1 clove garlic, crushed
3 cups vegetable stock
TOPPING
a few slices of French bread
grated cheese
chopped parsley

Soak the kidney beans in cold water to cover overnight, then drain and cook in boiling water for 10 minutes. Drain and set aside. Cut the leeks into rings and rinse well in a colander under running water.

Arrange the beans, leeks, carrots, potatoes and onion in an ovenproof dish. Sprinkle with seasoning and the grated cheese. Stir the crushed garlic into the stock and pour it over the vegetable mixture.

Cover and cook in a preheated 300° oven for $2\frac{1}{2}$ hours. Top with the French bread, arranging the slices in an overlapping pattern and sprinkle with a little grated cheese. Increase the oven temperature to 400° and cook for a further 30 minutes, or until the cheese has melted. Sprinkle with a little chopped parsley and serve. SERVES 4

Lentil-stuffed Zucchini

— Janet Hunt —

6 medium-size zucchini
1 onion
2 tomatoes (optional)
2 stalks celery
$\frac{1}{4}$ cup butter or margarine
$\frac{1}{2}$ cup red split lentils
salt and pepper
1–2 teaspoons chopped fresh mixed herbs
or $\frac{1}{2}$–1 teaspoon dried mixed herbs
$\frac{1}{2}$ cup grated Cheddar cheese

Blanch the zucchini in boiling salted water for 2 to 3 minutes. Drain well, cool slightly and cut the zucchini in half lengthwise. Scoop out and chop the flesh.

Chop the onion and the tomatoes, if used, and finely slice the celery. Melt half the butter or margarine in a saucepan and stir in the onion, tomato, celery, and chopped zucchini. Cook all the vegetables together briefly, then add the lentils and enough water to cover.

Bring to a boil, reduce the heat and simmer for about 20 minutes, until the lentils and vegetables are tender and all the water has been absorbed. Season with salt and pepper to taste and sprinkle with herbs. Use the mixture to fill the zucchini skins and arrange the stuffed zucchini side by side in a greased ovenproof dish. Sprinkle with cheese and dot with the remaining butter. Broil the zucchini for 5 to 10 minutes, or until golden brown. Serve with young green beans or spinach. SERVES 4

Broccoli and Egg Salad

— Janet Hunt —

1 lb broccoli
salt
2 large tomatoes
6 scallions
about $\frac{1}{4}$ cup mayonnaise
2 hard-cooked eggs, sliced
a little paprika

Break the broccoli into sprigs and cook them in a little boiling salted water until just tender. Drain and rinse the broccoli in cold water, then drain thoroughly and place in a serving bowl.

Quarter the tomatoes; trim and chop the scallions and add them to the broccoli. Mix in enough mayonnaise to moisten the salad ingredients to taste and top with the sliced eggs. Sprinkle with paprika and serve. SERVES 4

Chestnut Roll

— Janet Hunt —

PASTRY
$\frac{1}{2}$ cup butter or margarine
2 cups wholewheat flour
pinch of salt
5–6 tablespoons cold water
milk for glazing
FILLING
$\frac{1}{2}$ lb chestnuts
2 tablespoons butter or margarine
$\frac{1}{2}$ cup chopped mushrooms
1 leek, finely sliced
$\frac{1}{2}$ clove garlic, crushed
1–2 tablespoons water
salt and pepper
watercress for garnish

Rub the butter or margarine into the flour and salt until the mixture resembles fine bread crumbs. Add enough water to bind the ingredients to a dough, knead lightly and wrap in foil or plastic wrap. Chill the dough in the refrigerator for at least 30 minutes.

To make the filling, slit the shells of the chestnuts and cook them in boiling water for 15 minutes. Drain and allow to cool, then peel away both the outer shells and the inner skin. Melt the butter or margarine in a pan and cook the mushrooms briefly; remove and set them aside. Put the sliced leek and garlic together into the pan and cook gently for 5 minutes. Chop the chestnuts coarsely and add them to the pan. Pour in just enough water to moisten the ingredients, cover the pan and simmer for 10 minutes or until the nuts and leeks are tender. Add more water if necessary, but not too much as the mixture must be dry. Stir in the mushrooms and remove the pan from the heat. Drain thoroughly and season to taste with salt and pepper.

On a lightly floured surface, roll out the pastry to a neat oblong measuring roughly 12 × 9 in and spread the chestnut and vegetables over it, leaving a small space around the edges. Roll up the pastry from the longest edge, like a jelly roll. Dampen the edges with a little water, press them together to seal and place the roll on a lightly greased baking sheet. Brush the top with milk.

Bake the chestnut roll in a preheated 400° oven for 30 to 40 minutes, until the pastry is cooked. Serve in thick slices garnished with watercress and accompanied by a creamy white sauce and a cucumber salad, if liked. SERVES 4

Gloucester Pie

Carol Bowen

8 slices bread, crusts removed
6 tablespoons butter
$\frac{1}{4}$ lb Brick cheese, thinly sliced
$\frac{1}{2}$ lb tomatoes, peeled and sliced
$\frac{1}{2}$ cup milk
1 egg, beaten
1 teaspoon prepared mustard
salt and pepper
watercress sprigs for garnish

Butter the slices of bread with three-quarters of the butter. Sandwich together, in pairs, with the cheese and tomatoes. Cut each sandwich into four triangles and arrange in a shallow ovenproof dish.

Beat together the milk, egg, mustard and seasoning to taste. Pour over the bread and leave to soak for 30 minutes. Dot the top with the remaining butter and bake in a preheated 375° oven for 25 to 30 minutes or until the top is crisp and golden. Serve garnished with watercress sprigs. SERVES 4

Spiced Egg Ragoût

Carol Bowen

$\frac{1}{4}$ cup butter or margarine
$\frac{1}{2}$ lb pearl onions, halved
1 lb potatoes, cut into fingers (or fries)
1 teaspoon chili seasoning
1 teaspoon ground cardamom
$\frac{1}{2}$ teaspoon ground coriander
$\frac{1}{2}$ teaspoon turmeric
2 tablespoons flour
1 (16-oz) can peeled tomatoes
1 clove garlic, crushed
$1\frac{1}{4}$ cups vegetable stock
$\frac{3}{4}$ cup plain yogurt
salt and pepper
8 hard-cooked eggs, shelled
GARNISH
croûtons (see page 17)
1 tablespoon chopped parsley

Melt the butter in a large saucepan. Add the onions and potatoes and cook until lightly brown. Add the chili seasoning, cardamom, coriander, turmeric and flour and cook for 1 minute, stirring all the time.

Stir in the tomatoes with their juice, the garlic, stock, yogurt and seasoning to taste. Bring to a boil, then cover the pan and simmer gently for about 40 minutes.

Cut the eggs in half lengthwise. Add to the sauce and leave over a low heat to warm through. Mix the croûtons with the chopped parsley and sprinkle over to garnish the dish. Serve with cooked rice or pasta. SERVES 4

Iced Camembert Tart

———— Audrey Ellis ————

PIE PASTRY
2 cups flour
pinch of salt
½ cup margarine
cold water to mix
FILLING
3 eggs, separated
¾ cup light cream
1 ripe Camembert cheese
1 envelope unflavored gelatin, dissolved in
2 tablespoons boiling water
GARNISH
parsley sprigs
1 tomato, sliced

To make the pastry, sift the flour into a bowl with the salt. Add the margarine and rub it in until the mixture resembles fine bread crumbs. Stir in enough water to make a dough.

Roll out the pastry to line an 8-in quiche or flan pan and bake ''blind'' (unfilled) in a preheated 375° oven for 30 minutes. Cool.

Beat together the egg yolks and cream in the top of a double boiler, then place over hot water and cook, stirring constantly, until thickened. Trim away the outer crust from the cheese. Cut the cheese into small dice, add to the egg mixture and stir until melted. Remove from the heat and stir in the gelatin. Beat the egg whites until stiff, fold into the cheese, and pour into the pastry case.

Chill the tart until the filling is set, then serve cut in wedges, garnished with parsley sprigs and tomato slices. SERVES 4 TO 6

Walnut Cheese Ball

———— Audrey Ellis ————

1 (8-oz) package cream cheese
1½ teaspoons garlic salt or celery salt
1 tablespoon chopped parsley
1 tablespoon grated onion
1 tablespoon chopped green pepper
½ cup drained canned crushed pineapple
1 cup chopped walnuts
TO SERVE
lettuce leaves
cocktail crackers
olives
tomatoes

Beat the cream cheese until soft and gradually stir in the salt, parsley, onion, green pepper and crushed pineapple. Finally add half the nuts and combine well, then chill in the refrigerator until firm.

Sprinkle the remaining nuts on a sheet of foil. Shape the chilled mixture into a ball and roll in the nuts until evenly coated. Serve the walnut-coated cheese on a bed of lettuce and surround it with cocktail crackers, olives and tomatoes. SERVES 4

Gougère

— Janet Hunt —

CHOUX PASTRY
$\frac{3}{4}$ cup wholewheat flour
pinch of salt
$\frac{1}{4}$ cup butter or margarine
$\frac{3}{4}$ cup water
2 large eggs, lightly beaten
$\frac{1}{3}$ cup grated Cheddar cheese
FILLING
2 tablespoons oil
1 onion, finely chopped
$\frac{1}{2}$ clove garlic, crushed
2 large zucchini
4 large tomatoes
salt and pepper
1–2 tablespoons water
$\frac{1}{2}$ cup cooked peas
chopped fresh parsley or chives for garnish
(optional)

Sift the flour with the salt, reserving the bran from the flour for another recipe. Combine the butter and water in a small saucepan and heat gently until the fat melts. Bring the mixture to a boil and immediately add the flour. Beat the ingredients quickly with a wooden spoon until the mixture forms a dough and comes away from the side of the pan. Leave to cool for a few minutes, then gradually beat in the eggs, a little at a time, and continue beating until the mixture is thick and glossy in texture.

Place the dough in a pastry bag fitted with a large plain nozzle and pipe choux puffs around the inside edge of a round, greased ovenproof dish. Sprinkle with the grated cheese and bake in a preheated 400° oven for 30 to 40 minutes or until well risen.

Heat the oil in a pan and cook the chopped onion and garlic for 5 to 10 minutes. Slice the zucchini and the tomatoes and add them to the pan with salt and pepper to taste. Cook the vegetables briefly, then pour in enough water to moisten, cover and simmer for 15 to 20 minutes. Stir in the cooked peas and allow them to heat through.

Arrange the gougère on a warmed serving dish and fill the center with the vegetables. Sprinkle with chopped fresh parsley or chives, if liked, and serve cut into wedges. A cheese or tomato sauce (page 125) goes well with this dish. SERVES 4

Wholewheat Pizza

— Carol Bowen —

1 (0.6-oz) cake compressed yeast
$\frac{1}{2}$ teaspoon sugar
$\frac{3}{4}$ cup lukewarm water
$1\frac{3}{4}$ cups wholewheat flour
1 teaspoon salt
2 teaspoons olive oil
TOPPING
1 (16-oz) can peeled tomatoes, drained
and sliced
salt and pepper
1 tablespoon dried basil
$\frac{1}{2}$ teaspoon garlic salt
6 oz mozzarella cheese, sliced
8 ripe olives
1 tablespoon capers

Mix the yeast with the sugar and 2 tablespoons of the water. Leave until frothy.

Combine the flour and salt in a large mixing bowl. Make a well in the center and pour in the yeast liquid, olive oil and remaining water. Mix in the flour to make a smooth dough. Knead for 5 minutes, then leave to rise, covered, in a warm place until double in size.

Roll out the dough into a 9-in round and place on a greased baking sheet. Leave for 10 minutes, then arrange the topping ingredients on the dough and bake in a preheated 375° oven for 30 minutes. Serve immediately
SERVES 4 TO 6

Vegetable Lasagne

— Carol Bowen —

6 oz lasagne verdi
2 medium-size onions, sliced
$\frac{3}{4}$ lb tomatoes, peeled and sliced
$\frac{3}{4}$ lb zucchini, halved lengthwise and sliced
3 tablespoons oil
$\frac{1}{2}$ teaspoon dried basil
1 tablespoon tomato paste
salt and pepper
$\frac{1}{4}$ cup chopped walnuts
2 cups plain yogurt
2 eggs
$\frac{1}{4}$ teaspoon ground cumin
$\frac{3}{4}$ cup grated Cheddar cheese

Cook the lasagne in plenty of boiling salted water for 15 minutes. Drain. Fry the onions, tomatoes and half the zucchini in 1 tablespoon of the oil until the tomatoes soften. Stir in the basil, tomato paste and seasoning. Mix in the walnuts.

Grease a 2-quart ovenproof dish and layer the vegetable mixture and lasagne in it, ending with a layer of lasagne. Season the yogurt generously and beat in the eggs, cumin and cheese. Pour over the lasagne and top with the remaining zucchini. Brush with the remaining oil and bake in a preheated 400° oven for about 40 minutes or until the yogurt is set. Serve immediately.
SERVES 4

Parsnip Quiche

Janet Hunt

QUICHE CASE
1 (8-oz) package wholewheat crackers or
crispbread
about 6 tablespoons butter or margarine
½ cup grated Cheddar cheese
salt and pepper
FILLING
1 lb parsnips
2 eggs, beaten
½ cup grated Cheddar cheese
pinch of grated nutmeg
2 large tomatoes, sliced

Put the crackers or crispbread into a plastic bag and use a rolling pin to crush them to fine, even-sized crumbs. Melt the butter or margarine in a pan and stir in the crumbs, adding a little more fat if the mixture seems dry. Stir well, add the grated Cheddar and seasoning to taste and remove the pan from the heat. Grease an 8-in quiche or flan pan and line it with the mixture. Leave in a cool place to firm up.

Peel and chop the parsnips and cook them in boiling salted water for 15 to 20 minutes until tender. Mash them to a purée and leave to cool slightly. Mix in the beaten eggs, grated Cheddar, nutmeg and salt and pepper to taste. Spoon the mixture into the crumb crust and arrange the sliced tomatoes on top. Bake in a preheated 375° oven for 20 to 30 minutes until the filling is cooked and the crust crisp. SERVES 4

Scrambled Eggs with Tofu

Janet Hunt

2 tablespoons butter or margarine
10 oz tofu, diced
4 eggs
salt and pepper
pinch of paprika
chopped fresh chives for garnish

Melt the butter or margarine in a saucepan. Add the tofu to the pan, mashing it with the fat to make a crumb-like mixture. Cook for a few minutes.

Beat the eggs with salt and pepper to taste and pour the mixture over the tofu. Cook gently, stirring the eggs up from the bottom of the pan, until the mixture begins to set but is still soft. Remove the pan from the heat and allow the egg to set completely for about 1 minute before serving on toast or a bed of fresh, lightly steamed spinach. Sprinkle paprika and chopped fresh chives over the top. SERVES 4

Hummus

Carol Bowen

1 lb cooked or canned chick peas, drained
2 tablespoons olive oil
1 or 2 cloves garlic, crushed
2 teaspoons lemon juice
½ teaspoon paprika
1 tablespoon sesame seeds (optional)
salt

Mash the chick peas well. Add the oil, garlic and lemon juice and beat well, then add the paprika, sesame seeds (if used) and salt to taste. Alternatively, place all the ingredients in a food processor or blender and process until smooth.

Serve with a selection of raw vegetables, such as strips of carrot and celery, cauliflower florets and scallions. SERVES 4

Coriander Mushrooms

Carol Bowen

½ lb small button mushrooms
6 tablespoons olive oil
1 teaspoon crushed coriander seeds
2 tablespoons lemon juice
salt and pepper
chopped parsley

Wipe the mushrooms with a damp cloth and cut them into halves or quarters.

Heat 4 tablespoons of the oil in a large skillet. Add the coriander seeds and fry for about 2 minutes, stirring continuously. Stir in the mushrooms, then cover and cook for 3 to 5 minutes or until tender.

Transfer to a serving dish, and add the remaining oil, lemon juice and seasoning. Chill before serving sprinkled with chopped parsley. SERVES 2

Vegetables and Salad

This chapter is filled with mouth-watering ideas for all seasons: warming vegetable pie for the winter months, crisp and crunchy salads for the spring and summer, and some homely baked potato suggestions for autumnal evenings.

Stuffed Baked Potatoes

(ILLUSTRATED ON PREVIOUS PAGE)

Allow one large potato per person. Thoroughly scrub the potatoes and cut out any eyes or bruised bits. Prick the skin and brush with a little oil. Place the potatoes on a baking sheet. Bake in a preheated 400° oven for about 1½ hours. The cooking time will depend on the size of the potatoes. When cooked, split the potatoes down the middle and fill with any of the suggested fillings. If you like, cook two small potatoes per person and offer a selection of fillings.

Cream Cheese and Herbs Beat chopped fresh herbs, seasoning and finely chopped scallions into cream cheese. Shape into a roll, chill thoroughly, then slice thickly. Place two or three slices in each cooked potato.

Cottage Cheese and Ham Mix chopped cooked ham, seasoning and chopped parsley into cottage cheese. Spoon the mixture into the cooked potatoes before serving.

Bacon Rolls Roll up slices of bacon and secure with wooden toothpicks. Cook until golden, then place a couple on each cooked potato and serve immediately.

Seafood Filling Mix peeled cooked shrimp with flaked tuna fish and a little mayonnaise. Add lemon juice, seasoning and a little tomato paste to taste. Spoon this mixture into the cooked potatoes.

Provençal Filling Mix roughly chopped peeled tomatoes with finely chopped onion, pitted ripe olives and plenty of seasoning. Stir in a little olive oil and lemon juice to taste, then spoon into the cooked potatoes.

Salami and Gherkin Filling Arrange two or three cones or rolls of salami in each potato. Add gherkin fans and halved slices of tomato.

Sour Cream and Caviar Spoon a little sour cream into each potato and top with a little caviar. Add a couple of quartered lemon slices to each one.

Smoked Salmon Place a couple of rolls of smoked salmon in each potato. Top with a couple of small lemon wedges and some parsley. Serve with sour cream or mayonnaise and plenty of black pepper.

Mixed Vegetable Salad

(ILLUSTRATED ON PREVIOUS PAGE)

Arrange a selection of prepared vegetables on a platter. For example, prepare chopped peppers, both green and red, chopped or sliced cucumber, sliced tomatoes, coarsely grated carrots, sliced celery, shredded cabbage, lettuce or chicory, lightly cooked cut green beans (cooled), radishes and scallions. Serve the Herb Dressing separately.

Herb Dressing

(ILLUSTRATED ON PREVIOUS PAGE)

Stir ¼ cup chopped mixed fresh herbs into 1 cup mayonnaise. Add seasoning, mild mustard and a little sugar to taste. Chill lightly before serving.

Cauliflower au Gratin

Bridget Jones

(ILLUSTRATED ON PREVIOUS PAGE)

1 medium-size cauliflower
1¼ cups Béchamel Sauce (page 20)
1 cup grated Cheddar cheese
⅛ teaspoon dry mustard
salt and pepper

Trim the cauliflower and break it into florets if you like. Cook the whole cauliflower or the florets in boiling salted water for about 15 minutes. Drain thoroughly.

   Prepare the sauce according to the recipe instructions. Stir in most of the cheese, the mustard and seasoning to taste. Place the cauliflower in an ovenproof dish and cover with the sauce. Top with the reserved grated cheese, then bake in a preheated 400° oven for about 20 minutes or until the topping is golden. Serve immediately. SERVES 4

Note: This dish is delicious topped with chopped fresh herbs, chopped crisply fried bacon, or chopped cooked ham.

Braised Celery with Walnuts

— Diana Jaggar —

1 bunch celery, trimmed and washed
salt and pepper
1 medium-size onion, finely chopped
$\frac{1}{4}$ cup butter
$\frac{1}{2}$ cup walnut pieces
coarsely grated rind of 1 lemon

Cut the celery diagonally into $1\frac{1}{2}$-in sticks, then blanch in boiling salted water for 5 minutes. Cook the onion in 2 tablespoons of the butter, then add the celery and cook gently for 5 to 10 minutes, until tender but still crisp.

Meanwhile, fry the walnuts in the remaining butter for 1 to 2 minutes. Stir in the lemon rind, then add the nut mixture to the celery and toss well. Season to taste. SERVES 4

Cauliflower Amandine

— Diana Jaggar —

1 medium-size cauliflower
salt and pepper
6 tablespoons butter
1 cup blanched shredded almonds
chopped parsley for garnish

Break the cauliflower into florets. Trim, wash and cook them in boiling salted water for 10 to 15 minutes until cooked but still crisp. Drain.

Melt the butter in a skillet and cook the almonds until golden brown. Add the cauliflower and season to taste, then toss gently and turn into a serving dish. Sprinkle with parsley before serving. SERVES 4

Vegetable Pie

Marguerite Patten

1 lb potatoes
1–1¼ lb mixed root vegetables (not potatoes)
1–1½ cups grated cheese
SAUCE
2 tablespoons butter
2 tablespoons flour
1¼ cups milk or milk and vegetable stock
salt and pepper

Cook the potatoes in boiling salted water until tender. When cooked, drain and mash them. Meanwhile, peel the vegetables and cut them into small pieces. Cook in boiling salted water until tender.

To make the sauce, melt the butter in a saucepan and stir in the flour. Gradually pour in the milk, stirring all the time, and bring to a boil. Remove the pan from the heat and stir the mixed vegetables into the sauce. Stir in most of the grated cheese and season to taste.

Pour the vegetable mixture into an ovenproof dish and top with the mashed potato. Sprinkle the remaining cheese over the potato and bake in a preheated 400° oven for about 15 minutes, or until golden brown. Serve immediately. SERVES 4

Austrian Cabbage

Elizabeth Pomeroy

1 small head cabbage (about 1 lb)
2–4 tablespoons butter or bacon fat
1 small onion, chopped
1 teaspoon paprika
1 teaspoon caraway seeds
salt and pepper
¾ cup sour cream

Discard the coarse outer leaves of the cabbage and cut it into quarters, then remove the stalk from each piece. Shred the cabbage finely, wash and drain it thoroughly, then dry it in a clean dish towel.

In a flameproof casserole, melt the butter or fat and fry the onion gently until transparent. Add the shredded cabbage and cook lightly, stirring well. Sprinkle in the paprika, caraway seeds, salt and pepper, then stir in the sour cream.

Cover the casserole and continue cooking very gently on top of the stove or in a preheated 325° oven for 15 to 20 minutes, until the cabbage is tender. Serve with Hungarian Goulash (page 62), bratwurst sausages or mackerel. SERVES 4

Cider-baked Onions

Elizabeth Pomeroy

4 medium-size onions
3 tablespoons butter *or* 2 tablespoons olive oil
2 teaspoons chopped fresh lemon thyme *or*
1 teaspoon dried lemon thyme
2 teaspoons chopped fresh sage *or*
1 teaspoon dried sage
salt and pepper
3–4 tablespoons hard cider
chopped fresh thyme or other fresh herbs
for garnish

Peel the onions, cut off the roots and slice off the top. Cut the onions across in half. Melt the butter or heat the oil in a shallow flameproof casserole or gratin dish. Place the onions, center downwards, in the casserole and fry until golden. Remove from the heat, turn the onions upwards, sprinkle with the herbs and season well with salt and pepper. Pour in sufficient cider to cover the bottom of the casserole, then cover with a lid or foil.

Bake in a preheated 375° oven for 45 minutes to 1 hour, according to size, until tender. Just before serving, spoon the cooking liquid over the onions and sprinkle with fresh herbs. SERVES 4

Minted Tomato Ratatouille

Carol Bowen

1 lb tomatoes
½ lb zucchini
½ lb onions
¼ lb button mushrooms
1 green pepper, seeded
¼ cup oil
2 tablespoons chopped fresh mint
salt and pepper
grated Parmesan cheese

Peel and quarter the tomatoes, and remove the seeds, reserving the juices. Wipe the zucchini and cut them into ¼-in slices. Slice the onions and mushrooms. Slice the pepper thinly.

Heat the oil in a large saucepan and fry the zucchini and onions, stirring, until golden. Add half the tomatoes and their juices, the mushrooms, green pepper, mint and salt and pepper to taste. Cover and simmer gently for 15 minutes.

Stir in the remaining tomatoes and heat gently for about 5 minutes. Serve hot or cold, with Parmesan cheese. SERVES 4

Minty New Potatoes with Cucumber

—— *Diana Jaggar* ——

1 lb small new potatoes, washed and scraped
few mint sprigs
salt and pepper
$\frac{1}{2}$ large cucumber, peeled
$\frac{1}{4}$ cup butter
2 teaspoons chopped fresh mint
$\frac{1}{2}$ cup light cream (optional)

Cook the potatoes, with the mint sprigs, in boiling salted water for 10 to 15 minutes or until just tender. Quarter the cucumber lengthwise and cut across into cubes. Melt the butter in a pan and cook the cucumber for 5 minutes. Add the drained cooked potatoes and chopped mint. Season to taste and toss thoroughly. Add the cream, if used, and heat to just below boiling. Turn into a serving dish and serve immediately. SERVES 4 TO 6

Fantail Potatoes

—— *Diana Jaggar* ——

6 medium-size potatoes, peeled and shaped
into even-sized ovals
1 slice lemon
$\frac{1}{4}$ cup butter
1 onion, finely chopped
salt and pepper
$\frac{1}{4}$ cup grated Parmesan cheese
$\frac{1}{4}$ cup grated Cheddar cheese
parsley sprigs for garnish

Slice the potatoes thinly into vertical slices, leaving them attached at the base. Soak the potatoes in cold water with a slice of lemon added, until they are all sliced. Melt the butter in a skillet and fry the onion until soft.

Drain the potatoes and arrange them, cut side upwards, in an ovenproof dish. Spoon the onion and butter over and season to taste. Cook in a preheated 375° oven for 30 minutes, basting occasionally.

Mix the cheeses and sprinkle over the potatoes. Cook for a further 20 to 30 minutes until crisp and golden. Serve immediately. SERVES 6

Tuna Bean Salad

Rosemary Wadey

2 green-skinned apples, cored and chopped
1 tablespoon lemon juice
1 (7-oz) can tuna, drained and flaked
1 tablespoon finely chopped onion
3 stalks celery, sliced
1 (16-oz) can red kidney beans, drained
salt and pepper
4–5 tablespoons vinaigrette dressing
watercress for garnish

Dip the apple in the lemon juice, then place in a bowl with the tuna, onion, celery and red kidney beans. Season well, add the dressing and toss thoroughly. Leave to stand for about 30 minutes before serving on individual plates. Garnish with watercress and serve with French bread and butter. SERVES 4 TO 6

Salade Niçoise

Rosemary Wadey

a few lettuce leaves
1 (7-oz) can tuna, drained and flaked
1 green pepper, seeded and sliced
1 tablespoon finely chopped onion
3 large tomatoes, each cut into 6 wedges
$\frac{1}{2}$ lb green beans, cooked
1 tablespoon capers
6 tablespoons vinaigrette dressing
GARNISH
3 hard-cooked eggs
$\frac{1}{2}$ ($1\frac{3}{4}$-oz) can anchovy fillets, drained
a few ripe olives

Arrange the lettuce leaves on six small plates or dishes. Lightly toss together the tuna, green pepper, onion, tomatoes, beans, capers and dressing. Spoon the salad over the lettuce leaves. Cut the eggs into quarters and arrange them on the salads with the anchovy fillets and ripe olives. Serve with French bread. SERVES 6

Ham and Egg Salad

Marguerite Patten

2 or 3 hard-cooked eggs
1 head lettuce
4–6 oz cooked ham
1 (11-oz) can mandarin oranges
2 tablespoons mayonnaise
a little chopped parsley
1 bunch radishes, trimmed
1 sweet red or green pepper

Shell the hard-cooked eggs and cut them into neat slices.

Arrange the lettuce on a flat dish. Cut the ham into neat cubes and mix with the well-drained mandarin oranges and a little of the mayonnaise. Pile the ham mixture into the center of the lettuce; top with a spoonful of mayonnaise and parsley.

Wash, dry, then slice the radishes and arrange them on top of the sliced eggs around the salad. Cut the stalk end off the pepper, remove the seeds and core, then cut the flesh into neat rings. Arrange on the lettuce. SERVES 4

Nutty Cheese Salad

Jane Todd

4 apples
juice of 1 lemon
½ cup chopped walnuts
⅓ cup golden raisins
2 stalks celery, chopped
1½ cups finely shredded white cabbage
1 cup grated Cheddar cheese or
crumbled blue cheese
salt and pepper
½ cup plain yogurt or sour cream
chopped parsley for garnish (optional)

Quarter, core and slice the apples, place in a bowl and sprinkle with the lemon juice. Mix in the walnuts, raisins, celery, cabbage and cheese. Season to taste.

Add the yogurt or sour cream and stir gently until the mixture is evenly coated. Spoon into a serving dish and garnish with chopped parsley, if used. Chill lightly before serving. SERVES 4 TO 6

Cheese and Ham Cornets

Jane Todd

½ (8-oz) package cream cheese
¼ cup chopped walnuts
2 tablespoons chopped parsley or chives
1 tablespoon mayonnaise
salt and pepper
4 slices cooked ham
watercress for garnish

Beat the cream cheese to soften it. Mix in the chopped walnuts, parsley or chives and mayonnaise. Season to taste.

Form each slice of ham into a cornet shape and secure with a wooden toothpick. Divide the cream cheese mixture between the ham cornets and chill lightly.

Place the chilled ham cornets on a serving platter and garnish with watercress. SERVES 4

Garlic Sausage and Cheese Salad

Jane Todd

½ lb Gruyère or Swiss cheese
½ lb garlic sausage
¼ cucumber
¼ cup mayonnaise
pinch of dry mustard
pinch of paprika
salt and pepper
½ cup cooked pasta
few lettuce leaves (optional)
chopped parsley or chives for garnish

Cut the cheese, garlic sausage and cucumber into cubes. Mix the mayonnaise with the mustard, paprika and seasoning. Toss the cubed ingredients and pasta in the mayonnaise mixture.

Line a salad bowl with the lettuce leaves, if used, and spoon in the salad. Garnish with parsley or chives and chill lightly before serving. SERVES 4

Cracked Wheat Salad

—— Carol Bowen ——

1 cup bulgur (cracked wheat)
2 tablespoons finely chopped shallots or
scallions
6 tablespoons chopped parsley
6 tablespoons chopped mint
2 tablespoons olive oil
2 tablespoons lemon juice
salt and pepper
ripe olives
2 tomatoes, sliced

Place the cracked wheat in a bowl and cover with cold water. Leave to soak for 30 minutes. Drain, then wrap in a dish towel and squeeze to extract as much moisture as possible.

Mix the wheat with the shallots or scallions, parsley, mint, oil and lemon juice. Season to taste with salt and pepper. Place the mixture in a shallow serving dish and garnish with ripe olives and sliced tomatoes. SERVES 4

Simple Bean Sprout Salad

Crunchy, fresh bean sprouts can be used to make a delicious salad. Mixed with a variety of ingredients – chopped gherkins, chopped canned pimiento, chopped scallions, or green peppers, or even chopped mixed nuts – the sprouts can be dressed with a light mixture of oil and vinegar, seasoned yogurt or mayonnaise.

Lentil and Mung Bean Salad

—— Janet Hunt ——

1 small onion
1 small green pepper, seeded
$\frac{1}{4}$ cucumber
1 cup cooked brown lentils
1 cup cooked mung beans
LEMON AND HONEY DRESSING
2 tablespoons oil
2 tablespoons clear honey
2 tablespoons lemon juice
salt and pepper
about $\frac{1}{4}$ cup plain yogurt for serving

Chop the onion, green pepper and cucumber and mix them in a bowl with the lentils and mung beans. Mix the oil, honey, lemon juice and seasoning to make the dressing, then pour this over the salad. Leave to marinate for 1 to 2 hours.

Stir in enough yogurt to give the beans a creamy coating and serve the salad on a bed of shredded cabbage, if liked. SERVES 4

Hot Cabbage Salad

—— Janet Hunt ——

$\frac{1}{2}$ head white cabbage
3 carrots
1 onion
2 tablespoons vegetable oil
2 tablespoons raisins
1 teaspoon marjoram *or* $\frac{1}{2}$ teaspoon dried
marjoram
pinch of brown sugar
salt and pepper
$\frac{3}{4}$ cup plain yogurt
$\frac{1}{2}$ cup chopped nuts (optional)

Shred the cabbage. Slice the carrots and onion as finely as possible. Heat the oil in a large skillet and gently fry the vegetables and raisins for 3 to 4 minutes, stirring continuously.

Mix the herbs, sugar and seasoning to taste into the yogurt and stir the mixture into the vegetables with the chopped nuts, if used. Heat through very gently for a minute, then serve at once. SERVES 4

Crunchy Bacon Salad

Moya Maynard

4 slices white bread, cut $\frac{1}{2}$ in thick
$\frac{1}{4}$ cup butter or margarine
5 tablespoons oil
8 slices bacon
$\frac{1}{2}$ lb button mushrooms, thickly sliced
$\frac{1}{2}$ small onion
salt and pepper
pinch of dry mustard
1 tablespoon vinegar
$\frac{1}{3}$ cup pimiento-stuffed olives, sliced
2 tablespoons chopped parsley

Remove the crusts from the bread and cut the slices into large cubes. Melt the butter or margarine in a skillet with 2 tablespoons of the oil. Heat gently and fry the bread cubes, turning frequently, until crisp and golden. Remove and drain on paper towels.

Cut the bacon into large pieces, then fry them in the skillet until slightly crisp. Remove from the pan and drain well. Add the mushrooms to the pan and cook slowly until just soft. Remove from the pan, drain and place in a salad bowl.

Grate the onion and add to the mushrooms with the seasoning and mustard. Blend the remaining oil and vinegar into the mushroom mixture. Leave to cool, then stir in the olives, parsley, bacon and cubes of bread. Serve immediately. SERVES 4

Malayan Curried Salad

Moya Maynard

$\frac{1}{2}$ cup long-grain rice
$\frac{1}{2}$ cup mayonnaise
1–2 teaspoons concentrated curry sauce
1 (8-oz) can pineapple rings, drained
1 small green pepper, seeded and diced
1 cup diced cooked chicken
3 tablespoons raisins
chopped green pepper for garnish

Cook the rice in boiling salted water for 12 to 15 minutes until tender. Drain well and spread on paper towels to cool.

Mix the mayonnaise with the curry sauce. Cut the pineapple into small pieces and add to the mayonnaise with the green pepper, chicken and raisins. Stir to coat evenly.

Place the rice on a serving dish and top with the curried chicken mixture. Garnish with chopped green pepper. SERVES 3 TO 4

Artichokes Niçoise

Rosemary Wadey

1 (16-oz) can artichoke hearts, drained
2 tablespoons chopped onion
½ cup vinaigrette dressing
salt and pepper
1 (1¾-oz) can anchovy fillets, drained
12 ripe olives
watercress for garnish

Cut the artichoke hearts into halves or quarters, depending on size, and place in a bowl with the onion, dressing and seasoning. Cut the anchovies into 1-in lengths and add them to the artichokes together with the olives. Toss lightly and leave the salad to stand for about 20 minutes. Arrange in four small dishes and garnish with watercress. SERVES 4

Chinese Salad

Diana Jaggar

½ cucumber, peeled
½ lb bean sprouts, washed and drained
2 sweet red peppers, halved, seeded and finely sliced
1 (8-oz) can whole kernel corn, drained
2 teaspoon chopped parsley
chopped parsley for garnish
LEMON DRESSING
2 tablespoons lemon juice
¼ cup olive oil
2 tablespoons soy sauce
2 tablespoons light cream
salt and pepper
sugar to taste

Cut the cucumber into matchstick strips. Mix these with the bean sprouts, peppers, corn and parsley.

Put all the dressing ingredients into a screw-topped jar and shake well, adding seasoning and sugar to taste. Pour the dressing over the salad and toss well. Serve in individual bowls with a little extra parsley sprinkled on top. SERVES 4 TO 6

Bok Choy and Avocado Salad

—— *Janet Hunt* ——

1 small head bok choy
1 small green pepper, seeded
2 stalks celery
½ small head red cabbage
2 tomatoes
1 large avocado
⅓ cup raisins
½ cup flaked almonds, toasted, for garnish
TOFU DRESSING
6 oz tofu
2 tablespoons oil
2 tablespoons cider vinegar
soy sauce *or* salt and pepper

Chop the bok choy, pepper, celery and red cabbage. Quarter the tomatoes. Peel and halve the avocado, remove the seed and slice the flesh. Mix all the prepared ingredients together in a bowl and add the raisins. Mix all the dressing ingredients and pour over the salad. Stir well, then sprinkle with the flaked almonds before serving. SERVES 4

Three Bean Salad

—— *Janet Hunt* ——

¼ lb green beans
1 large onion
½ cup cooked kidney beans
½ cup cooked chick peas
1 small clove garlic, finely chopped
6 tablespoons vinaigrette dressing
¼ leek *or* 1 small green pepper
salt and pepper

Trim the green beans and cut them into 1-in pieces. Cook them in a little boiling salted water for 10 to 15 minutes, until just tender. Drain and leave to cool. Slice the onion. Mix the green beans, kidney beans, chick peas, onion and garlic together in a bowl, pour in the vinaigrette dressing and toss well. Leave the salad in a cool place for at least a few hours, preferably 1 to 2 days, so that the beans can absorb all the flavors. Just before serving, finely shred the leek or green pepper, removing the seeds from the pepper. Season the salad and sprinkle the shredded leek or pepper over the top. SERVES 4

Orange and Apple Salad

—— *Marguerite Patten* ——

1 orange
1 tangerine
a few lettuce leaves
1 apple
vinaigrette dressing
a few nuts

Peel the orange, removing the pith. Divide into neat sections, discarding the seeds. Peel and section the tangerine. Arrange the fruit on the lettuce leaves like the petals of a flower. Quarter, core and dice the apple. Coat the apple in vinaigrette dressing to taste, add the nuts and spoon the mixture into the center of the salad. SERVES 2 TO 3

Russian Salad

—— *Marguerite Patten* ——

about 1 lb mixed root vegetables
1 tablespoon oil
1 tablespoon vinegar
3–4 tablespoons mayonnaise
salt and pepper

Prepare the vegetables and cut them into neat dice. Put into boiling salted water and cook steadily until tender, then drain and allow to cool. Put the cooked vegetables into a bowl and mix in the oil and vinegar, then add the mayonnaise. Season to taste and serve. SERVES 4

Rice and Pasta

Rice and pasta can be quickly transformed into exciting dishes with an international flavour, from spicy Lamb Pilaff and Special Chow Mein to more familiar spaghetti dishes, and the recipes are all here to try.

Special Chow Mein, Pullao with Almonds and Pasta alla Carbonara

Pullao with Almonds

Bridget Jones

(ILLUSTRATED ON PREVIOUS PAGE)

$\frac{1}{4}$ cup butter
$\frac{1}{4}$ cup flaked almonds
1 onion, chopped
1 cinnamon stick
4 cardamoms
2 bay leaves
1 cup long-grain rice
$\frac{2}{3}$ cup dried apricots
$2\frac{1}{2}$ cups water
$\frac{1}{2}$ cup frozen peas

Melt the butter in a saucepan. Add the almonds and cook gently until they are golden, then remove from the pan with a slotted spoon and set aside. Add the onion and spices to the butter remaining in the pan and cook, stirring frequently, until soft but not browned.

Add the bay leaves and rice and stir in the apricots. Pour in the water and bring to a boil. Cover the pan and cook gently for 15 to 20 minutes or until the rice is tender and all the water has been absorbed. About 5 minutes before the end of the cooking time stir in the peas. Add the almonds when the rice has cooked and fluff up the grains with a fork. Serve immediately. SERVES 4

Pasta alla Carbonara

Bridget Jones

(ILLUSTRATED ON PREVIOUS PAGE)

1 lb pasta (spaghetti, noodles or shapes)
salt and pepper
$\frac{1}{4}$ cup butter
$\frac{3}{4}$ lb cooked ham, cut into strips
$\frac{1}{4}$ lb mushrooms, sliced
1 egg
$1\frac{1}{4}$ cups light cream
a little chopped parsley for garnish

Cook the chosen pasta in plenty of boiling salted water until just tender – about 10 to 15 minutes.

Meanwhile, melt the butter in a large skillet and add the ham. Cook until it is a dark pink, then add the mushrooms and toss well in the butter. Cook gently for a few minutes.

Beat the egg thoroughly and stir in the cream. Add seasoning to taste to the ham mixture. Drain the pasta and place it on a heated serving dish or individual plates. Pour the cream mixture over the ham and cook gently, stirring continuously, until heated through. Do not allow the mixture to overheat or it will curdle. Pour the mixture over the pasta and serve immediately, sprinkled with a little parsley if you like. SERVES 4 TO 6

Special Chow Mein

Bridget Jones

(ILLUSTRATED ON PREVIOUS PAGE)

$\frac{3}{4}$ lb Chinese egg noodles
2 tablespoons oil
$\frac{1}{4}$ lb boneless pork, diced (about $\frac{1}{2}$ cup)
$\frac{1}{4}$ lb boneless chicken meat, diced (about $\frac{1}{2}$ cup)
$\frac{1}{4}$ lb peeled and deveined shrimp
2 oz canned water chestnuts, sliced
1 bunch scallions, chopped
a little light soy sauce

Cook the noodles in plenty of boiling salted water for about 5 to 10 minutes or until they are just tender. Drain and set aside.

Heat the oil in a large skillet or wok and add the pork and chicken. Stir-fry until the meats are lightly browned, then add the shrimp and water chestnuts, and cook for a few minutes. Stir in the cooked noodles and toss them with the ingredients until they are heated through. Add the scallions and soy sauce to taste, then serve immediately. SERVES 4

Lamb Pilaff

Jane Todd

$\frac{1}{4}$ cup butter
3 onions, sliced
$1\frac{1}{2}$ lb ground lamb
$\frac{1}{3}$ cup pine nuts
$\frac{1}{3}$ cup raisins
1 cup long-grain rice
2 tomatoes, peeled and sliced
$3\frac{1}{2}$ cups chicken broth or water
2 tablespoons chopped parsley
$\frac{1}{2}$ teaspoon dried sage
$\frac{1}{4}$ teaspoon ground coriander
$\frac{1}{4}$ teaspoon ground cinnamon
salt and pepper
chopped parsley for garnish

Melt the butter in a flameproof casserole and cook the onions until softened. Add the lamb and continue cooking until browned. Stir in the pine nuts, raisins, rice and tomatoes. Pour in the broth or water, herbs, spices and seasoning, then bring to a boil and lower the heat. Cover and simmer gently for about 25 minutes, until the rice is tender and the liquid absorbed.

Remove the lid and fork the mixture over the heat to dry off any excess moisture. Turn into a serving dish and garnish with chopped parsley. Serve with a selection of salads. SERVES 6

Seafood Paella

Carol Bowen

2 chicken pieces, skinned and boned
3 tablespoons oil
$\frac{1}{2}$ lb lean boneless pork, cubed
$\frac{1}{2}$ lb piece garlic sausage, cubed
1 medium-size onion, chopped
3 tomatoes, peeled and chopped
2 cups long-grain rice
2 cups peas
1 sweet red pepper, seeded and chopped
salt and pepper
pinch of powdered saffron or turmeric
$3\frac{1}{2}$ cups chicken broth
2 tablespoons chopped parsley
$\frac{1}{2}$ lb peeled and deveined shrimp
12–15 cooked mussels
a few shrimp in shell for garnish

Cut the chicken meat into bite-sized pieces. Heat the oil in a deep skillet or paella pan and add the chicken, pork and sausage. Sauté for 5 minutes over a high heat. Add the onion and continue to cook gently over a low heat for 5 minutes, stirring from time to time. Stir in the tomatoes and cook for 3 minutes, then add the rice. Cook, stirring continuously, for a further 5 minutes.

Stir in the peas, red pepper, seasoning and saffron or turmeric, then add the broth. Bring to a boil, cover and simmer for about 20 minutes until all the liquid has been absorbed and the rice is tender. Stir from time to time during the cooking.

Place in an ovenproof dish and stir in the parsley, shrimp and mussels. Cover and cook in a preheated 325° oven for 5 to 10 minutes. Serve garnished with unpeeled shrimp. SERVES 4 TO 6

Chicken Pilaff

Carol Bowen

$\frac{1}{4}$ cup butter
2 tablespoons flour
1 (15-fl oz) can evaporated milk *or*
$1\frac{3}{4}$ cups milk
$1\frac{1}{4}$ cups chicken broth
salt and pepper
1 lb cooked chicken meat, cut into bite-sized
pieces (about 2 cups)
3 cups cooked long-grain rice
(about 1 cup uncooked)
$\frac{1}{4}$ lb button mushrooms, sliced
1 green pepper, seeded and chopped
1 sweet red pepper, seeded and chopped
1 tablespoon chopped parsley

Melt the butter in a medium-sized saucepan. Add the flour and cook for 1 minute, then gradually stir in the evaporated milk or ordinary milk and the broth to make a smooth sauce. Bring to a boil and simmer for 2 minutes, stirring. Season to taste.

Stir in the chicken, rice, mushrooms, peppers and parsley. Turn into a 7-cup casserole, cover and cook in a preheated 350° oven for 45 minutes. Taste and adjust the seasoning, then serve. SERVES 6

111

Danish Pilaff

Moya Maynard

2 tablespoons butter or margarine
1 tablespoon oil
1 medium-size onion, chopped
2 stalks celery, sliced
$\frac{1}{2}$ lb ham steak
1 cup long-grain rice
2–2$\frac{1}{2}$ cups chicken broth
$\frac{1}{3}$ cup golden raisins
1 medium-size green pepper
toasted flaked almonds for garnish

Place the butter and oil in a skillet, add the onion and celery and cook slowly until soft – about 10 minutes.

Cut the ham into small strips. Add to the pan and cook slowly, stirring, for about 5 minutes. Stir in the rice and cook for 2 minutes until the rice is opaque. Add 2 cups of the chicken broth and cook gently, stirring occasionally, for 20 minutes; add the extra broth if the rice becomes too dry.

Stir in the raisins. Cut the pepper into strips, removing seeds and pith, and add to the rice. Cook for a further 10 minutes. Spoon the pilaff onto a serving dish and sprinkle with the toasted almonds. SERVES 4

Vegetable Risotto

Moya Maynard

2 tablespoons corn oil
$\frac{1}{4}$ lb onions, sliced
2 carrots, diced
$\frac{1}{2}$–1 teaspoon dried pepper flakes
1 tablespoon imported yeast extract
1 quart boiling water
$\frac{3}{4}$ cup long-grain rice
2 tablespoons tomato paste
3 tablespoons golden raisins
1 cup peas
grated cheese for serving

Heat the oil in a skillet, add the onions and cook gently for about 5 minutes. Add the carrots and cook for a further 5 minutes. Stir in the pepper flakes, yeast extract and boiling water. Add the rice, tomato paste and raisins, then cook for about 20 minutes, stirring occasionally. Check the risotto during cooking and add a little extra water if necessary. Stir in the peas and cook for about 10 minutes.

Serve immediately, sprinkled with grated cheese. SERVES 4

Risotto with Leeks and Bacon

Carol Bowen

1 lb slab bacon, chopped
2 tablespoons oil
4 leeks, chopped
2 cups long-grain rice
1 (16-oz) can peeled tomatoes
salt and pepper
$\frac{1}{2}$ teaspoon cayenne
$\frac{1}{2}$ teaspoon ground cumin
1 teaspoon grated lemon rind
$3\frac{1}{2}$ cups chicken broth
1 tablespoon butter
grated Parmesan cheese (optional)

Cook the bacon in a large saucepan for 8 minutes, or until crisp and golden. Remove from the pan with a slotted spoon and set aside. Add the oil to the bacon fat in the saucepan and fry the leeks for about 12 minutes. Stir in the rice and fry for a further 5 minutes, stirring frequently. Add the tomatoes with their can juice, seasoning to taste, the cayenne, cumin, lemon rind and broth, and bring to a boil.

Return the chopped bacon to the pan, cover and simmer for 15 to 20 minutes, or until the rice is cooked and has absorbed all the liquid. Serve at once, dotted with the butter and sprinkled with the Parmesan cheese, if used. SERVES 4

Rice and Chicken Cakes

Audrey Ellis

$1\frac{1}{2}$ cups cooked long-grain rice
$\frac{1}{2}$ cup Béchamel Sauce (page 20)
$\frac{1}{2}$ cup chopped nuts (for example almonds, walnuts or peanuts)
$\frac{3}{4}$ cup chopped cooked chicken
$\frac{1}{3}$ cup golden raisins
1 teaspoon curry powder
2 egg yolks
salt and pepper
a little flour
1 egg, beaten
toasted bread crumbs for coating
oil for deep frying
GARNISH
lettuce heart
watercress sprigs
quartered lemon slices

Mix the cooked rice, sauce, nuts, chopped chicken, raisins, curry powder and egg yolks. Season well with salt and a little pepper. Form into 8 square cakes and chill for 2 to 3 hours.

Coat the cakes in flour, dip into beaten egg and coat with bread crumbs, taking care that the cakes are completely sealed. Heat the oil for deep frying to 375°, add the cakes, one or two at a time, and cook until crisp and golden. Drain on paper towels.

Garnish the cakes with a few leaves from the heart of a lettuce, watercress sprigs and quartered lemon slices. Serve immediately. SERVES 4

Rice Moussaka

Audrey Ellis

$\frac{3}{4}$ cup long-grain rice
salt and pepper
2 tablespoons oil
1 onion, chopped
$\frac{1}{2}$ lb ground beef
1 tablespoon tomato paste
4 tomatoes, chopped
$\frac{1}{2}$ cup beef broth
$2\frac{1}{2}$ cups Béchamel Sauce (page 20)
1 cup grated cheese
GARNISH
1 tomato, sliced
parsley sprig

Cook the rice in plenty of boiling salted water for 15 to 20 minutes, until just tender. Drain and set aside.

Meanwhile, heat the oil, add the onion and fry gently for a few minutes. Add the beef and cook, stirring, until browned. Stir in the tomato paste, chopped tomatoes and broth. Season to taste and simmer for 15 minutes.

Mix the Béchamel sauce with the cooked rice and half the grated cheese. Spoon half the mixture into an ovenproof dish and cover with the meat. Top with the remaining rice mixture and sprinkle with the rest of the cheese. Bake in a preheated 375° oven for 30 minutes, until lightly browned on top. Serve immediately, garnished with tomato slices and a sprig of parsley. SERVES 6

Cannelloni with Chicken Livers

Audrey Ellis

$\frac{1}{2}$ lb cannelloni tubes
salt and pepper
3 tablespoons oil
$\frac{1}{2}$ lb chicken livers, chopped
1 onion, finely chopped
$\frac{1}{2}$ cup chopped mushrooms
1 egg, beaten
2 tablespoons dry stuffing mix
3 tablespoons light cream
$1\frac{1}{4}$ cups Béchamel Sauce (page 20)
$\frac{1}{2}$ cup grated cheese
GARNISH
tomato slices
watercress sprigs

Cook the cannelloni in plenty of boiling salted water for 8 minutes, until just tender. Drain thoroughly.

Meanwhile, heat the oil in a skillet. Add the chicken livers and onion and fry for 10 minutes. Stir in the mushrooms and cook for 5 minutes. Off the heat, stir in the beaten egg, stuffing mix and seasoning to taste.

Fill the cannelloni tubes with the meat mixture (careful handling will be necessary to avoid splitting the cannelloni). Arrange in a greased ovenproof dish. Stir the cream into the sauce, spoon over the cannelloni and sprinkle with the cheese. Bake in a preheated 350° oven for 30 minutes. Serve immediately, garnished with tomato slices and watercress sprigs. SERVES 4

114

Chicken Rice Ring

— Carol Bowen —

1 cup long-grain rice
salt and pepper
2 tablespoons butter or margarine
1 green pepper, seeded and chopped
1 sweet red pepper, seeded and chopped
1 onion, chopped
½ cup canned whole kernel corn, drained
4 chicken pieces, cooked
paprika
SAUCE
½ cup mayonnaise
2 teaspoons curry paste
2 small onions, grated
2 teaspoons finely chopped parsley

Cook the rice in plenty of boiling salted water for 15 to 20 minutes, or until the grains are tender; drain.

Meanwhile, melt the butter or margarine in a saucepan and add the chopped peppers and onion, then cook gently for 5 minutes. Add the corn and continue to cook for 5 minutes. Fold the fried vegetables into the cooked rice and season to taste. Pack into a greased 5-cup ring mold, leave to cool then chill thoroughly.

Meanwhile, remove the skin and any bones from the chicken and cube the meat. Combine the mayonnaise, curry paste, grated onions, parsley and seasoning to taste. Fold in the cubed chicken meat and chill.

To serve, unmold the rice ring onto a plate and fill the center with the chicken mixture. Dust with a little paprika and serve. SERVES 4

Creamy Curried Pasta

— Carol Bowen —

½ lb pasta shapes
salt and pepper
1 onion, finely chopped
¼ cup dry vermouth or chicken broth
¾ cup mayonnaise
2 teaspoons mild concentrated curry paste
2 teaspoons apricot jam
2 teaspoons lemon juice
8 large link pork sausages, cooked and thinly sliced
GARNISH
halved tomato slices
chopped parsley

Cook the pasta in boiling salted water for 12 to 15 minutes, until tender. Drain well and allow to cool.

Place the onion and vermouth or broth in a saucepan and bring to a boil. Simmer for 3 minutes, then remove from the heat and allow to cool.

Combine the onion mixture with the mayonnaise, curry paste, apricot jam, lemon juice and seasoning. Pour over the pasta and toss well to coat. Finally fold in the cooked sausages. Turn the mixture into a serving dish and garnish it with the tomatoes and parsley. Chill for 30 minutes before serving. SERVES 4

Eggs Mulligatawny

Moya Maynard

¾ cup long-grain rice
3 cups chicken broth
6 large eggs, hard-cooked
watercress sprigs for garnish
SAUCE
1 (16-oz) can mulligatawny soup
(ready to serve)
1 tablespoon cornstarch
1 tablespoon tomato paste
2 tablespoons sweet chutney
⅓ cup golden raisins

Place the rice in a saucepan with the broth, bring to a boil, then reduce the heat and simmer for 12 to 15 minutes.

To make the sauce, pour the soup into a saucepan. Blend the cornstarch with a little water and add to the soup with the remaining ingredients. Bring slowly to a boil, stirring, and cook for about 5 minutes until the sauce thickens.

Drain the rice and arrange it on a heated dish. Cut the eggs into halves lengthwise and arrange on the rice. Spoon the sauce over the eggs and garnish with watercress. Serve with currant jelly and salted peanuts, if liked. SERVES 4

Spaghetti alla Marinara

Marguerite Patten

¼ lb spaghetti
salt and pepper
2 large tomatoes
2 tablespoons butter or margarine
1 onion, chopped
½ cup sliced mushrooms
½ cup flaked cooked white fish
¼ cup peeled and deveined shrimp (optional)
a little chopped parsley
½ cup grated cheese

Cook the spaghetti in plenty of boiling salted water until tender. Meanwhile, peel and chop the tomatoes. Melt the butter or margarine in a skillet, add the onion, mushrooms and tomatoes and cook gently until the onion is soft.

Add the cooked fish and shrimp, if used, and season to taste. Drain the spaghetti, then add it to the fish mixture. Toss and heat for a few minutes, then add chopped parsley and grated cheese and serve immediately. SERVES 2

Bolognaise Sauce

Jane Todd

3 slices bacon, chopped
2 tablespoons butter
1 onion, chopped
1 clove garlic, crushed
2 carrots, chopped
2 stalks celery, chopped
½ lb ground beef
¼ lb ground pork
¼ lb ground veal
1 (8-oz) can peeled tomatoes
¾ cup chicken broth
¾ cup red wine
2 tablespoons tomato paste
pinch of grated nutmeg
½ lb mushrooms, sliced
salt and pepper
¼ cup heavy cream

Cook the bacon in a saucepan until it has rendered its fat. Pour off most of the fat. Add the butter to the pan and melt it. Add the onion, garlic, carrots and celery and cook until the vegetables are beginning to soften. Add the meats and continue cooking, stirring, until browned and crumbly. Add the tomatoes with their juice, broth, wine, tomato paste, nutmeg, mushrooms and seasoning. Bring to a boil, reduce the heat and cover the pan. Simmer for 1 hour. Stir in the cream just before serving. SERVES 6

Cheese and Mushroom Noodles

Moya Maynard

3 tablespoons butter or margarine
1 medium-size onion, chopped
¼ lb mushrooms, halved
¼ lb American cheese slices
6 oz ribbon noodles
salt and pepper
1 teaspoon lemon juice
chopped parsley for garnish

Melt the butter or margarine in a skillet, add the onion and cook gently for about 10 minutes until soft. Add the mushrooms and cook for a further 2 minutes. Cut the cheese into matchstick lengths.

Meanwhile, cook the noodles in plenty of boiling salted water for about 8 minutes, or until just tender. Drain well and return the noodles to the pan. Stir in the cooked onion and mushroom mixture, the cheese, seasoning and lemon juice. Mix thoroughly and serve immediately, garnished with chopped parsley. SERVES 2

Kidney and Pasta Sauté

———— Marguerite Patten ————

6 lamb kidneys
1 tablespoon seasoned flour
1 tablespoon oil
2 tablespoons butter
1 small onion, sliced
3 slices bacon, chopped
1 (8-oz) can peeled tomatoes
1 tablespoon tomato paste
2 cups chicken broth
1 teaspoon Worcestershire sauce
1 tablespoon sherry wine
2 oz pasta shapes (about $\frac{1}{2}$ cup)
salt and pepper
chopped parsley for garnish (optional)

Skin, halve and core the kidneys, then dredge them in seasoned flour. Heat the oil and butter together in a saucepan, then add the onion and bacon and fry for 2 to 3 minutes. Add the prepared kidneys and continue cooking until the kidneys are sealed on the outside. Pour off any excess fat.

Stir in the tomatoes, tomato paste, chicken broth, Worcestershire sauce and sherry and bring to a boil. Add the pasta and salt and pepper to taste. Cover the pan and cook gently until the pasta is just tender – about 15 minutes. Remove the lid toward the end of the cooking time if the mixture is too moist. Serve piping hot, sprinkled with a little chopped parsley if liked. SERVES 4

Veal-stuffed Cannelloni

———— Jane Todd ————

8 cannelloni tubes
1 tablespoon oil
FILLING
$\frac{1}{2}$ cup butter
$\frac{1}{2}$ cup chopped mushrooms
$\frac{3}{4}$ lb ground veal
pinch of grated nutmeg
salt and pepper
about 6 tablespoons water
2$\frac{1}{2}$ cups Tomato Sauce (page 125)
grated Parmesan cheese

Cook the cannelloni in plenty of boiling salted water, with the oil added, until tender. Drain and rinse in cold water.

To make the filling, melt half the butter in a skillet and cook the mushrooms for 3 to 4 minutes. Stir in the veal, nutmeg and seasoning and continue to cook until the veal is browned. Add the water and allow the mixture to simmer for about 20 minutes, stirring occasionally to prevent it from sticking.

Allow the meat mixture to cool slightly, then use to fill the cannelloni – the easiest way to do this is to spoon the filling into a large pastry bag fitted with a plain nozzle and pipe it into the cannelloni. Even so, careful handling is necessary to avoid splitting the cannelloni.

Arrange the filled cannelloni in a greased ovenproof dish and pour over the tomato sauce. Sprinkle the surface generously with grated Parmesan cheese and dot with the remaining butter. Bake in a preheated 350° oven for 30 to 40 minutes, until bubbling and lightly browned. SERVES 4

Lasagne Verdi

———— Jane Todd ————

12 sheets lasagne verdi
salt and pepper
1 tablespoon oil
Bolognaise Sauce (page 116)
2$\frac{1}{2}$ cups Béchamel Sauce (page 20)
$\frac{1}{2}$ cup grated cheese
2 tablespoons grated Parmesan cheese

Bring a pan of salted water to a boil, add the lasagne with the oil and cook until just tender. Drain and rinse in cold water. Lay the sheets of lasagne on paper towels to dry. Meanwhile, make the Bolognaise Sauce and the Béchamel Sauce.

To assemble the lasagne, line the bottom of a lightly greased ovenproof dish with some of the lasagne. Spread with a layer of bolognaise sauce followed by a layer of béchamel sauce. Continue in this way, ending with a layer of béchamel sauce on top. Sprinkle the surface with a mixture of the cheeses and cook in a preheated 400° oven for 40 to 45 minutes, until browned and bubbling. Or cool, cover with plastic wrap and store in the refrigerator until ready to cook. Serve with a tossed green salad. SERVES 4

Fondue Cookery

What better way to entertain friends than to gather round for a delicious fondue? Not only is this a simple, fun way of entertaining, but it can be quite economical too.

Mixed Fondue with Peppered Tomato Sauce, Curried Mayonnaise, Deviled Mayonnaise and Yogurt Herb Sauce

Mixed Fondue

To prepare a mixed fondue, serve a selection of foods which can be deep fried. For example, offer fine slices of sirloin steak, sliced smoked sausage, small meatballs about the size of walnuts, thin slices of chicken breast, small bacon rolls and some fish — peeled cooked shrimp, small chunks of white fish or fish balls.

Arrange the chosen foods on platters or piled in dishes and garnish them with herbs, lemons and tomatoes — it is important to make the raw food look attractive. Serve a selection of sauces to accompany the cooked food, a salad and some bread. Garlic bread can also be served, if you like. Prepare a small amount of batter which can be used to coat the fish pieces before they are cooked.

Heat enough oil to two-thirds fill the fondue pot — do this on the stove before you serve the fondue. Transfer the pot to the spirit burner and keep the oil hot enough to cook the food. Guests help themselves to foods, spearing each piece with a fondue fork and dipping it in the hot oil (or in batter first, if necessary) until cooked. If the oil cools during the meal, quickly reheat it on the stove before any more items are cooked.

Choose from the following sauces, or serve bottled chutneys and relishes if you prefer.

Yogurt Herb Sauce Mix plenty of chopped fresh herbs, seasoning and about 2 oz cream cheese with $\frac{3}{4}$ cup plain yogurt. Chill lightly before serving.

Deviled Mayonnaise Mix $\frac{1}{4}$ teaspoon chili powder, $\frac{1}{2}$ teaspoon Worcestershire sauce, 2 tablespoons tomato paste and 1 tablespoon grated onion into 1 cup mayonnaise. Add seasoning to taste and chill thoroughly. Serve sprinkled with a little extra chili powder or paprika if you prefer.

Curried Mayonnaise Stir 1 tablespoon concentrated curry paste, 1 tablespoon grated onion, 2 finely chopped green chilies and the grated rind of 1 small lemon into 1 cup mayonnaise. Chill thoroughly and serve garnished with a little chopped fresh coriander and a couple of small whole red or green chilies.

Peppered Tomato Sauce Finely chop 1 large onion and 2 sweet green or red seeded peppers. Fry these in a little butter until soft but not browned. Add 1 (16-oz) can tomatoes and bring to a boil. Cover and simmer for 5 minutes, then taste and adjust the seasoning and stir in 2 tablespoons chopped parsley and a little paprika. Serve immediately.

Sauces for Fish Fondues

— Diana Jaggar —

Avocado Sauce Mash a ripe avocado with a little lemon juice and some vinaigrette dressing. Add a little mayonnaise, heavy cream, Worcestershire sauce, diced cucumber and seasoning to taste.

Tomato Chili Sauce Mix together mayonnaise, tomato relish, finely grated onion, 1–2 teaspoons hot pepper sauce, lemon juice, salt and pepper and whipped cream.

Hollandaise Sauce

— Marguerite Patten —

2 egg yolks
pinch of cayenne
salt and pepper
1-2 tablespoons lemon juice or white
wine vinegar
$\frac{1}{4}$–$\frac{1}{2}$ cup butter

Place the egg yolks and cayenne in the top of a double boiler with the seasoning and lemon juice or vinegar. Place over hot, not boiling, water and whisk until the sauce begins to thicken. Add the butter in very small pieces, whisking in each piece until completely melted before adding the next. Do not allow to boil or the sauce will curdle. If the sauce is too thick, add a little cream.
SERVES 4

Crispy Fried Fish Balls

Jill Spencer

¼ cup butter · ¼ cup flour
¾ cup milk
¾ lb finnan haddie (smoked haddock fillet),
cooked, skinned and flaked
grated rind of ½ lemon
salt and pepper
1 tablespoon chopped parsley
2 hard-cooked eggs, chopped
COATING
1 egg, beaten · bread crumbs for coating
oil for deep frying

Place the butter, flour and milk in a blender and switch on to maximum speed for 30 seconds. Pour into a saucepan and bring to a boil, whisking all the time. Simmer the sauce over a low heat for 1 minute. Stir in the remaining ingredients, making sure there are no bones in the fish, and spread the mixture in a shallow dish. Mark into 12 portions and chill until firm enough to handle.

Roll the portions into balls, using a little flour if necessary, then dip them in the beaten egg and coat them in bread crumbs. Heat the oil to 350° in a suitable fondue pot. Cook the fish balls at the table and serve a Tomato Sauce (page 125) as an accompaniment. SERVES 4

Fried Fish Fondue

Diana Jaggar

½ lb haddock or cod fillet, cooked
3 tablespoons butter · 3 tablespoons flour
¾ cup milk
3 tablespoons heavy cream
a little lemon juice
salt and cayenne
1 egg, beaten · bread crumbs for coating
1 lb whitebait
1 lb shrimp in shell
½ lb button mushrooms

For the fish balls, flake the haddock or cod, removing all the skin and bones. Melt the butter in a small saucepan and stir in the flour. Gradually pour in the milk and bring to a boil, stirring continuously, to make a thick sauce. Remove the pan from the heat and stir in the cream and flaked fish. Add a little lemon juice and seasoning to taste, then beat well. Allow to cool and chill thoroughly.

Shape spoonfuls of the fish mixture into walnut-sized balls (flour your hands first). Coat the fish balls in beaten egg and then in bread crumbs. Arrange these on individual plates with the whitebait, shrimp and mushrooms. Each guest spears a piece of seafood or mushroom and cooks it in hot oil in the fondue pot.

Serve cooked rice, a fresh salad, the Avocado Sauce and Tomato Chili Sauce (both opposite) to accompany the fish. SERVES 4

Fondue Bourguignonne

— Jill Spencer —

1¼ lb fillet or sirloin steak
oil for deep frying

Cut the beef into small cubes. Heat the oil in the fondue pot over a gentle heat. The oil should not come more than halfway up the sides of the pot. When the oil is hot enough, a cube of day-old bread should turn golden brown in 1 minute of cooking.

Arrange the meat on individual plates; each person spears a piece and cooks it to taste in the hot oil. Serve baked potatoes, salads and French bread to accompany the fondue with a selection of sauces. SERVES 4

Cucumber and Sour Cream Sauce Peel and dice half a cucumber, then mix it with ½ cup sour cream, ¼ cup mayonnaise, 1 tablespoon chopped chives and seasoning to taste. Chill lightly before serving.

Tomato Sauce Finely chop 1 large onion and cook it in ¼ cup butter until soft but not browned. Add a bay leaf, salt and pepper, 1 teaspoon oregano and 1 tablespoon (16-oz) flour. Cook for a minute, then stir in 2 cans tomatoes and 2 tablespoons tomato paste. Simmer for 20 minutes, remove the bay leaf and blend in a food processor or blender before serving.

Bacon and Corn Fondue

— Jill Spencer —

¾ cup dry white wine
1 lb Swiss cheese, grated
2 teaspoons cornstarch
¾ cup canned whole kernel corn, drained
¼ lb slab bacon, chopped and fried
1 tablespoon chopped parsley
freshly ground black pepper

Pour most of the wine into a fondue pot and heat gently. Gradually stir in the cheese and cook gently, stirring continuously, until smooth and melted.

Blend the cornstarch with the remaining wine until smooth and stir into the fondue with the corn, bacon, parsley and pepper to taste. Serve cubes of French bread to dip in the fondue. SERVES 3 TO 4

Spicy Meatballs

— Jill Spencer —

1 onion, finely chopped
1 tablespoon oil
1 lb ground beef
salt and pepper
¼ teaspoon grated nutmeg
¼ teaspoon garlic salt
1 egg, beaten
cooking oil

Cook the onion in the hot oil until soft – about 5 to 10 minutes. Mix it with the beef, seasoning, nutmeg, garlic salt and beaten egg. Using floured hands, shape the meat mixture into walnut-sized balls. Arrange the meatballs on individual plates.

Pour enough oil into the fondue pot to half fill it, then heat it to 350°. Guests spear the meatballs and cook them in the hot oil. Serve with Green Pepper and Pickle Sauce (below), mustard, peach chutney and mango chutney. SERVES 4

Green Pepper and Pickle Sauce

— Jill Spencer —

1 onion, chopped
2 green peppers, chopped
4 large dill pickles, sliced
2 tablespoons butter
¼ cup water
salt and pepper
¼ teaspoon chili sauce

Cook the onion, green pepper and pickles together in the butter until golden. Add the remaining ingredients, bring to a boil and simmer for 10 minutes, stirring occasionally.

Traditional Cheese Fondue

Jill Spencer

1 clove garlic
$\frac{3}{4}$ cup dry white wine
1 teaspoon lemon juice
$2\frac{1}{2}$ cups grated Emmental cheese
$2\frac{1}{2}$ cups grated Gruyère cheese
1 tablespoon cornstarch
3 tablespoons kirsch
pinch of white pepper
pinch of grated nutmeg
pinch of paprika

Rub the inside of a fondue pot with the cut clove of garlic. Pour the wine into the pot with the lemon juice and heat gently. Gradually add the cheeses, stirring continuously, and heat gently until all the cheese has melted.

When the mixture begins to bubble, blend the cornstarch and kirsch together and add to the fondue. Continue to cook gently, again stirring continuously, for a further 2 to 3 minutes and season to taste with pepper, nutmeg and paprika. Serve cubes of French bread to dip in the fondue. SERVES 4

Horseradish Fondue

Jill Spencer

1 tablespoon butter
2 cups grated Cheddar cheese
$\frac{1}{4}$ cup milk
1 tablespoon Worcestershire sauce
2 teaspoons dried grated horseradish
salt and pepper
$\frac{1}{2}$ tablespoon flour
1 tablespoon water
1 tablespoon dry white wine

Place the butter and cheese together in a fondue pot and allow to melt over a low heat, stirring frequently. Stir in the milk, Worcestershire sauce, horseradish and seasoning. Blend the flour with the water and stir into the fondue. When smooth and thick add the white wine and reheat, stirring all the time.

Serve artichoke hearts, cubes of cooked ham and cauliflower florets to dip in the fondue. SERVES 2

Asparagus Fondue

Jill Spencer

$\frac{3}{4}$ cup dry white wine
1 lb Swiss cheese, grated
1 tablespoon cornstarch
1 (12-oz) can asparagus spears
2 tablespoons chopped parsley
freshly ground black pepper
cayenne

Pour the wine into the fondue pot and heat gently. Gradually add the cheese and cornstarch, mixed, and stir constantly until all the cheese has melted. Drain the asparagus and cut it into 1-in lengths. Stir the asparagus into the fondue with the remaining ingredients. Use cubes of cooked ham and French bread to dip in the fondue. SERVES 4

Onion and Mushroom Fondue

Jill Spencer

$\frac{1}{4}$ cup butter
2 shallots, finely chopped
$\frac{1}{2}$ cup chopped mushrooms
$1\frac{1}{4}$ cups dry white wine
3 cups grated Gruyère cheese
3 cups grated Emmental cheese
pinch of dry mustard
pinch of grated nutmeg
1 tablespoon cornstarch
2 tablespoons kirsch
chopped parsley for garnish

Melt the butter in a fondue pot and cook the shallots and mushrooms in it for 5 to 10 minutes. Pour in the white wine and heat gently. Gradually add the cheeses, stirring continuously until melted. Add the mustard and nutmeg, then blend the cornstarch with kirsch and stir into the fondue. Cook for a further 10 minutes, stirring all the time, until thickened. Garnish with the parsley and serve with small button mushrooms, cubes of bread and pickled onions to dip. SERVES 4 TO 6

Farmhouse Fondue

Jill Spencer

1 clove garlic
1 lb Cheddar cheese, grated
$\frac{3}{4}$ cup milk
salt and pepper
pinch of dry mustard
pinch of grated nutmeg
2 tablespoons dry white wine (optional)

Rub the inside of a fondue pot with the cut clove of garlic. Add the cheese and melt it slowly over a very gentle heat, stirring continuously. Stir in the remaining ingredients. Cook until thickened and creamy, stirring all the time.

Serve cubes of French bread to dip in the fondue.
SERVES 4

Cider Fondue

Jill Spencer

2 cups hard cider
1$\frac{1}{2}$ lb Gruyère or Swiss cheese, grated
1 tablespoon flour
3 tablespoons applejack or Calvados
salt and pepper
pinch of grated nutmeg

Heat the cider in a fondue pot. Gradually add the cheese and flour, mixed together, and heat gently until all the cheese has melted, stirring continuously.

Stir in the remaining ingredients and cook for a few minutes until the fondue has thickened. Serve quartered apples (dipped in a little lemon juice to prevent discoloration) and cubes of French bread to dip in the fondue. SERVES 6

Barbecues and Picnics

Whether it's a simple barbecue in your own garden or an elaborate picnic party, outdoor eating is great fun. All the ideas you need to ensure that your summer extravaganzas are a success are here – from fantastic filled rolls to aromatic grills.

Picnic Rolls, Pork and Apple Barbecue and Seafood Kabobs

Pork and Apple Barbecue

Bridget Jones

(ILLUSTRATED ON PREVIOUS PAGE)

4 lean pork chops
2 tart apples, cored and thickly sliced
a little lemon juice
salt and pepper
a few sage leaves
oil for cooking
a little light brown sugar
sage sprigs for garnish

Trim any excess fat off the chops. Dip the apple slices in a little lemon juice to prevent them from discoloring. Season the chops and cook them on the barbecue with sage leaves to give flavor. Turn the chops to cook the second side and make sure that the meat is cooked through. Brush the chops with oil during cooking, but do not make them too greasy.

When the chops are almost cooked, place the apple slices over the coals and cook until browned underneath. Turn over and sprinkle a little brown sugar on top, then cook for a few minutes longer. Serve these with the chops, garnished with a few fresh sage sprigs. SERVES 4

Seafood Sauce

Carol Bowen

6 tablespoons thick mayonnaise
1 tablespoon tomato paste
2 tablespoons lemon juice
1 tablespoon Worcestershire sauce
1 teaspoon grated lemon rind
1 teaspoon finely chopped onion
2 teaspoons chopped parsley
salt and pepper

Blend all the ingredients together with a wooden spoon until smooth and well mixed. Place in the refrigerator and chill for at least 1 hour before serving. SERVES 4

Tuna Steaks with Mustard

Carol Bowen

$\frac{1}{4}$ cup butter, melted
1 tablespoon prepared mustard
1 tablespoon lemon juice
salt and pepper
4 tuna or cod steaks
lemon slices for garnish

Combine the melted butter with the mustard, lemon juice and seasoning to taste. Brush half this mixture over the steaks, on both sides, then grill the fish over medium coals for 10 minutes. Turn, brush with the remaining mixture and grill for a further 10 minutes.

Serve hot, with any of the remaining mustard mixture and lemon slices to garnish. SERVES 4

Seafood Kabobs

Carol Bowen

6 slices bacon
$\frac{1}{2}$ lb flounder fillets
salt and pepper
3 crayfish tails, peeled
8 large cooked shrimp, peeled and deveined
1 large lemon, cut into 4 thick slices
MARINADE
1 lemon
$\frac{1}{2}$ cup olive oil
1 clove garlic, crushed
$\frac{1}{4}$ teaspoon salt
bay leaf

Prepare the marinade first by carefully paring the rind from the lemon. Add the rind to the juice squeezed from the lemon, the oil, garlic, salt and bay leaf. Mix together thoroughly.

Place the bacon slices on a board and stretch them with the back of a round-bladed knife. Cut each slice into two. Skin the flounder fillets and divide the fish into twelve pieces. Place each piece of fish on half a bacon slice, season and roll up, enclosing the fish completely. Secure each with a wooden toothpick. Cut each crayfish tail into four pieces. Place the bacon and fish rolls, shrimp and crayfish in the marinade and leave for 2 hours, turning occasionally.

Cut each lemon slice into four pieces. Remove the toothpicks from the bacon and fish rolls and put them with the shrimp and crayfish on four long or eight short skewers, alternating with the pieces of lemon. Cook the kabobs over medium coals for about 10 minutes, turning and brushing occasionally with the marinade. Serve with Seafood Sauce (left). SERVES 4

133

Malaysian Dindings Duck

Carol Bowen

1 tablespoon ground coriander
2 teaspoons ground fenugreek
2 teaspoons ground cumin
2 teaspoons turmeric
1 teaspoon ground cinnamon
$\frac{1}{2}$ teaspoon ground cardamom
$\frac{1}{4}$ teaspoon ground cloves
$\frac{1}{4}$ teaspoon grated nutmeg
1 teaspoon mild chili powder
1 teaspoon freshly ground black pepper
$\frac{1}{2}$ teaspoon salt
1 small piece fresh ginger root, grated
juice of 1 lemon
2 small onions, minced
2 cloves garlic, crushed
$1\frac{1}{3}$ cups shredded coconut
1 cup boiling water
1 (5-lb) duck

Mix all the spices and seasonings together in a bowl with the ginger, lemon juice, onions and garlic. Soak the coconut in the boiling water for 5 minutes, then add to the spice mixture. Stir well to make a thick paste.

Split the duck open through the breastbone and open out flat. Secure the duck flat with skewers if necessary. Spread the paste all over the duck and cook over medium coals for $1\frac{1}{2}$ to 2 hours. Turn and baste occasionally. Serve with a crisp salad. SERVES 4

Honey Barbecued Chicken

Carol Bowen

$\frac{1}{4}$ cup butter
1 medium-size onion, chopped
1 clove garlic, crushed (optional)
1 (16-oz) can peeled tomatoes
2 tablespoons Worcestershire sauce
2 tablespoons honey
salt and pepper
4 large *or* 8 small chicken drumsticks
watercress sprigs for garnish

Place the butter, onion, garlic, tomatoes with their can juice, Worcestershire sauce, honey and seasoning in a small saucepan. Heat gently for 30 minutes.

Brush the drumsticks with the sauce and cook over medium coals for 10 to 15 minutes on each side, depending upon size, brushing frequently with the sauce. Serve any remaining sauce separately with the cooked chicken. Garnish with watercress and accompany with a rice and vegetable salad. SERVES 4

Ground Beef Shasliks

Carol Bowen

1 lb lean ground beef
1 teaspoon salt
½ teaspoon freshly ground black pepper
1 tablespoon grated onion
1 tablespoon Worcestershire sauce
4 large onions
8 bay leaves
oil to baste

Combine the beef, salt, pepper, grated onion and Worcestershire sauce in a bowl. Wet your hands and shape the meat into small balls about the size of a large walnut. Blanch the onions in boiling water for 2 to 3 minutes, then cut into quarters.

Thread the meatballs, onion quarters and bay leaves onto four skewers, alternating the ingredients. Brush with oil and cook over medium coals for 15 to 20 minutes, or until cooked. Serve with grilled tomatoes and a crisp salad. SERVES 4

Rolled Veal and Ham Kabobs

Carol Bowen

4 veal cutlets
4 thin slices cooked ham
1 small green pepper, seeded
1 tablespoon Dijon-style mustard
24 stuffed green olives
¾ cup plain yogurt
2 tablespoons lemon juice
¼ cup oil
salt and pepper

Place the veal cutlets between two sheets of dampened wax paper. Beat until very thin. Divide each veal cutlet into four pieces. Cut each slice of ham into four pieces and the pepper into 12 pieces.

Spread each portion of veal with mustard, top with a slice of ham and roll up with the ham inside. Thread the veal rolls onto four skewers, alternating with the pieces of green pepper and the olives.

Mix the yogurt, lemon juice, oil and seasoning to taste together in a small bowl. Spoon over the kabobs and allow to marinate for about 2 hours.

Cook over medium coals for 10 to 15 minutes, basting frequently with the marinade. Serve any unused marinade with the cooked kabobs. SERVES 4

Skewered Noisettes of Lamb

— Carol Bowen —

4 noisettes of lamb (boned loin chops)
2 teaspoons prepared mustard
1 clove garlic, chopped
few rosemary sprigs, crushed
8 shallots or small onions
8 small tomatoes
olive oil
salt and pepper

Trim the noisettes of lamb and spread each side lightly with mustard. Sprinkle with a little chopped garlic and crushed rosemary.

Peel and parboil the onions until they are almost tender. Thread the onions onto skewers with the lamb noisettes and tomatoes. Brush with oil and season with salt and pepper. Grill over medium coals for 30 minutes, turning frequently. Serve with boiled rice. SERVES 4

Vacation Burgers with Cucumber Salad

— Audrey Ellis —

CUCUMBER SALAD
1 cucumber, peeled
2 teaspoons salt
$\frac{3}{4}$ cup sour cream
4 scallions, finely chopped
BURGERS
1 lb ground beef
salt and pepper
oil for brushing
GARNISH
shredded lettuce
8 scallions
1 small onion, sliced into rings
1 tomato, sliced · 4 gherkins

To make the cucumber salad, dice the cucumber and place it in a strainer. Sprinkle with the salt and leave for 15 to 20 minutes, then dry on paper towels. Place the cucumber in a serving dish, top with the sour cream and garnish with the scallions.

Mix the beef with seasoning to taste and shape it into four burgers. Brush the burgers with a little oil and cook under the broiler or over a barbecue until browned on the outside and juicy in the middle. Allow 4 to 6 minutes on each side, according to taste.

Arrange the lettuce on four plates. Place a burger on each and add two scallions. Garnish the burgers with onion rings, slices of tomato and gherkin fans. SERVES 4

137

Picnic Rolls

(ILLUSTRATED ON PAGES 130/131)

Allow three hot dog buns per person and fill them generously with any of the following combinations. Pack the rolls carefully in plastic wrap or close together in a covered container. Take a jar of mayonnaise, sour cream or salad dressing along to moisten the filling just before the rolls are eaten.

Ham Salad Place a large slice of ham, rolled or folded, some tomato wedges and trimmed scallions in each bun. Add a few sprigs of watercress or garden cress and a little seasoning.

Cottage Cheese and Cucumber Cup a large lettuce leaf in the split bun and fill it with cottage cheese, seasoned to taste. Arrange sliced cucumber on top and sprinkle a little chopped mint down the middle.

Egg and Cheese Half fill the bun with grated cheese, then top with quartered hard-cooked eggs and wedges of tomato. Season to taste and add a few sprigs of parsley if you like.

Salami and Coleslaw Cup two slices of salami in each bun and fill them with a little coleslaw. Top with a couple of halved tomato slices.

Smoked Mackerel Cream Mix flaked smoked mackerel with mayonnaise, seasoning and some chopped parsley. Arrange cupped lettuce leaves in the buns and fill with the mackerel mixture. Garnish with lemon wedges.

Shrimp Cocktail Mix cooked peeled shrimp with mayonnaise, a little tomato paste and seasoning to taste. Add a dash of Worcestershire sauce and spoon the mixture into cupped lettuce leaves in the buns. Top with a couple of cooked, unpeeled shrimp and parsley.

Golden Wrapped Eggs

—————— *Carol Bowen* ——————

$\frac{3}{4}$ lb bulk pork sausage meat
1 teaspoon dried mixed herbs
4 hard-cooked eggs, shelled
1 (12-oz) package frozen puff pastry, thawed
beaten egg for glazing

Mix the sausage meat with the herbs until well blended. Divide into four portions and shape each portion around a hard-cooked egg to cover it completely.

Divide the pastry into four portions and roll out each piece on a lightly floured surface to a 6-in square. Reserve any pastry trimmings. Place an egg in the center of each square, moisten the edges of the pastry with water and wrap the pastry around the egg, completely enclosing it.

Place, sealed edges down, on a dampened baking sheet and decorate the tops with pastry leaves made from the reserved pastry trimmings. Make a small slit in the top of each to allow any steam to escape.

Glaze each pastry-wrapped egg with beaten egg and bake in a preheated 425° oven for 25 to 35 minutes or until golden brown. Serve cold with a mixed salad. SERVES 4

Picnic Pie

—————— *Carol Bowen* ——————

PASTRY
$2\frac{1}{2}$ cups wholewheat flour
salt and pepper
$\frac{1}{3}$ cup margarine
$\frac{1}{3}$ cup lard or shortening
beaten egg for glazing
FILLING
2 large chicken pieces
$\frac{1}{2}$ cup soft white bread crumbs
grated rind of 1 lemon
pinch of dried thyme
1 tablespoon chopped parsley
1 large onion, chopped
3 slices lean bacon, chopped
$\frac{1}{2}$ cup chopped mushrooms
$\frac{1}{4}$ cup cold water

To make the pastry, place the flour in a bowl with a pinch of salt. Add the margarine and lard, cut into small pieces, and rub the fat in with the fingertips until the mixture resembles fine bread crumbs. Add enough cold water to bind to make a stiff dough.

Divide the pastry in half and roll out one piece on a lightly floured surface. When rolled out, the pastry should be large enough to line a deep 8-in pie pan.

To prepare the filling, remove the skin from the chicken pieces, cut the chicken meat away from the bone and cut it into small pieces. Place the bread crumbs in a bowl with the lemon rind, thyme and parsley. Add the chicken meat. Mix the onion, bacon and mushrooms together in another bowl.

Arrange half the onion mixture over the pastry-lined pan, season generously, cover with the chicken and bread crumb mixture, then top with the remaining onion mixture. Season again and sprinkle with the water.

Roll out the remaining pastry until large enough to cover the pie pan. Dampen the pastry rim with water and cover with the pastry lid. Trim and flute the edges. Use any pastry trimmings to make leaves to decorate the pie. Make a small hole in the center of the pie to allow any steam to escape. Glaze with the beaten egg.

Bake in a preheated 350° oven for about $1\frac{1}{2}$ hours, until the filling is cooked. If the pastry starts to become too brown during cooking, cover the top with a piece of foil. Allow to cool, then serve with a crisp, fresh salad. SERVES 6

Puff Cheese Whirls

Audrey Ellis

$\frac{1}{2}$ lb frozen puff pastry, thawed
$\frac{2}{3}$ cup crumbled blue cheese
$1\frac{1}{2}$ oz cream cheese
1 teaspoon Worcestershire sauce
$\frac{1}{8}$ teaspoon cayenne

Roll out the pastry thinly to an oblong about 12×8 in. Crumble the blue cheese into a bowl and beat in the cream cheese, Worcestershire sauce and cayenne. Spread this mixture evenly over the pastry and roll up tightly starting from one long edge, like a jelly roll. Chill until firm.

Cut the roll into $\frac{1}{4}$-in slices and lay these flat, and well apart, on non-stick baking sheets (or baking sheets lined with parchment paper).

Bake in a preheated 425° oven for 10 to 12 minutes, or until golden brown. Cool and remove to a wire rack before completely cold. MAKES 20 TO 24

Chicken Liver and Bacon Triangles

Audrey Ellis

4 slices bacon
6 oz chicken livers
salt and pepper
2 tablespoons rich gravy or broth
1 tablespoon apricot or peach chutney
1 lb frozen puff pastry, thawed
1 egg, beaten

Finely chop the bacon and roughly chop the chicken livers. Fry the bacon in a heavy-based skillet until the fat runs. Add the chicken livers, season and stir over moderate heat until just firm. Add the gravy and chutney and remove from the heat to cool.

Roll out the pastry thinly and cut out 12 (4-in) squares. Divide the filling between the pastry squares. Brush the edges with beaten egg, fold over diagonally to make triangular puffs and press the edges well together. Brush the tops with the remaining beaten egg, place on a dampened baking sheet and bake in a preheated 425° oven for 20 to 25 minutes, until well risen and golden brown. Cool on a wire rack. MAKES 12

Highlander's Game Pâté

— Audrey Ellis —

½ lb beef liver
¼ cup butter
1 lb boneless cooked hare or rabbit
4 thick slices bacon
2 cloves garlic, crushed
salt and pepper
1 tablespoon fine oatmeal
2 tablespoons Scotch whisky
2 teaspoons dried rosemary
2 bay leaves

Cut the liver into large pieces. Melt the butter and use to cook the liver lightly, until just firm. Allow to cool. Grind the liver with the cooked game meat. Finely dice the bacon, or grind it with the meats for a finer texture.

Mix all the ingredients except the bay leaves (including the butter used to cook the liver) and press the mixture into a greased terrine. Smooth the surface and press the bay leaves on top of the pâté.

Cover with a lid or foil and cook in a preheated 350° oven for about 1 hour. Cook, then serve with oatcakes and butter. SERVES 4 to 6

Anchovied Terrine of Pork

— Audrey Ellis —

¾ lb pork liver
¾ lb fresh pork sides
8 canned anchovy fillets
2 tablespoons butter
1 teaspoon anchovy oil (from the can)
½ cup finely chopped onion
salt and pepper
1 teaspoon grated nutmeg
1 tablespoon flour
¾ cup dry white wine
2 eggs, lightly beaten
6 slices bacon

Finely grind the liver, pork and anchovies. Melt the butter with the oil, and cook the onion until pale golden. Mix in the meat mixture, seasoning and nutmeg.

Blend the flour with a little wine to form a thin paste, then combine it with the eggs and remaining wine. Pour into the meat mixture and blend together well with a fork. Use the bacon to line the bottoms of two 8 × 4-in foil dishes. Pack the meat mixture into the dishes.

Stand the containers in a bain-marie (a roasting pan half filled with warm water) and cook in a preheated 350° oven for 1½ hours. Remove and cool. SERVES 8 TO 10

Sausage Meatloaf in Pastry

—— Carol Bowen ——

2 tablespoons butter
1 large onion, chopped
1 lb sliced bacon
3 cups soft white bread crumbs
$\frac{1}{4}$ cup shredded beef suet
1 tablespoon chopped parsley
salt and pepper
1 egg, beaten
$\frac{3}{4}$ lb bulk pork sausage meat
$\frac{1}{2}$ lb cooked chicken meat, sliced
1 (12-oz) package frozen puff pastry, thawed
beaten egg for glazing

Melt the butter in a saucepan and fry the onion until it is soft, about 5 minutes. Reserve eight of the bacon slices, then chop the rest quite finely. Add to the onion and cook for a further 5 minutes. Place the bread crumbs in a bowl and add the suet, parsley, drained bacon and onion mixture and seasoning to taste. Bind together with the egg.

Stretch the reserved bacon slices with the back of a knife and use six to line the bottom and sides of a 9 × 5 × 3 in loaf pan. Spread half the sausage meat on the bottom of the pan and cover with half the sliced chicken. Top with the bacon mixture, the remaining chicken and remaining sausage meat. Lay the remaining two bacon slices on top, cover with foil and stand the pan in a bain-marie (a roasting pan half filled with warm water). Bake in a preheated 350° oven for 1½ hours. Allow to cool, then turn the meatloaf out of its pan.

Roll out the pastry on a lightly floured surface to give a rectangle large enough to enclose the meatloaf. Brush with a little of the beaten egg. Place the cooled meatloaf on the pastry, then fold the dough to enclose it completely in a neat package. Trim and seal the edges, reserving any pastry trimmings. Glaze the pastry again with beaten egg and decorate with the pastry trimmings.

Place on a dampened baking sheet and bake in a preheated 425° oven for 35 to 40 minutes, until golden brown and well risen. Cool and serve sliced with a selection of salads. SERVES 8

Bacon and Sage Braid

—— Carol Bowen ——

3 tablespoons butter or margarine
2 onions, chopped
$\frac{1}{2}$ lb Canadian bacon, cut into $\frac{1}{4}$-in pieces
$\frac{1}{4}$ lb mushrooms, thinly sliced
$\frac{1}{2}$ lb bulk pork sausage meat
1 egg, beaten
$\frac{1}{2}$ teaspoon dried thyme
1 tablespoon chopped parsley
2 teaspoons chopped chives
1 teaspoon chopped fresh sage
salt and pepper
1 (12-oz) package frozen puff pastry, thawed
beaten egg for glazing
watercress sprigs for garnish

Melt the butter or margarine in a saucepan. Add the onions and cook for 5 minutes. Add the bacon and fry gently for 10 minutes. Stir in the mushrooms and continue cooking for a further 5 minutes. Transfer to a bowl and mix in the sausage meat, egg, herbs and seasoning.

Roll out the pastry on a lightly floured surface to an oblong approximately 12 × 8 in. Fold in half lengthwise and make diagonal cuts 2 in. in from the joined long edge of the pastry. Place on a dampened baking sheet and open out the pastry. Spoon the prepared filling in a roll shape down the length of the pastry. Fold over the pastry strips in a lattice design and secure together with a little beaten egg. Glaze the top with beaten egg and bake in a preheated 425° oven for 30 to 40 minutes until cooked, crisp and golden. Serve garnished with watercress sprigs. SERVES 4 TO 6

Hot Puddings

Why not round off a light meal with a perfect steamed pudding or a full-flavoured fruit pie for a change? Look through the following pages and you will find recipes for all your old favourite puddings along with some heart-warming new ones.

Pears in Red Wine, Nutty Fruit Crumble and Upside-down Pudding

Nutty Fruit Crumble

— Bridget Jones —

(ILLUSTRATED ON PREVIOUS PAGE)

about 2 lb fresh fruit – for example,
apples, blackberries, blueberries,
plums or rhubarb
sugar
TOPPING
1 cup flour
⅓ cup butter
¼ cup sugar
1 cup chopped walnuts or hazelnuts

Prepare the fruit according to its type; mix two or three different types if you like. For example, mix apples with blackberries, rhubarb with sliced bananas, plums with a little orange rind. Lay the prepared fruit in an ovenproof dish and sprinkle with sugar to taste.

Sift the flour into a bowl and rub in the butter until the mixture resembles fine bread crumbs. Stir in the sugar and nuts and sprinkle this mixture over the fruit.

Cook in a preheated 375° oven for about 45 minutes, or until the topping is brown and the fruit is cooked through. Serve with custard sauce or cream. SERVES 4 TO 6

Pears in Red Wine

— Bridget Jones —

(ILLUSTRATED ON PREVIOUS PAGE)

8 firm pears
juice of 1 lemon
1 bottle red wine
1 cinnamon stick
4 cloves
⅓ cup sugar
pared rind of 1 orange

Peel the pears but leave their stalks in place. Brush the fruit with lemon juice to prevent it from discoloring. Pour the wine into a large saucepan and add the remaining ingredients together with the pears.

Gradually heat the wine to simmering point. Cook gently, basting the pears all the time and turning them over once or twice to make sure that they cook. When the pears are soft, remove them from the pan and arrange them in a serving dish or individual dishes.

Boil the wine until it is reduced to a thick syrupy glaze, then spoon it over the pears and serve immediately with whipped cream. SERVES 4

Upside-down Pudding

— Bridget Jones —

(ILLUSTRATED ON PREVIOUS PAGE)

fresh or canned fruit – for example pineapple
rings, cherries, bananas, pears or plums
½ cup butter or margarine
½ cup sugar
2 eggs
1 cup self-rising flour

Grease a deep 9-in cake pan or straight-sided baking dish with butter and arrange the chosen fruit in the bottom, in a decorative pattern.

Cream the butter or margarine with the sugar until light and fluffy. Gradually beat in the eggs and fold in the flour. Spoon this mixture over the fruit and bake in a preheated 350° oven for about 1 hour. To serve, ease a knife around the side of the cake to free it from the container, then unmold onto a serving plate or dish. Serve with whipped cream or custard sauce. SERVES 6

Plum Pudding

——— Carol Bowen ———

2$\frac{1}{2}$ cups soft wholewheat bread crumbs
1 cup flour
$\frac{2}{3}$ cup golden raisins
$\frac{2}{3}$ cup raisins
$\frac{2}{3}$ cup currants
$\frac{1}{2}$ cup shredded beef suet
$\frac{1}{3}$ cup chopped mixed candied peel
$\frac{1}{3}$ cup glacé cherries
$\frac{2}{3}$ cup firmly packed light brown sugar
1 small tart apple, peeled, cored and grated
$\frac{1}{3}$ cup chopped blanched almonds
pinch of grated nutmeg
1 teaspoon molasses
2 large eggs, beaten
1 cup dark beer
$\frac{1}{4}$ cup brandy

Grease a 5-cup pudding basin or steaming mold. Thoroughly mix all the ingredients together in a large mixing bowl. Place the mixture in the prepared basin, smooth it down and level off the top. Cover with greased parchment paper and greased foil, pleated to allow for expansion. Secure with string. Steam the pudding steadily for 6 hours. Cool and store in a damp-free place.

To serve, steam for a further 3 hours, then unmold onto a serving plate. Flame with extra brandy and accompany with brandy butter. SERVES 6 TO 8

Sussex Pond Pudding

——— Carol Bowen ———

2 cups self-rising flour
1 teaspoon salt
$\frac{1}{3}$ cup shredded beef suet
$\frac{1}{4}$ cup sugar
$\frac{1}{3}$ cup currants
about $\frac{3}{4}$ cup water
FILLING
$\frac{1}{2}$ lb (1 cup) butter
$\frac{1}{3}$ cup mixed dried fruit
$\frac{1}{3}$ cup chopped mixed candied peel
$\frac{2}{3}$ cup glacé cherries
2 tablespoons mincemeat
1 apple, peeled, cored and coarsely grated

Mix the flour, salt, suet, sugar and currants together. Add the water and mix to a soft dough. Knead on a lightly floured surface until smooth. Divide in half and roll out each piece to a 6-in round.

To make the filling, cream the butter and add the dried fruit, peel, cherries, mincemeat and apple. Chill lightly, then form into a ball. Place the mixture in the center of one round of dough, dampen the edge, cover with the second round and pinch the two edges together. Enclose in a piece of greased foil and secure with string. Steam in a steamer or on a trivet in a saucepan half full of water for 2$\frac{1}{2}$ to 3 hours. Remove the foil and serve on a warmed dish. SERVES 4

Lemon Raisin Pudding

Audrey Ellis

1 cup self-rising flour
pinch of salt
$\frac{1}{4}$ cup shredded beef suet
2 tablespoons sugar
$\frac{1}{3}$ cup golden raisins
grated rind and juice of 1 lemon
1 egg
5–6 tablespoons milk
$\frac{1}{4}$ cup lemon cheese or curd
pared lemon·rind for decoration

Sift the flour and salt into a bowl and stir in the suet, sugar, raisins and lemon rind. Beat the egg, lemon juice and milk together, add to the dry ingredients and mix to give a soft dropping consistency. Divide between six greased timbale molds, cover with greased foil and steam for 30 minutes.

Warm the lemon curd and add a very little boiling water to give a thin pouring sauce. Unmold the puddings, spoon a little of the lemon curd sauce over each one and decorate with strips of pared lemon rind. SERVES 6

Yorkshire Apple Pie

Audrey Ellis

1 lb frozen puff pastry, thawed
1$\frac{1}{2}$ lb tart apples
2 cups diced Cheddar cheese
$\frac{1}{3}$ cup raisins
2–3 tablespoons brown sugar
grated rind and juice of $\frac{1}{2}$ lemon
1 egg, beaten

Roll out the pastry and cut out two 9-in rounds. Place one round of pastry on a dampened baking sheet.

Peel, core and slice the apples and arrange them on the pastry base, leaving a border $\frac{1}{2}$ in all around. Place the cheese and raisins on the apple and sprinkle with the sugar, lemon rind and juice. Brush the exposed pastry edges with beaten egg, place the remaining pastry round on top and seal the edges together well. Brush the pie with beaten egg and use any pastry trimmings to decorate. Brush again with egg to glaze. Score the top surface of the pastry lightly with a sharp knife, but do not cut a steam vent.

Bake in a preheated 400° oven for about 40 minutes, until well risen and golden brown. SERVES 6

Grand Marnier Soufflé

Diana Jaggar

$\frac{1}{2}$ cup sugar
ladyfingers or sponge cake slices
6 tablespoons Grand Marnier
$\frac{3}{4}$ cup milk
finely grated rind of $\frac{1}{2}$ lemon
thinly pared rind of 1 orange
2 tablespoons butter
2 tablespoons flour
3 eggs, separated
a little confectioners' sugar

Dust a greased soufflé dish with some sugar. Line with ladyfingers soaked in one third of the liqueur. Bring the milk, remaining sugar, lemon and orange rinds to a boil. Set aside for 10 minutes. Melt the butter in a saucepan, add the flour and cook for 1 minute. Add the strained milk. Bring slowly to a boil, beating continuously until smooth. Cool, then beat in the egg yolks and remaining liqueur.

Beat the egg whites until stiff; stir 1 tablespoon into the sauce and fold in the rest. Turn into the dish. Bake in a preheated 350° oven for 40 to 45 minutes. Dust the top of the soufflé with confectioners' sugar, then bake for a few more minutes. Serve immediately. SERVES 4 to 6

Normandy Apple Pie

Diana Jaggar

2 egg yolks
$\frac{1}{2}$ cup sugar
3 tablespoons butter
$\frac{1}{4}$ cup lard or shortening
2 tablespoons water
2 cups flour, sifted
$\frac{3}{4}$ teaspoon cinnamon
$\frac{1}{2}$ cup finely ground walnuts
1–1$\frac{1}{2}$ lb tart apples, peeled, cored
and quartered
$\frac{3}{4}$ cup heavy cream, lightly whipped
sugar for dredging

Cream together the egg yolks, sugar, butter, lard and water. Gradually add the flour, cinnamon and walnuts to make a paste. Knead, then chill for 30 minutes. Roll out two thirds of the pastry and use to line an 8-in fluted flan ring. Arrange the prepared apples, core side down, in the flan case. Roll out the remaining pastry to make a lid. Dampen the edges, lift the lid into position and press together. Cut a 3-in circle out of the center of the lid. Brush the pastry with cold water and dredge with sugar. Bake in a preheated 350° oven for 35 to 40 minutes until crisp. Serve with piped whipped cream. SERVES 6

Bread and Butter Pudding

—— Carol Bowen ——

3 tablespoons butter, softened
8 large slices bread, crusts removed
$\frac{1}{3}$ cup currants
$\frac{1}{3}$ cup golden raisins
$2\frac{1}{2}$ cups milk
$\frac{1}{4}$ cup sugar
2 eggs
2–3 drops vanilla extract
a little grated nutmeg
2 tablespoons light brown sugar

Butter each slice of bread on both sides and cut into four triangles. Place a layer of bread in the bottom of a 6-cup ovenproof dish. Sprinkle with half the currants and raisins. Top with the remaining bread triangles and dried fruit.

Heat the milk with the sugar in a saucepan until dissolved. Beat the eggs with the vanilla in a small bowl. Pour the milk onto the egg mixture and whisk until well mixed. Strain through a fine sieve over the bread and fruit mixture and leave to soak for 10 to 15 minutes. Sprinkle with nutmeg, then bake in a preheated 350° oven for $1\frac{1}{2}$ hours, until just set and golden. Sprinkle with the brown sugar before serving. SERVES 4 TO 6

Apple Charlotte

—— Carol Bowen ——

10 slices white bread
5 tablespoons butter
$\frac{1}{4}$ teaspoon cinnamon
$\frac{1}{3}$ cup firmly packed dark brown sugar
$1\frac{1}{4}$ lb tart apples, peeled, cored and
thinly sliced
juice of 1 lemon

Trim and reserve the crusts from the bread. Lightly butter the trimmed bread slices with 3 tablespoons of the butter. Line a deep 1-quart baking dish with the bread slices, buttered side inwards, reserving a few bread slices for the lid.

Make bread crumbs from the reserved crusts, then measure 1 cup of crumbs. Melt the remaining butter in a small saucepan. Add the crumbs and cook until golden. Stir in the cinnamon and sugar. Allow to cool.

Toss the apples in the lemon juice to prevent discoloration, then layer them in the dish with the bread crumbs. Cover with the reserved bread slices, buttered side up. Cover with foil and secure with string. Bake in a preheated 400° oven for about $1\frac{1}{4}$ hours. Allow to cool a little before unmolding onto a warmed serving dish or serving it straight from the dish. Serve with cream or custard sauce. SERVES 4

Apple Fritters

—— *Carol Bowen* ——

4 large apples, peeled, cored and cut into
$\frac{1}{4}$-in thick rings
$\frac{1}{2}$ cup vanilla sugar
oil for deep frying
confectioners' sugar for sprinkling
FRITTER BATTER
1 cup flour
$\frac{1}{4}$ teaspoon salt
1 tablespoon oil
1 egg, separated
$\frac{2}{3}$–1 cup milk or milk and water

Dip the apple rings in vanilla sugar and leave to dry slightly on paper towels.

Prepare the fritter batter by sifting the flour and salt together into a bowl. Make a well in the center and pour in the oil and egg yolk. Gradually draw the flour into the egg, adding the milk a little at a time, beating to produce a smooth batter. Beat the egg white until it stands in firm peaks and fold into the batter mixture.

Heat the oil to 375° and coat the apple rings in the batter. Fry the apple rings in the oil for about 4 minutes or until golden and cooked through. Drain on paper towels. Sprinkle with confectioners' sugar and serve. SERVES 4

Apple and Pear Dumplings

—— *Carol Bowen* ——

2 apples
2 pears
1 quantity Pie Pastry (page 87)
$\frac{1}{3}$ cup mixed dried fruit
1 tablespoon clear honey
2 tablespoons chopped mixed nuts
beaten egg or milk for glazing

Grease a baking sheet. Peel and core the apples and pears, leaving the fruit whole.

Roll out the pastry on a lightly floured board or work surface and cut out two rounds of dough slightly larger than the apples. Cut the remaining pastry into 1-in wide strips.

Mix the dried fruit, honey and nuts together in a bowl. Place each apple on a round of dough and fill the centers with half of the fruit mixture. Carefully fold the pastry around the apples, securing the dough together by dampening the edges with a little water. Place seam side down on the baking sheet.

Fill the centers of the pears with the remaining fruit mixture. Dampen the pastry strips with water, then carefully wind them around the pears to enclose them completely. Place upright on the baking sheet. Use any pastry trimmings to make decorative leaves for the apples and pears. Glaze with beaten egg or milk and bake in a preheated 400° oven for 35 to 40 minutes or until golden. Serve with custard sauce or cream. SERVES 4

Almond Apples

Marguerite Patten

4 medium-size tart apples
½ cup chopped blanched almonds
6 tablespoons sugar
2 egg yolks
1 cup soft white bread crumbs
¼ cup cornstarch
2 tablespoons butter

Peel and core the apples Mix the almonds with half the sugar. Beat the egg yolks with the rest of the sugar and stir in half of the bread crumbs. Coat the apples with this mixture.

Put the cornstarch on a plate or in a paper bag and roll the apples in this; use two spoons if the cornstarch is on a plate. Melt the butter in an ovenproof dish, arrange the apples in the dish and fill the centers with the almond and sugar mixture. Sprinkle with the remaining bread crumbs, and bake in preheated 350° oven until tender, about 45 minutes. SERVES 4

Stacked Crêpes

Marguerite Patten

1 quantity crêpe batter
FILLING
lemon cheese or curd
TOPPING
1 egg white
¼ cup sugar
2 tablespoons blanched almonds

Make the crêpe batter. Cook just enough batter at a time in a lightly greased, hot skillet to make thin crêpes. As they are cooked, pile the crêpes in a folded napkin to keep warm. Sandwich the cooked crêpes together with lemon curd.

To make the meringue topping, beat the egg white until very stiff. Very gradually, beat in a little of the sugar, then fold in the remainder of the sugar. Spread the meringue over the top of the pile of filled crêpes. Decorate with almonds, then put in a preheated 475° oven for 1 to 2 minutes only, or until the meringue is lightly browned. Serve warm. SERVES 4 TO 6

Crêpe Batter

Marguerite Patten

1 cup flour
pinch of salt
2 eggs
1 cup milk or milk and water
1 tablespoon olive oil

Sift the flour and salt into a bowl. Add the eggs and enough liquid to give a sticky consistency. Beat well, then gradually add the rest of the liquid, beating all the time. Add the oil last.

Crêpes Suzette

Jill Spencer

1 quantity Crêpe Batter
oil for frying
4 sugar cubes
1 orange
2 tablespoons butter
2 tablespoons sugar
1 tablespoon orange juice
1 tablespoon Curaçao
2–3 tablespoons brandy

Make the crêpe batter. Brush the bottom of a small heavy-based skillet with oil. Allow the oil to become hot, then pour in sufficient batter to cover the pan bottom thinly, tilting the pan for even spreading. Cook the crêpes for 1 to 2 minutes, then turn over to cook the other side.

Rub the sugar cubes over the orange skin to remove the zest. Crush the sugar cubes and mix them with the butter, sugar, orange juice and Curaçao.

Place the orange-flavored butter in a heavy-based skillet or chafing dish and allow it to melt. Fold the crêpes into four and place them, overlapped, in the pan. Baste with the butter sauce and heat through.

Pour over the brandy, allow to become warm, then ignite. When the flames have subsided, sprinkle with blanched, grated orange rind and serve immediately. SERVES 4

Orange and Almond Pudding

Audrey Ellis

$\frac{1}{2}$ cup soft margarine
$\frac{1}{2}$ cup sugar
2 eggs, beaten
grated rind and juice of 1 orange
1 cup self-rising flour, sifted
$\frac{1}{2}$ cup ground almonds
orange slices for decoration (optional)
SAUCE
2 teaspoons cornstarch
$1\frac{1}{4}$ cups orange juice
1 tablespoon light corn syrup

Cream the margarine and sugar together until soft and light. Gradually beat in the eggs and orange rind and juice, then fold in the flour and almonds. Pour the mixture into a greased 5-cup pudding basin or steaming mold, cover with greased foil and steam over simmering water for $1\frac{1}{2}$ hours.

Meanwhile, make the sauce. Moisten the cornstarch with a little of the orange juice. Place the remaining juice in a saucepan with the syrup and bring to boiling point. Add the moistened cornstarch and bring back to a boil, stirring constantly. Simmer for 2 minutes and serve poured over the pudding. Decorate with orange slices, if you like. SERVES 4

Rice Pudding

Marguerite Patten

$\frac{1}{3}$ cup round-grain rice
$2\frac{1}{2}$ cups milk
2–4 tablespoons sugar
a little butter (optional)

Rinse the rice, put it into an ovenproof dish and cover with the milk. Add the sugar. Cook for at least 2 hours in a preheated 275° oven, stirring once after the first 30 minutes. The larger quantity of rice gives a much more solid pudding.

If you are in a great hurry, you can cook the milk pudding for a shorter time at a higher temperature but the flavor is not as good.

Just before serving, stir in the butter, if used. SERVES 4

Cool Desserts

Here is a chapter full of recipes to wreck all intentions of a diet: light, fruity fools, unusual flans, glorious cheesecakes and luscious ices. For when you're feeling really adventurous there is even a recipe for a Frozen Christmas Pudding.

Fresh Fruit Salad, Raspberry Fool and Caramelized Oranges

Fresh Fruit Salad

Bridget Jones

(ILLUSTRATED ON PREVIOUS PAGE)

a selection of fresh fruit – for example, apples,
bananas, melon, kiwi fruit, oranges,
strawberries, grapes, pineapple and peaches
lemon juice
$\frac{1}{2}$ cup sugar
$\frac{3}{4}$ cup water

Prepare the fruit according to its type. Slice or cube the fruit as appropriate. Sprinkle any pieces which may discolor with lemon juice.

Place the sugar and water in a saucepan and heat gently, stirring continuously, until the syrup boils. Cook for a few minutes, then pour the syrup over the fruit, allow to cool and chill thoroughly. Serve with whipped cream.

Caramelized Oranges

Bridget Jones

(ILLUSTRATED ON PREVIOUS PAGE)

1 cup sugar
$\frac{1}{2}$ cup water
8 oranges

Place the sugar and water in a saucepan. Heat slowly, stirring continuously until the sugar dissolves, then bring to a boil and cook until the syrup has reduced and caramelized.

Meanwhile, prepare the oranges: cut off all the peel (do not discard it) and pith and slice the fruit. Remove any seeds and reshape the oranges on a heatproof serving dish or arrange the slices in a bowl. Cut a little of the rind into long fine threads and cook these in water until soft, then arrange them over the fruit.

When the caramel is golden, pour it over the fruit. Take care not to let the sugar overcook or it will become bitter. Chill for several hours or overnight. Serve with whipped cream. SERVES 4

Raspberry Fool

Bridget Jones

(ILLUSTRATED ON PREVIOUS PAGE)

1 lb ($1\frac{1}{2}$ pints) raspberries
$\frac{1}{2}$ cup sugar
$1\frac{1}{4}$ cups heavy cream
a few whole raspberries for decoration

Place the fruit in a saucepan with the sugar and heat gently until the juice runs. Cook for 15 minutes, then purée the fruit in a blender and press it through a fine sieve to remove all the seeds. Leave to cool completely.

Whip the cream until stiff, then carefully fold in the raspberry purée. Swirl the fool in individual glasses and chill thoroughly. Decorate with a few whole raspberries and serve with delicate cookies. SERVES 4

Vacherin Chantilly Glacé

Diana Jaggar

$1\frac{3}{4}$ cups sugar
$1\frac{1}{4}$ cups water
pared rind and juice of 1 lemon
$\frac{1}{2}$ lb ($1\frac{1}{2}$ cups) strawberries
$\frac{1}{2}$ cup confectioners' sugar
juice of 1 large orange
6 egg whites
whipped cream and fresh strawberries
for decoration

Simmer $\frac{1}{2}$ cup sugar, the water and lemon rind for 5 minutes. Cool and strain. Purée the strawberries with the confectioners' sugar in a blender, sieve, then add the orange and lemon juices and sugar syrup. Freeze in a shallow container. When half frozen, beat well, then beat one egg white until stiff and fold into the sherbet. Freeze until hard.

Beat the remaining egg whites until stiff. Add $\frac{1}{4}$ cup of the remaining sugar and beat hard for $3\frac{1}{2}$ minutes. Fold in the remaining sugar. Reserve a quarter of the meringue in the refrigerator and, using a large star nozzle, pipe about two-thirds of the remainder into an 8-in round on a baking sheet lined with parchment paper. Pipe the remaining one-third into a second, wide border around the edge of the round. Cook in a preheated 225° oven until slightly colored – about 2 hours. Pipe the reserved meringue on top of the second border while the case is still hot. Return to the oven for a further 1 hour to dry. When cool, pile the sherbet into the meringue case; decorate. SERVES 6

Caramel Oranges with Cointreau

Diana Jaggar

6 large seedless oranges
1½ cups sugar · 1¼ cups water
3 tablespoons Cointreau
CARAMEL
¾ cup sugar · ¼ cup water

Pare the rind thinly from four of the oranges and cut it into long julienne strips. Blanch the rind for 15 minutes, drain and rinse it in cold water. Bring the sugar and water to a boil, add the orange strips and simmer them for 30 minutes. Add the Cointreau and set aside to cool.

Cut away all the remaining skin and pith from the oranges. Slice each orange thinly and reshape, holding the fruit together with a toothpick. Strain the syrup over the oranges, reserving the orange strips. Chill.

Meanwhile, make the caramel by dissolving the sugar in the water. Cook steadily to a rich brown color, without stirring. Pour immediately onto a well-oiled surface or wax paper. Leave to harden, then crush in a mortar or with a rolling pin. Sprinkle over the oranges, with the reserved strips of rind. SERVES 6

Fresh Peach and Almond Tart

Diana Jaggar

½ cup butter
½ cup sugar
grated rind of 1½ lemons
1 small egg plus 1 yolk
1½ cups flour, sifted
1 cup ground almonds
3 large ripe peaches, halved
¾ cup sugar, dissolved
in 1¼ cups water
2 (3-oz) packages cream cheese
2 tablespoons light cream
blanched almonds and angelica for
decoration

Mix the butter, 6 tablespoons of the sugar, one third of the lemon rind and eggs until well mixed. Work in the flour and ¾ cup of the ground almonds and knead to a smooth paste. Wrap and chill for at least 1 hour. Line a flan ring with this almond pastry. Bake "blind" in a preheated 350° oven for 30 minutes. Cool.

Poach the peaches in the sugar syrup, then remove their skins. Reduce the syrup to a glazing consistency; cool. Beat the cream cheese with the remaining lemon rind, cream, remaining sugar and ground almonds. Spread over the pastry base. Arrange the peach halves on top. Brush with syrup glaze and decorate. SERVES 6

Ginger Soufflé

Carol Bowen

4 eggs, separated
$\frac{1}{2}$ cup firmly packed light brown sugar
$\frac{1}{2}$ teaspoon ground ginger
2 cups milk · 1 envelope unflavored gelatin
6 tablespoons imported ginger wine
$\frac{1}{2}$ cup sour cream
$\frac{1}{4}$ cup finely chopped preserved ginger
$1\frac{1}{4}$ cups heavy cream, whipped
crystallized ginger and chopped almonds
for decoration

Prepare a 6-in soufflé dish (or six $\frac{3}{4}$-cup soufflé dishes) by tying a double-thick band of wax paper around the dish, extended 2 in above the rim. Grease both dish and paper.

Beat the egg yolks, sugar and ground ginger together in a bowl. Scald the milk in a saucepan and pour onto the egg mixture, beating constantly. Return to the saucepan and heat, stirring, until the custard thickens and lightly coats the back of the spoon. Do not allow to boil. Dissolve the gelatin in 3 tablespoons of water in a bowl over a saucepan of hot water. Stir into the cooled custard with the ginger wine. Chill until almost set, then stir in the sour cream and preserved ginger. Fold in half the whipped cream. Beat the egg whites until stiff and fold into the custard. Pour into the dish and chill.

To serve, remove the collar and decorate with the remaining cream, ginger and almonds. SERVES 6

Little Orange Soufflés

Carol Bowen

4 large oranges
4 eggs, separated
$\frac{1}{4}$ cup sugar
1 tablespoon Cointreau, Grand Marnier or
frozen concentrated orange juice, thawed
1 tablespoon confectioners' sugar, sifted

Carefully slice the tops from the oranges and scoop out the flesh. Reserve the shells and zig-zag the top edge for decoration, if liked. Remove the rind from the caps of the oranges and cut into very thin julienne strips. Cook the orange strips in a little boiling water for 5 minutes; drain and cool. Extract the juice from the orange flesh and place it in a saucepan. Boil until just 1 tablespoon orange juice remains.

Place the egg yolks and sugar in a bowl and beat until very thick and creamy. Add the orange rind, warm orange juice and Cointreau, Grand Marnier or concentrated orange juice. In another bowl, beat the egg whites until they stand in firm peaks. Fold into the orange mixture using a metal spoon. Spoon equal quantities of the soufflé mixture into each orange case. Place on a baking sheet and bake in a preheated 450° oven for 10 minutes. While the oranges are still in the oven, sprinkle the tops with the confectioners' sugar. Bake for a further 2 to 3 minutes, then serve at once. SERVES 4.

Walnut and Strawberry Galette

— Carol Bowen —

¾ cup butter or margarine
½ cup sugar
grated rind of ½ lemon
1½ cups flour
1 cup roughly chopped walnuts
FILLING
1¼ cups whipping cream
1 tablespoon confectioners' sugar
1½ lb (about 1 quart) strawberries, hulled

Grease three baking sheets. Cream the butter or margarine and sugar together until light and fluffy. Beat in the lemon rind and fold in the flour. Knead until smooth and chill for 30 minutes.

Divide the dough into three portions and roll out each portion to a 7-in round. Pinch the edges of the rounds to form a decorative shape. Place on the prepared baking sheets and sprinkle the top of each with chopped nuts, pressing them down gently. Bake in a preheated 350° oven for 20 to 25 minutes or until golden. Allow to cool slightly on the sheets, then transfer to a wire rack to cool completely.

Whip the cream with the confectioners' sugar until it stands in soft peaks. Slice 1 lb of the strawberries and fold into two-thirds of the cream. Use to sandwich the rounds together. Pipe or spoon the remaining cream in swirls on top of the galette and decorate with the remaining whole strawberries. Chill for 30 minutes before serving. SERVES 6

Black Currant and Ginger Cheesecake

— Carol Bowen —

½ cup butter
3 cups crushed ginger snaps
2 (8-oz) packages cream cheese
¼ cup sugar
6 tablespoons light cream
1¼ lb (5 cups) black currants or blueberries
1 envelope unflavored gelatin
1¼ cups heavy cream
1 egg white, stiffly beaten

Lightly grease a 9-in springform cake pan with a little of the butter. Melt the remainder in a small saucepan. When melted, add the ginger snap crumbs and mix well to coat evenly. Use to line the bottom of the pan and chill until set.

In a mixing bowl, beat the cream cheese and sugar together until smooth and creamy. Stir in the light cream and 1 lb of the black currants. Dissolve the gelatin in 2 tablespoons of hot water and stir it into the black currant mixture. Spoon this mixture over the chilled crumb crust. Chill until set – about 1 hour.

Meanwhile, whip the double cream until it stands in soft peaks, then fold in the beaten egg white. Using a spoon, swirl this cream mixture over the top of the chilled cheesecake. Use the remaining black currants to sprinkle over the cream and decorate the edge of the cheesecake. Chill for about 15 minutes before serving. SERVES 6

Creamy Cheesecake

— Jane Todd —

$\frac{1}{2}$ cup plus 1 teaspoon butter, melted
3 cups graham cracker crumbs
1 teaspoon ground cinnamon
2 (8-oz) packages cream cheese
$\frac{1}{4}$ cup sugar
6 tablespoons light cream
1 envelope unflavored gelatin, dissolved in
2 tablespoons hot water
$1\frac{1}{4}$ cups heavy cream
1 egg white, stiffly beaten
DECORATION
whipped cream (optional)
fresh fruit (optional)

Lightly grease a 9-in springform cake pan with the teaspoon of butter.

In a medium mixing bowl, combine the cracker crumbs, the remaining melted butter and the cinnamon with a wooden spoon. Line the bottom of the pan with this mixture, pressing it firmly against the bottom. Set aside.

In another mixing bowl, beat the cream cheese and sugar together with a wooden spoon until smooth and creamy. Stir in the light cream and gelatin mixture. Whip the heavy cream until it stands in soft peaks and fold into the cheese mixture with the egg white. Spoon the mixture over the crumb crust. Place in the refrigerator to chill for about 1 hour, or until set.

Decorate the cheesecake with whipped cream and fresh fruit, if used, before serving. SERVES 6 TO 8

Chocolate and Orange Mousse

— Jane Todd —

12 (1-oz) squares semisweet chocolate
1 tablespoon unsalted butter
grated rind of 1 orange
1 tablespoon Cointreau
4 eggs, separated
chocolate curls for decoration

Break the chocolate into pieces and place them in the top of a double boiler. Place over simmering water and leave until the chocolate has melted, stirring occasionally.

Remove the pan from the heat and stir in the butter, orange rind and Cointreau. Mix in the egg yolks. Beat the whites until stiff, then fold in the chocolate mixture.

Spoon the mousse into individual dishes and chill for at least 1 hour. Decorate with chocolate curls, if used, and serve with crisp cookies. SERVES 6

Black Forest Cake

— Jill Spencer —

3 eggs
$\frac{1}{2}$ cup sugar
$\frac{3}{4}$ cup flour
2 tablespoons cocoa powder
FILLING
1 (16-oz) can pitted Bing cherries
1 tablespoon arrowroot
a little kirsch
$1\frac{1}{4}$ cups heavy cream
grated chocolate for decoration

Beat the eggs and sugar together until pale and thick. Sift the flour and cocoa together and gently fold into the mixture, using a metal spoon. Pour into a lined and greased deep 8-in cake pan. Bake in a preheated 375° oven for 35 to 40 minutes. Unmold and cool on a wire rack.

Drain the juice from the cherries and blend a little into the arrowroot. Bring the remainder of the juice to a boil, then pour onto the blended arrowroot and return to the heat to thicken, stirring continuously. Add the cherries to the syrup and allow to cool.

Cut the cake into two layers and sprinkle the base with a little kirsch. Whip the cream and place it in a pastry bag fitted with a large star nozzle. Pipe a circle of cream around the outside edge of the base. Fill the center with half the cherry mixture. Sprinkle the second layer of cake with a little kirsch and place on top of the filling. Spread a little cream around the edge of the cake and press grated chocolate over it. Pipe swirls of cream on top of the cake and fill the center with the remaining cherries. Sprinkle a little grated chocolate on the swirls of cream. SERVES 6

161

Coconut Peach Sundae

— *Carol Bowen* —

2½ cups heavy cream
1⅓ cups shredded coconut
½ cup confectioners' sugar, sifted
1 egg, separated
4 (1-oz) squares semisweet chocolate, grated
SUNDAE
4 fresh peaches or 8 canned peach halves
1 recipe Melba Sauce (below)
whipped cream and toasted coconut flakes
for decoration

Place the cream and coconut in a saucepan and cook, over a low heat, for about 10 minutes. Stir in the sugar and allow to cool. When cool, beat in the egg yolk and pour into freezer trays. Freeze until half frozen. Whisk the half-frozen ice cream to remove all the ice crystals, then fold in the chocolate. Beat the egg white until stiff and fold into the ice cream. Freeze until firm.

Meanwhile, if using fresh peaches, poach them in boiling water with a little sugar until they are tender – about 4 minutes. Cool, peel, halve and remove the pits.

To assemble the sundaes, place a scoop of coconut ice cream in the bottom of each of four tall glasses. Top each with two peach halves and melba sauce. Decorate with whipped cream and toasted coconut flakes. Serve with crisp cookies. SERVES 4

Melba Sauce To prepare a melba sauce, purée ½ lb (1½ cups) raspberries and press the purée through a sieve. Sprinkle in 4 to 5 tablespoons confectioners' sugar, according to taste, and stir until dissolved.

Banana Splits with Hot Fudge Sauce

— *Carol Bowen* —

1 (1-oz) square semisweet chocolate
1 tablespoon butter
2 tablespoons warm milk
⅔ cup firmly packed brown sugar
1 tablespoon light corn syrup
2–3 drops vanilla extract
BANANA SPLITS
4 large ripe bananas, peeled
4 portions vanilla ice cream
½ cup heavy cream
¼ cup finely chopped walnuts
fresh cherries for decoration (optional)

First prepare the sauce by melting the chocolate in the top of a double boiler over simmering water. Add the butter and stir until smooth and glossy. Gradually blend in the milk. Add the sugar and syrup, place the pan directly over the heat and heat gently to dissolve the sugar. Bring to a boil and cook for 5 minutes. Add the vanilla and keep warm.

Meanwhile, split each banana in half and quickly sandwich together with the ice cream in four individual dishes. Whip the cream until it stands in soft peaks. Spoon or pipe decoratively over the bananas and ice cream. Sprinkle with the nuts and decorate with the cherries, if used. Serve with the hot fudge sauce. SERVES 4

Frozen Plum Pudding

—— Carol Bowen ——

2 cups mixed dried fruit
$\frac{2}{3}$ cup chopped colored glacé cherries
$\frac{1}{3}$ cup chopped mixed candied peel
$\frac{1}{2}$ cup flaked almonds
3 tablespoons sherry wine or dark rum
1 tablespoon cocoa powder, sifted
$\frac{1}{2}$ teaspoon apple pie spice
1 egg, separated
$\frac{1}{2}$ cup confectioners' sugar, sifted
$1\frac{1}{4}$ cups heavy cream
DECORATION
whipped cream
glacé cherries
angelica

Put the dried fruit, cherries, peel and almonds in a bowl and add the sherry or rum. Leave to soak for 6 hours or overnight.

Add the cocoa to the fruit mixture with the spice and mix well. Add the egg yolk and confectioners' sugar and beat until well combined. Whip the cream until it stands in soft peaks and fold into the fruit mixture. Beat the egg white until it stands in firm peaks and fold into the cream mixture. Pour into a dampened 5-cup freezerproof mold and freeze until firm, about 4 to 6 hours.

When ready to serve, dip the mold briefly into warm water and invert it onto a serving dish. Leave for about 1 hour in the refrigerator so that the pudding softens a little. Decorate with whipped cream, glacé cherries and angelica. Top with a sprig of holly and cut into wedges to serve. SERVES 6 TO 8

Brown Bread Ice Cream

—— Carol Bowen ——

$1\frac{1}{4}$ cups heavy cream
$\frac{3}{4}$ cup light cream
$\frac{3}{4}$ cup confectioners' sugar, sifted
2 cups soft brown bread crumbs
1 tablespoon dark rum (optional)
2 eggs, separated
sliced strawberries for decoration (optional)

This traditional English ice cream recipe is far more delicious than it sounds.

Whip the heavy cream until just stiff, then gradually whip in the light cream. Fold in the confectioners' sugar and bread crumbs. Lightly beat the rum, if used, with the egg yolks and stir into the cream mixture.

Beat the egg whites until they stand in stiff peaks and fold into the cream mixture. Pour the mixture into freezer trays or into a 5-cup decorative ice cream mold and freeze for about 3 to 4 hours or until firm. Unmold and serve with sliced strawberries and crisp cookies. SERVES 4 TO 6

Baking

Home-baked breads and cakes are always far superior to those you can buy, so why not treat the family to a hot fresh loaf, a special fruit cake or some crunchy biscuits? All these basic recipes are here, and many more too.

Battenburg, Jelly Roll, Lattice Tart and Bread Rolls

Bread Rolls

(ILLUSTRATED ON PREVIOUS PAGE)

Make up a single quantity of the bread dough according to the instructions for white bread. When the dough has risen once, instead of dividing it between two loaf pans as instructed, cut it into about 18 or 20 equal portions. Shape each portion into a roll, making some into tiny loaves, twists and braids or knots, as illustrated. Place the shaped rolls on greased baking sheets, cover with oiled plastic wrap and leave to rise in a warm place until doubled in size.

Glaze the rolls with a little beaten egg and water and sprinkle poppy seeds, sesame seeds or chopped nuts over the top. Bake in a preheated 450° oven for 15 to 20 minutes. Cool the rolls on a wire rack.

Lattice Tart

Bridget Jones

(ILLUSTRATED ON PREVIOUS PAGE)

1½ quantities pie pastry (page 87)
1 cup jam

Roll out half the pastry and use to line an 8-in loose-bottomed quiche or flan pan. Prick the pastry all over with a fork and spread the jam over the pastry.

Roll out the remaining pastry to form an oblong measuring 8 in down one side. Cut this piece of pastry into strips measuring about ½ in wide and lay these across the jam in a lattice pattern.

Bake in a preheated 400° oven for about 40 minutes, or until golden brown and cooked. Serve hot or cold. SERVES 6

Farmhouse Loaf

Jill Spencer

1 cup self-rising flour
1 cup wholewheat flour
pinch of grated nutmeg
½ teaspoon baking soda
6 tablespoons butter or margarine
½ cup sugar
⅓ cup raisins
3 tablespoons glacé cherries
3 tablespoons golden raisins
3 tablespoons chopped mixed candied peel
grated rind of 1 lemon
1 egg, beaten
½–⅔ cup milk

Place the flours, nutmeg and baking soda in a mixing bowl and rub in the butter until the mixture resembles fine bread crumbs. Add the sugar, fruits, peel and lemon rind, then mix in the egg and milk to give a soft, dropping consistency. Place in a lined and greased 5 × 3 in loaf pan. Bake in a preheated 350° oven for 50 to 60 minutes. Unmold and cool on a wire rack. Serve sliced and spread with butter. MAKES ONE 5 × 3 IN LOAF

White Bread

— Mary Berry —

1 tablespoon lard or shortening
6 cups flour
1 tablespoon salt
YEAST LIQUID
1 teaspoon sugar
$2\frac{1}{2}$–3 cups warm water
2 teaspoons active dry yeast

First prepare the yeast liquid: dissolve the sugar in the water and sprinkle the yeast on top, then leave until frothy – about 10 minutes.

Rub the lard into the flour and salt and mix in the yeast liquid. Work to a firm dough, until the sides of the bowl are clean. Turn onto a lightly floured surface and knead thoroughly for about 10 minutes.

Place the dough in a lightly greased plastic bag, tie the bag loosely and leave to rise until double in size. Remove the bag and turn the dough onto a lightly floured surface. Knead lightly. Grease two 5 × 3 in loaf pans. Divide the dough in half, stretch each piece into an oblong the same width as the pans and fold over in three. With the seam underneath, smooth over the top and place the loaf in the pan, tucking in the folded ends so that they face the bottom of the pan. Place the pans inside greased plastic bags and leave the dough to rise until it comes to the top of the pans.

Bake the bread loaves in a preheated 450° oven for 30 to 40 minutes. Tip them out of the pans and leave to cool on a wire rack. MAKES TWO 5 × 3 IN LOAVES

Cheese and Celery Loaf

— Mary Berry —

4 cups self-rising flour
2 teaspoons salt
3 tablespoons butter
3 large stalks celery, chopped
1 clove garlic, crushed
$1\frac{1}{2}$ cups grated sharp Cheddar cheese
1 egg
$1\frac{1}{2}$ cups milk

Grease a 9 × 5 × 3 in loaf pan. Sift the flour and salt into a bowl and rub in the butter until the mixture resembles fine bread crumbs.

Add the celery, garlic and cheese to the flour mixture. Beat the egg and milk together, add gradually to the dry ingredients and mix to form a soft dough. Knead the dough lightly and quickly on a floured surface, then shape it into an oblong. Place in the loaf pan and bake in a preheated 425° oven for about 55 minutes.

Unmold and cool on a wire rack. Serve freshly cooked, with butter. MAKES ONE 9 × 5 IN LOAF

Quick Wholewheat Bread

———————— Janet Hunt ————————

12 cups wholewheat flour
$\frac{1}{8}$ teaspoon salt
2 (0.6 oz) cakes compressed yeast
1 quart lukewarm water
1 teaspoon brown sugar, honey or
molasses

Mix the flour and salt together in a warmed bowl. Cream the yeast with about one third of the water and the sugar, honey or molasses, then set it aside in a warm place for 5 minutes, until frothy.

Make a well in the center of the flour and pour in the yeast liquid, followed by the rest of the water. Mix the flour into the liquid with a wooden spoon, adding a little more warm water if it seems too dry. Stir thoroughly for several minutes; use your hands if you find it easier. Thoroughly grease two 9 × 5 × 3 in loaf pans and turn the dough into them. Leave the pans in a warm draft-free spot until the dough has risen to the top of each pan (this can take anything up to 1 hour). Bake the bread in a preheated 450° oven for 5 minutes, then lower the heat to 400° and continue to bake for 30 minutes more. Tip the bread out of the pan and test to see if it is done by tapping the base of each loaf with your knuckles – if it sounds hollow, put it on a wire rack to cool; if not, do not replace it in its pan, but return it to the oven, stand it upside down and bake the loaf for a further 5 minutes. MAKES TWO 9 × 5 IN LOAVES

Soda Bread

———————— Janet Hunt ————————

4 cups wholewheat flour
1 teaspoon baking soda
1 teaspoon cream of tartar
pinch of salt
about $1\frac{1}{2}$ cups milk and warm water

Mix the flour, soda, cream of tartar and salt. Stir in enough liquid to give a moist dough – you may need to adjust the quantity to get the right consistency.

Turn the dough onto a floured board, dust it with flour and, using your hands, pat it into one large or two small rounds – the traditional shape for soda bread. Put the bread on a lightly greased baking sheet, flatten it slightly and cut a large cross in the top of each loaf. Bake in a preheated 375° oven for 40 minutes or until the bread is firm to the touch and sounds hollow when tapped. Cool on a wire rack. Eat while fresh as this bread does not keep very well. MAKES ONE LARGE OR TWO SMALL LOAVES

Onion and Herb Loaf

———————— Carol Bowen ————————

1 (0.6 oz) cake compressed yeast
$\frac{1}{2}$ teaspoon sugar
$\frac{1}{2}$ cup lukewarm water
$\frac{1}{2}$ cup milk
1 tablespoon butter or margarine
$2\frac{1}{2}$ cups wholewheat flour
1 teaspoon salt
1 teaspoon finely chopped sage
2 teaspoons finely chopped savory
1 small onion, peeled and minced

Cream the yeast with the sugar and 2 tablespoons of the water to form a smooth paste. Set aside in a warm place for about 15 to 20 minutes, or until the yeast mixture has risen and is frothy.

Bring the milk to just under boiling point, remove from the heat, then add the butter or margarine and the remaining water. Set aside and leave until lukewarm.

Put the flour and salt into a warmed bowl. Sprinkle with the herbs and onion. Make a well in the center of the flour and pour in the yeast and milk mixtures. Draw the flour into the liquid and mix until the dough comes away from the sides of the bowl.

Turn onto a lightly floured surface and knead for 10 minutes. Form the dough into a ball and return it to the clean bowl. Cover with a damp cloth or plastic wrap and leave to rise in a warm place for 1 to $1\frac{1}{2}$ hours, or until the dough has doubled in bulk.

Lightly grease a 5 × 3 in loaf pan and set aside. Turn the dough onto a lightly floured surface and knead for 8 to 10 minutes. Form the dough into a loaf and place it in the pan. Cover with a damp cloth or plastic wrap and leave to rise for 30 to 45 minutes, or until the dough has doubled in bulk again. Bake in a preheated 400° oven for 1 hour. Cool on a wire rack. MAKES ONE 5 × 3 IN LOAF

Chopped Peanut Loaf

———— Audrey Ellis ————

1 cup wholewheat flour
1 cup all-purpose flour
2 teaspoons baking powder
$\frac{1}{4}$ teaspoon salt
$\frac{1}{2}$ cup peanut butter
1 egg
3 tablespoons clear honey
1 cup milk
2 tablespoons margarine, melted
1 teaspoon grated lemon rind
$\frac{1}{2}$ cup chopped salted peanuts

Mix the flours, baking powder and salt in a large bowl. Rub in the peanut butter until the mixture is crumbly. Lightly beat the egg and add to the flour mixture with the honey, milk, melted margarine and lemon rind. Stir until just combined, then fold in the chopped peanuts.

Spoon the mixture into a 9 × 5 × 3 in loaf pan and bake in a preheated 350° oven for 1 hour. Cool for 10 minutes in the pan, then tip onto a wire rack. MAKES ONE 9 × 5 IN LOAF

Welsh Currant Bread

———— Mary Berry ————

6 tablespoons margarine
3 cups flour
$\frac{1}{2}$ cup firmly packed light brown sugar
1 teaspoon salt
1 teaspoon apple pie spice
4 cups mixed raisins, currants, golden raisins and candied peel
1 egg, beaten
honey for glazing
YEAST LIQUID
1 cup flour
1$\frac{1}{2}$ teaspoons active dry yeast
1 teaspoon sugar
1–1$\frac{1}{4}$ cups warm water

Put the flour for the yeast liquid into a large bowl and make a well in the middle. Mix the yeast, sugar and water in the well in the flour. Set aside until frothy – about 20 minutes.

Rub the margarine into the 3 cups of flour, then mix in the sugar, salt, spice and fruit. Add the egg and the flour mixture to the yeast liquid. Mix well. Knead the dough thoroughly on a lightly floured surface. Place in a greased plastic bag, loosely tied, and allow to rise until double in size.

Lightly knead the dough to knock out the air bubbles. Divide in half and shape to fit two greased 5 × 3 in pans. Place each pan in a greased plastic bag and allow the dough to rise to 1 in above the top of the pans. Bake in a preheated 350° oven for 50 to 60 minutes. Tip onto a wire rack and glaze with honey while still hot. MAKES TWO 5 × 3 IN LOAVES

Battenburg Cake

Jill Spencer

¾ cup butter or margarine
¾ cup sugar
3 large eggs
1½ cups self-rising flour
1 tablespoon cocoa powder
1 tablespoon hot water
grated rind of 1 lemon
lemon cheese or curd
1 lb almond paste
sugar

Mix the cake as for the Basic Layer Cake (right). Divide the batter in half. To one half add the cocoa blended in hot water, and to the other add the lemon rind. Line and grease a 7-in square cake pan and divide down the middle with a strip of folded parchment paper. Place the chocolate mixture in one side and the lemon in the other. Bake in a preheated 325° oven for 40 to 50 minutes.

Trim the edges of the cooled cake and cut each half in two lengthwise, making four strips. Join alternate colors together in two layers, sandwiching them with lemon curd.

Roll the almond paste into an oblong 8 × 15-in on a sugared surface. Spread the outside of the assembled cake with lemon curd and place it in the middle of the almond paste. Carefully ease the almond paste around the cake with the join underneath. Trim and finish as shown in the picture.

Meringues

Jill Spencer

2 egg whites
½ cup sugar
FILLING AND DECORATION
1¼ cups heavy cream
a few glacé cherries
angelica leaves

Beat the egg whites until stiff. Gradually beat in half the sugar then carefully fold in the remainder using a metal spoon. Transfer the mixture to a pastry bag fitted with a large star nozzle and pipe small meringues onto greased baking sheets. Dry out in a preheated 225° oven for 3½ hours. Cool on a wire rack.

Whip the cream until stiff and use to sandwich the meringues together, then decorate with pieces of cherry and angelica leaves. MAKES ABOUT 12

Basic Layer Cake

Jill Spencer

½ cup butter or margarine
½ cup sugar
2 large eggs
1 cup self-rising flour
3–4 tablespoons raspberry jam
confectioners' sugar

Cream the butter and sugar together until light and fluffy. Beat in the eggs one at a time, adding a little of the flour with the second egg. Fold in the remaining flour using a metal spoon. Place the batter in a lined and greased deep 8-in cake pan or two 7-in layer cake pans. Bake in a preheated 325° oven, 35 to 40 minutes for the 8-in cake, and 25 to 35 minutes for the 7-in cakes. Unmold and cool on a wire rack.

Split the larger cake into two layers and sandwich the cakes or two layers with the raspberry jam. Lay a doily on top of the cake and dredge with confectioners' sugar. Carefully lift off the doily to leave a design on the surface of the cake.

Jelly Roll

Mary Berry

3 large eggs, at room temperature
6 tablespoons sugar, warmed
¾ cup self-rising flour, sifted
sugar for dredging
⅓ cup raspberry jam, warmed

Line and grease a 9 × 12-in jelly roll pan. Beat the eggs with the sugar until light and creamy and the beater leaves a trail when lifted out of the mixture. Fold in the flour, using a metal spoon.

Turn into the prepared pan and smooth the batter level with a spatula. Bake in a preheated 425° oven for 7 to 10 minutes, until the cake begins to shrink from the edges of the pan and is pale golden.

Unmold onto a sheet of wax paper dredged with sugar. Trim the edges of the cake, spread it with warmed jam and roll up tightly. Dredge with more sugar and cool on a wire rack.

Cherry Cake

Mary Berry

1⅓ cups glacé cherries
¾ cup self-rising flour
¾ cup all-purpose flour
pinch of salt
¾ cup butter
¾ cup sugar
finely grated rind of 1 lemon
3 eggs, beaten
¾ cup ground almonds
a little milk (if necessary)

Grease a 7-in round deep cake pan and line it with greased parchment paper. Rinse, dry and halve the cherries. Sift the flours and salt together twice, then toss the cherries into a little of the flour. Cream the butter, sugar and lemon rind together until the mixture is pale and creamy. Add the beaten eggs a little at a time, beating well after each addition and keeping the mixture stiff. Add a tablespoon of the flour with the last amount of egg. Fold in the flour, cherries and ground almonds, adding a little milk to make a fairly stiff consistency; the stiff consistency will help to keep the cherries suspended evenly in the cake.

Turn the mixture into the prepared pan and bake in a preheated 350° oven for about 1 hour 20 minutes, or until a skewer inserted in the center of the cake comes out clean.

Leave the cake to cool in the pan for 5 minutes, then unmold it onto a wire rack to finish cooling. When cold remove the cooking paper and wrap the cake in foil or store it in an airtight tin.

British Christmas Cake

Mary Berry

$2\frac{1}{4}$ cups flour
$\frac{1}{4}$ teaspoon salt
1 teaspoon apple pie spice
$\frac{1}{2}$ lb (1 cup) butter
$1\frac{1}{3}$ cups firmly packed brown sugar
4 eggs, lightly beaten
1–2 tablespoons molasses
2 cups raisins
2 cups golden raisins · 2 cups currants
$\frac{1}{3}$ cup chopped candied peel
$\frac{1}{2}$ cup glacé cherries, quartered
$\frac{1}{2}$ cup chopped blanched almonds
2 tablespoons brandy

Line the bottom and side of an 8-in round deep cake pan with a double layer of parchment paper, then tie a double band of brown paper, 1 in wider than the depth of the pan, around the outside.

Sift the flour, salt and spice into a large bowl. Cream the butter and sugar together and gradually beat in the eggs. Stir in the molasses, then the flour, dried fruit, peel, cherries and almonds. Turn the mixture into the prepared pan and bake in a preheated 300° oven for 3 hours, then reduce the oven to 275° and bake for a further 1 to $1\frac{1}{2}$ hours, or until a skewer inserted into the cake comes out clean.

Cool the cake in the pan for 10 minutes, then on a wire rack. Remove the paper. Turn the cake upside down, pierce it with a skewer and spoon over the brandy. Store, when cold, wrapped in wax paper and foil, in an airtight tin.

Christmas Cake Icing

Mary Berry

ALMOND PASTE
3 cups ground almonds
$\frac{3}{4}$ cup granulated sugar
$1\frac{1}{2}$ cups confectioners' sugar, sifted
3 egg whites
a few drops of almond extract
3 tablespoons apricot jam, sieved
ROYAL ICING
4 egg whites
2 lb (8 cups) confectioners' sugar, sifted
4 teaspoons lemon juice
2 teaspoons glycerine

Mix the almonds and sugars in a bowl, then blend in the egg whites and almond extract to make a soft paste. Knead until smooth and divide into three equal portions. Roll out one piece on a sugared board to an 8-in round. Roll the remaining two thirds to a strip the same depth as the cake, and long enough to go all the way around the edge. Brush the side of the cake with apricot jam. Place the long strip around the side and press firmly to join. Place the round of paste on top of the cake. Allow to dry for at least 3 days before icing.

To make the royal icing, beat the egg whites until they become frothy. Add the sugar, a tablespoon at a time, and beat well after each addition. Finally beat in the lemon juice and glycerine. To prevent the icing from hardening, cover the bowl with a damp cloth.

Spread the icing thickly over the top and around the side of the cake, then draw it up in peaks with the handle of a teaspoon. Leave to set for a day, then arrange any decorations on top.

Coffee Ginger Cake

Mary Berry

4 eggs
6 tablespoons sugar
$\frac{3}{4}$ cup flour, sifted

FILLING

3 cups confectioners' sugar, sifted
1 tablespoon coffee flavoring
2 tablespoons rum · $\frac{3}{4}$ cup butter
$\frac{1}{3}$ cup chopped crystallized ginger

ICING

1$\frac{1}{2}$ cups confectioners' sugar, sifted
1 tablespoon coffee flavoring
$\frac{1}{2}$ cup chopped blanched almonds

Grease two layer cake pans and line the bottoms with greased parchment paper. Beat the eggs and sugar until the mixture is pale and thick. Carefully fold in the flour. Divide the mixture between the pans and bake in a preheated 375° oven for 20 to 25 minutes or until each cake springs back when lightly pressed. Cool on a wire rack. Slice each cake into two layers.

Blend together the confectioners' sugar, coffee flavoring and rum. Cream the butter until it is soft, then gradually add the sugar mixture and beat well. Mix the chopped ginger with three-quarters of the filling and use to sandwich the four layers together. Spread more filling thinly over the side of the cake.

Make a fairly thick glacé icing with the confectioners' sugar, coffee flavoring and a little water. Use to cover the top of the cake. Lightly toast the almonds and press them against the sides of the cake. Use any remaining filling to pipe rosettes around the top edges of the cake.

Tipsy Ring

Jill Spencer

$\frac{1}{2}$ cup butter or margarine
$\frac{1}{2}$ cup sugar
7 tablespoons imported ginger wine
2 eggs
1 cup self-rising flour
$\frac{1}{4}$ cup cocoa powder

ICING AND DECORATION

6 (1-oz) squares semisweet chocolate
$\frac{1}{4}$ cup butter
$\frac{3}{4}$ cup heavy cream
a few pieces of crystallized ginger

Cream the butter with the sugar and 4 tablespoons of the ginger wine until pale and fluffy. Gradually beat in the eggs. Sift the flour with the cocoa and fold into the creamed mixture using a metal spoon. Turn into a well greased 9-in ring mold and bake in a preheated 325° oven for 40 to 45 minutes. Unmold and cool on a wire rack. While the cake is still warm, drizzle the remaining ginger wine over it, until absorbed.

Melt the chocolate with the butter for the icing. Allow to cool slightly, then drizzle the icing over the cake. Whip the cream until stiff and, using a pastry bag fitted with a large star nozzle, pipe the cream along the top of the cake. Decorate with pieces of crystallized ginger.

Honey Squares

Jill Spencer

½ cup thick honey
¾ cup butter or margarine
½ cup firmly packed light brown sugar
⅔ cup golden raisins
¾ cup chopped blanched almonds
grated rind of 2 oranges
juice of ½ orange
2 eggs, lightly beaten
1¾ cups self-rising flour
1 teaspoon baking powder
½ teaspoon ground cinnamon

TOPPING

1 cup blanched almonds
5 tablespoons thick honey
⅓ cup golden raisins
⅛ teaspoon ground cinnamon
grated rind of 1 orange

Melt the honey, butter or margarine and sugar together with the raisins, almonds, orange rind and juice over a gentle heat; cool slightly. Beat in the eggs. Sift the dry ingredients and beat in to give a smooth batter.

Pour into a lined and greased 7 × 10½-in shallow pan and bake in a preheated 325° oven for 40 to 50 minutes. Cool slightly in the pan, then mix all the ingredients for the topping. Warm slightly if necessary, spread on top of the cake and leave to cool. Cut into squares. MAKES 12

Lemon Honey Cakes

Jill Spencer

½ cup butter or margarine
⅓ cup firmly packed brown sugar
⅓ cup thick honey
grated rind and juice of 1 lemon
2 egg, lightly beaten
2 cups self-rising flour
1 teaspoon baking powder

ICING

2 cups confectioners' sugar, sifted
2–3 tablespoons lemon juice
pared lemon rind for decoration

Melt the butter or margarine, sugar and honey together with the lemon rind and juice over a gentle heat, stirring occasionally. Leave to cool slightly, then beat in the eggs. Sift the flour and baking powder together and beat into the melted mixture to give a smooth, thick batter.

Divide between greased, deep muffin or cup cake tins and bake in a preheated 375° oven for 15 to 20 minutes. Cool on a wire rack. Beat the confectioners' sugar and lemon juice together until smooth, then pour it over the cakes and top with lemon rind. MAKES 12 TO 14

Almond Macaroons

Jill Spencer

2 egg whites
$\frac{1}{2}$ cup sugar
1 cup ground almonds
1 teaspoon ground rice
few drops of almond extract
halved almonds

Beat the egg whites until stiff. Gradually beat in the sugar and continue beating until the mixture is thick and glossy. Stir in the ground almonds, ground rice and a few drops of almond extract.

Place the mixture in a pastry bag fitted with a large plain nozzle. Place sheets of rice paper on baking sheets and pipe small rounds of the mixture onto the paper. Place an almond on top of each macaroon and bake in a preheated 325° oven for 15 to 20 minutes. Carefully remove as much of the rice paper as possible from around the macaroons and cool them on a wire rack. MAKES ABOUT 20

Peanut Cookies

Jill Spencer

$\frac{1}{4}$ cup butter or margarine, softened
$\frac{1}{3}$ cup firmly packed brown sugar
$\frac{1}{2}$ cup roughly chopped salted peanuts
grated rind of 1 orange
$\frac{3}{4}$ cup self-rising flour
$\frac{1}{4}$ cup orange juice

Cream the butter or margarine and sugar until light and fluffy, then mix in all the remaining ingredients to form a soft dough. Take small pieces of dough, about the size of a walnut, and roll them into balls. Place well apart on greased baking sheets, flatten with a fork and bake in a preheated 350° oven for 10 to 12 minutes. Remove and cool on a wire rack. MAKES ABOUT 12

Orange Shortbread

Mary Berry

1 cup flour
$\frac{1}{2}$ cup cornstarch
$\frac{1}{2}$ cup butter
$\frac{1}{4}$ cup sugar
grated rind of 1 orange
sugar for dredging

Sift the flour and cornstarch together. Cream the butter until soft, then add the sugar and beat until the mixture is pale and creamy. Gradually work the orange rind and flours into the mixture.

Lift the shortbread onto a large baking sheet. Roll it out to give an 8-in round. Pinch the edges and prick the shortbread with a fork. Cut into sections with the blunt edge of a knife, then dredge with a little sugar.

Chill for 15 minutes, then bake in a preheated 325° oven for 35 minutes or until pale golden. Cool on the baking sheet for a few minutes, then transfer to a wire rack to cool. MAKES 12

Flapjacks

Mary Berry

$\frac{1}{2}$ cup margarine
$\frac{1}{3}$ cup light corn syrup
6 tablespoons sugar
$2\frac{1}{4}$ cups rolled oats
$\frac{1}{4}$ teaspoon salt

Grease a $7\frac{1}{2}$-in square, shallow pan. Put the margarine and syrup in a pan over a low heat until the margarine has melted. Remove from the heat and add the sugar, oats and salt. Mix thoroughly.

Turn the mixture into the prepared pan and bake in a preheated 325° oven for 30 to 40 minutes, until golden brown.

Leave to cool in the pan for 5 minutes. Cut the flapjacks into bars and cool completely on a wire rack. MAKES 12

Preserving

There is nothing more satisfying than the sight of a shelf
stocked with freshly potted preserves. Jams and jellies,
chutneys and pickles are all included in this chapter, ready
for the day when you have both the time and inclination
as well as the ingredients to make them.

Making Jams and Jellies

For a successful preserve, it is important to use good quality fruit. Select fruit which is not quite ripe as it contains the most pectin – the substance which is essential for making the jam set. Follow the chart on the opposite page for the quantities of water and sugar and refer to the pectin/acid column to check whether there is any need to add lemon juice or apple pulp or commercial pectin. Wrap all the trimmings (peel, seeds, cores and pits) securely in cheesecloth and cook them with the fruit, then thoroughly squeeze out the package to extract all the pectin.

Prepare the fruit according to its type, slicing or halving the pieces, then cook it in a large pan with the liquid, or just a little of the sugar to bring out the juice, until the fruit is soft. Add the bulk of sugar when the fruit is cooked, preferably warming the sugar first so the temperature of the mixture is not drastically reduced. Cook slowly, stirring continuously, until the sugar has dissolved completely, then bring to a rolling boil and boil hard until jell point is reached

There are three ways of testing for setting – the thermometer test, the saucer test and the flake test. Using a candy thermometer is the most accurate method. The thermometer should be placed well into the jam, but it should not touch the bottom of the saucepan. Most jams and jellies set at 220°. The next most reliable is the saucer test: drop a little of the hot preserve onto a cool saucer and leave it to set for a few minutes. If jell point is reached, the surface should wrinkle when pushed with the finger. The flake test is the least accurate – drop a little of the preserve off the edge of a wooden spoon; as it drops it should form flakes.

Pour the preserve into thoroughly cleaned, heated jars (you can heat the jars by filling them with boiling water or in a warm oven or dishwasher), then cover with the lids. Process jams in a boiling water bath for 10 minutes. Store the preserve in a cool, dry place.

Apple Pulp Rinse and roughly chop 1 lb tart apples. Place them in a saucepan with 1 cup water, bring to a boil and cook, covered, for about 20 to 25 minutes or until the fruit is reduced to a pulp. Press this pulp through a sieve and use the purée for adding pectin to jams prepared from fruits which have a low pectin content. This quantity is sufficient to set 3 lb fruit.

Quantities for Jams and Jellies

Fruit	Water per 1 lb	Sugar per 1 lb	Pectin/Acid
Apple	$1\frac{1}{4}$ cups	$1\frac{1}{2}$ cups	juice of 1 lemon
Apricot	$\frac{3}{4}$ cup	2 cups	juice of $\frac{1}{2}$ lemon
Blackberry	2 tablespoons	2 cups	juice of 1 lemon
Black currant	$1\frac{1}{4}$ cups	$2\frac{1}{2}$ cups	—
Gooseberry	$1\frac{1}{4}$ cups	2 cups	juice of $\frac{1}{2}$ lemon
Greengage	$\frac{1}{4}$ cup	2 cups	—
Loganberry	1–2 tablespoons	2 cups	—
Plum, damson	$\frac{3}{4}$ cup	2 cups	juice of 1 lemon
Plum, others	2–4 tablespoons	2 cups	juice of $\frac{1}{2}$ lemon
Quince	2 cups	$2\frac{1}{2}$ cups	juice of 1 lemon
Raspberry	1–2 tablespoons	2 cups	—
Rhubarb	2–4 tablespoons	2 cups	apple pulp
Strawberry	2 tablespoons	$1\frac{1}{2}$ cups	juice of 1 lemon *or* apple pulp

Ginger Marmalade

Bridget Jones

8 lemons
2 large oranges
9 cups water
$\frac{1}{4}$ lb fresh ginger root
6 cups sugar

Pare the rind from the lemons and oranges and cut it into thin strips. Squeeze the juice from the fruit and mix it in a large kettle with the rinds and water. Thinly peel the ginger, slice and finely shred it, then add it to the pan.

Chop the remainder of the lemons and oranges, including the pith, and tie them up in a piece of clean cheesecloth. Add the bag to the pan and bring the mixture to a boil. Reduce the heat, cover the pan and simmer for 2 hours or until the ginger and fruit rinds are completely tender. Take the pan off the heat and leave it to stand until the cheesecloth is cool enough to handle, then squeeze all the juices out of it into the marmalade.

Pour the sugar into the pan and stir the mixture over a gentle heat until the sugar has completely dissolved. Bring to a boil and boil hard to jell point. Use a slotted spoon to remove the scum from the top of the marmalade, then allow it to stand for about 15 to 20 minutes. Stir it thoroughly before pouring it into warmed jars. Cover and process in a boiling water bath for 10 minutes. MAKES ABOUT 5 LB

181

Apricot and Loganberry Jam

Bridget Jones

2 lb fresh apricots
$1\frac{1}{4}$ cups water
1 lb ($1\frac{1}{2}$ pints) loganberries
6 cups sugar
2 tablespoons butter

Halve and pit the apricots. Crack the pits and remove the kernels. Mix the fruit with their kernels in a large kettle and pour in the water. Bring to a boil and reduce the heat, then cook the apricots, uncovered, for 5 to 10 minutes until they are just soft.

Add the loganberries to the pan and gradually stir in the sugar. Stir the mixture over a gentle heat until the sugar has dissolved completely, bring to a boil and boil hard until jell point is reached.

Stir in the butter to disperse the scum and transfer the jam to warmed jars. Cover and process in a boiling water bath for 10 minutes. MAKES ABOUT 5 LB

Apple and Mandarin Jam

Bridget Jones

1 lb mandarins
1 lb tart apples
$2\frac{1}{2}$ cups water
juice of 2 lemons
$3\frac{1}{2}$ cups sugar

Halve the mandarins and carefully remove all the seeds. Chop the flesh and peel quite finely, removing any further seeds. Peel, core and slice the apples. Mix the apple peelings and core with seeds from the mandarins and tie them securely in a piece of clean cheesecloth.

Put all the chopped fruit in a large kettle and pour in the water. Add the cheesecloth package and bring to a boil. Cover the pan, reduce the heat and simmer the mixture gently for 1 hour or until the fruit is soft.

Allow to cool until the cheescloth can be handled, then squeeze all the juices out of it into the jam. Pour in the lemon juice and sugar and heat the jam gently, stirring continuously, until the sugar has completely dissolved. Bring to a boil and boil hard to jell point.

Pour the jam into warmed jars. Cover and process in a boiling water bath for 10 minutes. MAKES ABOUT 2 LB

Cherry and Apple Jam

Bridget Jones

2 lb (2 quarts) cherries
2 lb tart apples
juice of 2 lemons
5 cups water
5 cups sugar
1 tablespoon butter

Pit the cherries and place the pits in a large kettle. Peel, core and thickly slice the apples, then sprinkle the slices with the lemon juice and set them aside. Add the apple trimmings to the pan with the cherry pits and pour in the water. Bring to a boil and cook, uncovered, until the liquid is reduced to about one third of its original quantity. This will take about 1 hour.

Press the resulting pulp through a fine sieve and return it to the rinsed-out kettle. Add the prepared cherries and apples and bring the mixture to a boil. Cover the pan and simmer gently, stirring occasionally, for 10 to 15 minutes, until the fruit is soft.

Pour in the sugar and heat gently, stirring, until the sugar has dissolved. Bring the jam to a rapid boil and boil hard to jell point. Stir in the butter to disperse any scum and pour the jam into warmed jars. Cover and process in a boiling water bath for 10 minutes. MAKES ABOUT 5 LB

Black Currant Butter

Bridget Jones

1 lb tart apples
2 lb (2 quarts) black currants
$2\frac{1}{2}$ cups water
sugar
juice of 2 large lemons

Rinse and roughly chop the apples and place them in a large kettle with the black currants and water. Bring to a boil, cover the pan and reduce the heat. Simmer the fruit for 2 hours.

Allow it to cool slightly, then press it through a fine sieve and measure the resulting pulp. For every 2 cups pulp allow $1\frac{1}{2}$ cups sugar. Return the pulp to the kettle with the sugar and lemon juice and stir the mixture over a gentle heat until the sugar has dissolved. Bring to a boil and boil for 30 to 40 minutes, stirring frequently, until the butter has thickened to a creamy consistency and a spoon dipped into it will leave a ribbon trail on the surface.

Transfer the butter to warmed pots and top each with a disk of wax paper, waxed side down. Leave it to cool and cover the pots with pieces of cellophane or airtight lids. MAKES ABOUT 2 LB

Apricot and Date Jam

Bridget Jones

2 lb fresh apricots
$\frac{1}{2}$ lb fresh dates
$2\frac{1}{2}$ cups water
grated rind of 1 orange
5 cups sugar
2 tablespoons butter

Halve and pit the apricots. Crack the pits and take out the kernels. Place the fruit and their kernels in a large kettle. Halve and pit the dates, removing and discarding their skins, and place them in the kettle. Pour in the water, add the orange rind and bring to a boil. Reduce the heat and simmer the fruit, uncovered, for 30 minutes.

Add the sugar to the jam and stir it over a low heat until the sugar has completely dissolved. Bring to a boil and boil rapidly until jell point is reached. Add the butter to the pan, stirring it in to disperse the scum.

Pour the jam into warmed jars. Cover and process in a boiling water bath for 10 minutes. MAKES ABOUT 3 LB

Lemon Curd

Bridget Jones

(ILLUSTRATED ON PREVIOUS PAGE)

grated rind and juice of 3 large lemons
$\frac{1}{2}$ cup butter, cut into pieces
3 large eggs, beaten
$1\frac{1}{2}$ cups sugar

Mix all the ingredients in the top of a double boiler or in a large bowl over a pan of gently simmering water. Do not allow the water to boil or the curd may overheat and curdle.

Stir the mixture until the sugar has dissolved, then continue cooking, stirring frequently, until the eggs are cooked and the mixture has thickened enough to coat the back of a wooden spoon.

Pour the curd into clean, warmed jars and cover the surfaces with wax paper disks, waxed sides down. Allow to cool before topping the jars with airtight lids. MAKES ABOUT 2 LB

Mincemeat

Bridget Jones

$1\frac{1}{3}$ cups raisins
$1\frac{1}{3}$ cups golden raisins
$1\frac{1}{3}$ cups currants
1 cup shredded beef suet
$\frac{2}{3}$ cup chopped mixed candied peel
1 cup blanched almonds
1 lb tart apples
1 large carrot
grated rind and juice of 1 orange
juice of 2 lemons
$1\frac{1}{3}$ cups firmly packed dark brown sugar
$\frac{1}{2}$ teaspoon freshly grated nutmeg
$\frac{1}{2}$ teaspoon ground cinnamon
$\frac{3}{4}$ cup brandy or rum
$\frac{1}{4}$ cup dry sherry wine

Mince or finely chop the raisins and currants and mix them with the suet and peel in a large bowl. Chop the almonds and add them to the fruit. Peel, core and grate the apples and grate the carrot, then stir both into the fruit with the orange rind and juice, the lemon juice and sugar.

Stir in the spices and pour over the brandy or rum and the sherry, mixing throughly to combine all the ingredients. Leave the mincemeat to stand for a couple of days, stirring it every day. Transfer it to jars and cover these with airtight lids. Allow to mature for at least 3 weeks before use. MAKES ABOUT 4 LB

Blackberry Jelly

Bridget Jones

5 lb ($4\frac{1}{2}$ quarts) blackberries
3 lemons
$2\frac{1}{2}$ cups water
sugar

Pick over and rinse the blackberries. Place them in a large kettle. Squeeze the juice from the lemons and add it to the pan. Chop the remainder of the lemons and stir them into the blackberries.

Pour in the water and bring to a boil. Reduce the heat, cover the pan and simmer the fruit for 1 to $1\frac{1}{2}$ hours, until reduced to a pulp. Allow to cool, strain through a jelly bag overnight and measure the resulting extract.

Pour the extract into a large saucepan and add 2 cups sugar for each $2\frac{1}{2}$ cups. Heat slowly until the sugar has dissolved, stirring continuously, then bring to a rapid boil and boil hard to jell point.

Skim the surface of the jelly with a slotted spoon to remove all the scum and pour it into warmed jars. Cover with lids or melted paraffin wax.

Elder and Gooseberry Jelly

———— Elizabeth Pomeroy ————

4 lb (5 quarts) green gooseberries
2½–4 cups water
sugar
4–8 elder flower heads according to size

Cover the gooseberries with water – there is no need to top and tail them – then simmer the fruit, uncovered, for about 2 hours. Strain the gooseberries through a jelly bag, preferably overnight.

To each 2½ cups of juice add 2 cups warmed sugar. Heat gently, stirring, until the sugar has dissolved. Tie the elder flowers in a cheesecloth bag and add them to the syrup. Heat to boiling point and boil briskly for 10 minutes until jell point is reached. Remove the elder flowers, pour the jelly into jars and cover.

Honey Marmalade

———— Bridget Jones ————

4 large lemons
5 cups water
3 cups sugar
⅔ cup thick honey

Slice the lemons lengthwise into quarters, discarding the seeds, and cut the quarters widthwise into fine slices. Place the fruit in a large kettle with the water and bring the mixture to a boil. Cover the pan, reduce the heat and simmer for 1½ hours.

Add the sugar and honey and stir the mixture over a low heat until the sugar has completely dissolved. Bring to a boil and boil rapidly until jell point is reached

Carefully remove the scum from the surface of the marmalade with a slotted spoon, then allow it to stand for about 15 minutes. Stir the preserve thoroughly before pouring it into warmed jars. Cover and process in a boiling water bath for 10 minutes. MAKES ABOUT 3 LB

Note: To make a fine marmalade, begin by paring the rind from the lemons and shredding it finely. Squeeze out the juice and place it in the pan with the rind. Chop the remainder of the fruit, tie it securely with the seeds in a piece of cheesecloth and add this to the pan. Pour in the water, bring to a boil and continue as above, but before you add the sugar, allow the marmalade to cool until the cheesecloth can be handled. Squeeze the juices from the bag into the marmalade, pour in the sugar and proceed as in the main recipe.

Dark Orange and Lemon Marmalade

———— Bridget Jones ————

2 large oranges
4 large lemons
7 cups water
4 cups granulated sugar
1⅓ cups firmly packed dark brown sugar

Finely chop the fruit, removing the seeds, and place it in a large kettle with the water. Bring to a boil, cover the pan and reduce the heat. Simmer for 1½ hours.

Add all the sugar to the pan and stir the mixture over a low heat until the sugar has completely dissolved. Bring to a rolling boil and continue to boil until jell point is reached.

Remove the scum from the surface of the marmalade with a slotted spoon. Allow it to stand for 15 minutes. Stir the marmalade, transfer it to heated jars and cover. Process in a boiling water bath for 10 minutes. MAKES ABOUT 4 LB

Lime Marmalade

———— Bridget Jones ————

6 limes
2 lemons
6 cups water
6 cups sugar

Cut the limes into quarters lengthwise and then into long, very fine slices, removing all the seeds. Cut up the lemons in the same way and mix both fruits in a large kettle. Pour in the water and bring to a boil. Cover the pan, reduce the heat and simmer for 1½ hours.

Add the sugar to the softened fruit and stir the mixture over a low heat until the sugar has completely dissolved. Bring the marmalade to a rolling boil and continue to boil until jell point is reached.

Remove the scum from the surface of the marmalade with a slotted spoon. Leave it to stand for 10 minutes. Stir it thoroughly before pouring it into warmed jars. Cover and process in a boiling water bath for 10 minutes. MAKES 5 LB

Sweet Vinegar Pickles

—— Marguerite Patten ——

a selection of fresh vegetables (for example
cauliflower, pearl onions and
small cucumbers)
allow 1 tablespoon pickling spice to each
2½ cups white vinegar
sugar

Choose good quality, firm vegetables which are not
discolored. Prepare them according to their type, cut
large vegetables into small pieces and place them in a
large bowl. Sprinkle generously with salt and leave to
stand overnight. Drain, rinse and dry thoroughly.

Place the vinegar and spices in a kettle, bring to a
boil and simmer for 15 minutes. Strain the vinegar and
sweeten it to taste with sugar. Pack the vegetables into
jars and pour in the vinegar, making sure there is enough
to cover the vegetables. Cover and process.

Pickled Red Cabbage

—— Marguerite Patten ——

1 head red cabbage
salt
spiced vinegar

Shred the cabbage, discarding any damaged outer leaves,
and layer it with salt in a large bowl. Leave to stand
overnight, drain, rinse and dry thoroughly.

Pack the cabbage loosely into jars and cover with cold
spiced vinegar. Cover tightly and use within 10 weeks as
the color often fades.

Tomato Chutney

Marguerite Patten

1 teaspoon pickling spice
$\frac{1}{2}$ lb onions, finely chopped
1$\frac{1}{4}$ cups vinegar
$\frac{1}{2}$ lb tart apples, peeled, cored and chopped
2 lb green or red tomatoes, peeled and sliced
$\frac{1}{2}$ teaspoon salt
$\frac{1}{4}$ teaspoon pepper
1$\frac{1}{8}$ teaspoons dry mustard
$\frac{1}{2}$ teaspoon ground ginger
1$\frac{1}{3}$ cups golden raisins
1 cup sugar

Put the pickling spice into a piece of cheesecloth. Put the onions into a saucepan with 2 to 3 tablespoons of the vinegar, and simmer gently until nearly soft. Add the apples, tomatoes, spices, salt, pepper, mustard, ginger and raisins. Simmer gently until the mixture is quite soft, stirring from time to time.

Add the remaining vinegar and the sugar. When the sugar has dissolved, boil steadily until the chutney is the consistency of jam. Remove the spices. Pour the hot chutney into warm jars, cover and process. MAKES ABOUT 4 LB

Mustard Pickles

Marguerite Patten

2 lb prepared mixed vegetables (for example, cauliflower, onions, cucumber, small green tomatoes and green beans)
salt
2$\frac{1}{2}$ cups vinegar
1 tablespoon pickling spice
1 tablespoon dry mustard
2 teaspoons turmeric
$\frac{1}{4}$ cup sugar
1 tablespoon flour *or* 2 teaspoons cornstarch
2 teaspoons ground ginger

Cut or break the vegetables into small pieces (about 1 in). Place in a bowl and sprinkle generously with salt, then leave to stand overnight. Wash well under cold water and drain thoroughly.

Boil the vinegar and pickling spice together steadily for 10 minutes. Mix all the dry ingredients with a very little vinegar to make a smooth paste. Pour in the strained hot vinegar, and stir well. Return to the pan, and cook until just thickened. Add the vegetables and cook for a further 5 minutes. Pour into sterilized jars and cover tightly. Process.

Apple Chutney

Bridget Jones

3 lb tart apples
1 lb onions
$\frac{1}{3}$ cup raisins
2 oz fresh ginger root
1 small green pepper
1 tablespoon dry mustard
2 teaspoons ground coriander
3 cloves garlic, crushed
1$\frac{2}{3}$ cups firmly packed light brown sugar
2$\frac{1}{2}$ cups vinegar

Peel, core and chop the apples; chop the onions and raisins and grate the ginger. Remove the stalk, seeds and pith from the pepper and chop the flesh. Mix all these prepared ingredients together in a large kettle, add the mustard, coriander, garlic and sugar and pour in the vinegar.

Bring the mixture to a boil, stirring occasionally so that all the ingredients are thoroughly combined. Cover the pan, reduce the heat and simmer for 1 hour. Stir the ingredients frequently during cooking to make sure they do not stick to the pan.

Transfer the chutney to warmed jars and cover immediately with lids. Allow to mature for a few weeks if possible. Process before long storage. MAKES ABOUT 5 LB

Cucumber Relish

Carol Bowen

2 large cucumbers
1 bunch celery
1 large sweet red pepper
1 large green pepper
1 lb onions
2 scallions
1 quart white vinegar
1 teaspoon curry powder
1 teaspoon dry mustard
$\frac{1}{2}$ teaspoon cayenne
$\frac{1}{2}$ teaspoon paprika
$\frac{1}{2}$ teaspoon ground ginger
2 cups sugar

Wash the cucumbers and cut into short lengths. Scrub and trim the celery. Discard the core and seeds from the peppers and cut them into quarters. Peel and quarter the onions. Chop the scallions, then pass all the prepared ingredients through a food processor or meat grinder.

Put the vinegar in a heavy-based saucepan with the spices. Bring to a boil. Add the minced ingredients and sugar and bring back to a boil. Simmer the relish for 20 to 30 minutes, until thick. Pack into jars, cover and process. MAKES ABOUT 4$\frac{1}{2}$ LB

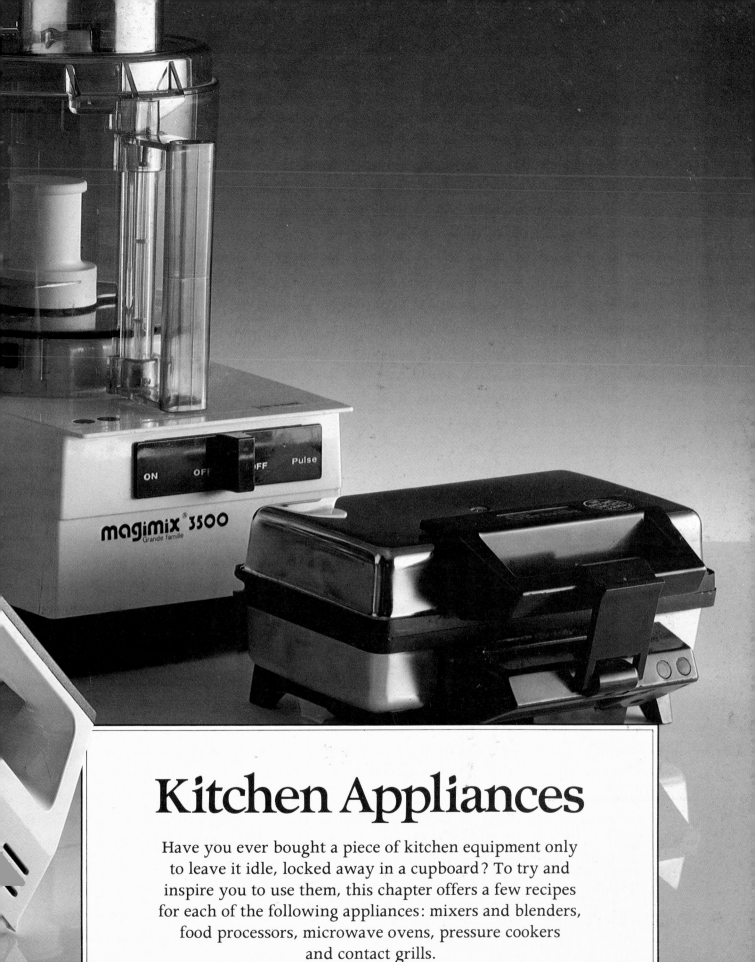

Kitchen Appliances

Have you ever bought a piece of kitchen equipment only
to leave it idle, locked away in a cupboard? To try and
inspire you to use them, this chapter offers a few recipes
for each of the following appliances: mixers and blenders,
food processors, microwave ovens, pressure cookers
and contact grills.

Mixers and Blenders

Recipes by Jill Spencer

Most modern kitchens have a food mixer or blender, or both. The size of these appliances varies widely, from small hand-held mixers and one-speed blenders to large stand-mounted food mixers which can accommodate any number of attachments. Moderately sized models are quite adequate for most family cooking – making cakes, pastry and small amounts of bread dough; beating eggs, sauces or ice creams; preparing soups or making fruit purées. For mixing heavy fruit cakes, large batches of bread and royal icing, a large food mixer is essential.

Similarly, for preparing pâtés or carrying out other tasks which strain the blender, a powerful appliance with several settings is best.

The section offers a few recipes, both sweet and savory, using the mixer and blender. In addition, remember to make use of the mixer and blender for all those small chores which are otherwise so time-consuming: beating eggs and cream or making batters; chopping herbs or grinding spices; making smooth sauces and dips or preparing pâtés and stuffings.

Cream of Lettuce Soup

2 tablespoons butter
2 heads lettuce, washed and shredded
1 onion, finely chopped
1½ tablespoons flour
1 quart milk
salt and pepper
2 egg yolks
¼ cup light cream

Melt the butter in a saucepan and add the lettuce and onion. Cover and cook gently for 5 minutes. Add the flour and milk and, beating all the time, bring to a boil. Reduce the heat and simmer for 15 to 20 minutes.

Allow to cool, then pour the soup into the blender and process until smooth. Return the soup to the saucepan and add seasoning to taste.

Mix the egg yolks and cream together and pour into the soup. Heat gently without allowing the soup to boil. Serve hot or chilled, sprinkled with croûtons flavored with garlic (see page 17). SERVES 4

Beef Olives

3 onions, roughly chopped
1 slice bread, crusts removed
a few parsley sprigs
1 teaspoon dried mixed herbs
6 oz ($\frac{3}{4}$ cup) ground pork
1 apple, peeled, cored and finely chopped
salt and pepper
1 egg, beaten
8 thin slices beef top round
2 tablespoons oil
4 tomatoes, peeled and chopped
1$\frac{1}{4}$ cups red wine or beef broth
mashed potatoes for serving (optional)
wedges of tomato and cress for garnish

Place one of the onions, the bread and parsley in the blender and blend for 30 seconds. Add this mixture to the herbs, pork, apple, seasoning and beaten egg. Spread the stuffing evenly over the slices of meat. Roll up the beef and secure with string. Heat the oil and sauté the beef olives until brown. Transfer the meat to an ovenproof casserole. Add the remaining onions to the fat left in the skillet. Sauté for 5 minutes, then place them in the casserole and add the tomatoes. Pour in the wine or broth, cover and cook in a preheated 350° oven for 1 to 1$\frac{1}{2}$ hours. Remove the beef olives from the casserole and keep hot on a serving dish. If you like, the meat can be arranged in a ring of pipe mashed potato. Pour the sauce and vegetables into the blender and process until smooth. Reheat and pour over the beef olives. Garnish with tomato wedges and cress and serve immediately.
SERVES 4

Stuffed Lamb Chops

4 loin lamb chops
2 slices white bread, crusts removed
a few mint sprigs
a few rosemary sprigs
$\frac{1}{2}$ small onion, roughly chopped
grated rind of $\frac{1}{2}$ lemon
beaten egg for binding
GARNISH
watercress sprigs
tomato wedges

Slit the chops horizontally through to the bone, to form a pocket.

Place the bread in the blender with the remaining ingredients and process until a fairly moist stuffing is formed. Use to fill the pockets in the chops, then wrap each one in foil. Cook in a preheated 375° oven for 20 to 25 minutes. Serve garnished with watercress and tomato.
SERVES 4

Strawberry Cream Sorbet

¾ lb (1½ pints) strawberries, hulled
¼ cup sugar
¾ cup strawberry-flavored yogurt
a few drops of lemon juice
¾ cup heavy cream
2 egg whites, beaten
DECORATION
strawberries
mint leaves

Place the strawberries, sugar and yogurt in the blender and process until smooth. Add lemon juice to taste.

Pour into a rigid plastic container and freeze for 1 hour or until half frozen. Turn out into a bowl and break up with a fork. Whip the cream lightly and fold into the strawberry mixture with the beaten egg whites. Return to the freezer until firm. Spoon into glasses and decorate with strawberries and mint leaves. SERVES 4

Apricot Sherbet

1 (16-oz) can apricots, drained
2 eggs, separated
2 tablespoons sugar
¼ cup ground almonds
¼ cup light cream

Place the apricots in the blender and process to a purée. Place the egg whites in the mixer bowl and beat until stiff. Beat in the sugar.

Combine the egg yolks, ground almonds and cream. Fold into the egg whites, together with the apricot purée. Pour into a shallow, rigid plastic container and freeze for 4 hours, or until firm. Scoop out into serving dishes. SERVES 4

Banana Teabread

1 lb ripe bananas
½ cup butter or margarine
¾ cup sugar
2 eggs
2 cups self-rising flour
grated rind of 1 lemon
⅓ cup glacé cherries, chopped
⅔ cup raisins

Mash the bananas, reserving a whole one for decoration. Place all the ingredients in the mixer bowl and beat slowly until well mixed. Place in a lined and greased 9 × 5 × 3 in loaf pan.

Bake in a preheated 325° oven for 1½ to 1¾ hours. Unmold and cool on a wire rack. Decorate with the reserved banana cut into slices and dipped into lemon juice. Slice and spread generously with butter. MAKES ONE 9 × 5 IN LOAF

Butterscotch Brownies

½ cup butter or margarine
1 cup firmly packed brown sugar
2 eggs
½ cup chopped walnuts
¾ cup self-rising flour
¼ teaspoon baking powder
⅓ cup cocoa powder
DECORATION
confectioners' sugar
walnut halves

Place all the ingredients in the mixer bowl and beat until well mixed. Place in a lined and greased 7-in square cake pan. Bake in a preheated 350° oven for 40 to 50 minutes. Unmold and cool on a wire rack.

Dredge with confectioners' sugar, then cut into squares. Place a walnut half on each square. MAKES ABOUT 16 SQUARES

Food Processors

Recipes by Jill Spencer

A food processor is probably one of the most efficient and helpful appliances to have in the kitchen. Whether you want to chop an onion or herbs, grate or slice some cheese or vegetables, or mix a small fruit cake, then most food processors will perform the task with speed – and very little dish washing as a result. A small quantity of bread dough can be kneaded in most machines and some allow for larger quantities of dough and cakes to be processed.

Blending, chopping, mincing, slicing, grating and shredding are all processes which an average model will undertake. Most food processors have a bowl with a lid which has a feed tube. Disks for slicing, shredding, grating or making French fries are easily attached and a double-bladed knife is used for most processes – chopping, mincing, blending and mixing. Some machines have plastic blades for mixing cakes and certain models can be used for beating egg whites and whipping cream, although this facility is not available with all processors.

Unlike many kitchen gadgets, a food processor is easily assembled for use and it is not difficult to wash. It can be kept out on the work surface, taking up very little space, and the attachments can be stored on a wall-mounted rack. Juice extractors are available for some processors. Depending on the model, a food processor can have a simple on/off switch, sometimes incorporated into the lid so that the machine cannot be used open, or it can have several settings, including a pulse control. This last is useful when preparing foods which can be over-processed very easily.

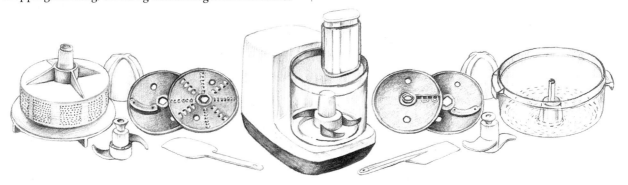

Fish Croquettes

1 lb mixed cooked fish (shrimp, cod, and so on)
3 tablespoons butter
3 tablespoons flour
$1\frac{1}{4}$ cups milk
1 egg yolk
2 tablespoons chopped parsley
salt and pepper
1 egg, beaten
fine bread crumbs for coating
oil for deep frying

Remove any skin and bones from the fish and chop it in the food processor.

Place the butter, flour and milk in a saucepan and bring to a boil, whisking all the time. Allow to cool slightly, then beat in the egg yolk, parsley, seasoning and fish. Spread the mixture on a plate or flat dish and chill thoroughly. Divide the mixture into eight portions and shape into croquettes. Coat the croquettes first in egg, then in bread crumbs. Heat the oil to 350°. Fry the croquettes for 5 to 6 minutes and drain them on paper towels. Serve immediately. SERVES 4

Nutty Chicken Salad

$\frac{1}{2}$ cup salted peanuts
1 clove garlic
6 tablespoons oil
$\frac{1}{2}$ cup unsweetened apple juice
freshly ground black pepper
1 small head lettuce, washed
1 lb cooked chicken, cut in pieces (2–$2\frac{1}{2}$ cups)
GARNISH
1 (2-oz) can anchovy fillets
$\frac{1}{3}$ cup stuffed olives

Grind the peanuts finely in the food processor. Add the garlic and oil and continue to mix until creamy. Pour in the apple juice and season with freshly ground black pepper. Process thoroughly to form a smooth dressing.

Line a serving dish with lettuce leaves. Toss the chicken in the dressing, then pile it on top of the lettuce.

Garnish with anchovy fillets and stuffed olives. SERVES 4

Italian Sauce

a few sprigs of fresh basil
$\frac{3}{4}$ cup Parmesan cheese, broken into chunks
3–4 tablespoons peanut or olive oil
$\frac{1}{4}$ cup walnuts
1 clove garlic
salt and pepper

Finely chop the basil and Parmesan together in the food processor; continue blending to make a paste. Pour the oil slowly onto the paste, blending all the time until well combined. Add the nuts, garlic and seasoning and process to form a soft paste.

Use as a topping for soups, or toss into freshly cooked pasta. SERVES 4

Sage Derby Coleslaw

3 oz imported Sage Derby cheese or similar, chilled
$\frac{1}{2}$ cup blanched almonds
2 oz cucumber
$\frac{3}{4}$ lb head white cabbage
1 green pepper, seeded
2 apples
a little lemon juice
$\frac{3}{4}$ cup mayonnaise
salt and pepper
2 tablespoons chopped parsley

Roughly chop the cheese in the food processor, then transfer it to a large mixing bowl. Chop the almonds finely and add to the cheese. Peel the cucumber and roughly chop it, then add to the salad.

Cut the cabbage into wedges and shred them in the food processor. Cut the green pepper lengthwise into quarters and slice finely. Add the cabbage and pepper to the cheese, almonds and cucumber.

Peel, core and quarter the apples. Slice and sprinkle with lemon juice to prevent discoloration. Add to the salad.

Stir the mayonnaise, seasoning and chopped parsley into the coleslaw and mix well. SERVES 6 TO 8

Zucchini Salad

$\frac{1}{4}$ lb button mushrooms
1 lb zucchini, thinly peeled
$\frac{1}{2}$ lb garlic sausage
small bunch of parsley
grated rind and juice of 1 lemon
5 tablespoons salad oil
$\frac{1}{2}$ teaspoon salt
1 teaspoon sugar
$\frac{1}{2}$ teaspoon dry mustard
freshly ground black pepper
3 tomatoes, peeled and cut into wedges

Slice the mushrooms and zucchini in the food processor. Cut the garlic sausage into strips. Mix these ingredients together in a bowl.

Place the parsley in the food processor and chop it finely. Add all the remaining ingredients apart from the tomatoes and process until a smooth dressing is formed. Pour it over the salad. Cover and leave the salad to stand for 1 hour.

Toss the tomatoes into the salad just before serving. SERVES 4

Peanut Butter Spread

1 cup salted peanuts
$\frac{1}{4}$ cup butter
salt

Finely chop the peanuts in the food processor. Add the butter and process to form a smooth paste. Blend in salt to taste.

Store the spread in the refrigerator and use as required. MAKES 6 OZ

Peach Ice Cream

2 cups milk
$\frac{3}{4}$ cup sugar
2 eggs
$1\frac{1}{4}$ cups heavy cream
6 peaches

Beat the milk, sugar and eggs together until well combined. Stand the bowl over a saucepan of hot water and cook until slightly thickened, stirring occasionally. Allow to cool.

Stir in the cream and pour into a shallow freezer container. Freeze until slushy.

Skin the peaches, remove the pits and process them to a purée. Add the partially frozen mixture and mix well. Re-freeze until partially frozen, then process the ice cream until smooth and light in color. Return the ice cream to the freezer and freeze until solid. Remove from the freezer and place in the refrigerator 1 hour before serving. Serve with fresh peaches. SERVES 6

Coeur à l'Orange

1 cup cottage cheese
$1\frac{1}{4}$ cups heavy cream
$\frac{1}{3}$ cup fresh orange juice
$\frac{1}{4}$ cup sugar
2 egg whites
DECORATION
slices of orange
mint leaves (optional)

Process the cottage cheese until really smooth. Lightly whip the cream and orange juice together until soft but not stiff. Add to the cheese with the sugar and process until well combined. Beat the egg whites until stiff and fold into the cream mixture with a metal spoon. Divide the mixture between eight special heart-shaped molds with holes in the base for draining or eight individual ramekin dishes with a piece of cheesecloth tied over each, turned upside down. Allow to drain overnight before serving. Either serve in the molds or unmold and decorate with slices of orange and mint leaves. SERVES 8

Lime Splice

$\frac{1}{2}$ lb ginger snaps
$\frac{1}{4}$ cup butter, melted
grated rind and juice of 1 lime
lime juice concentrate
2 teaspoons cornstarch
$\frac{1}{4}$ cup sugar
1 egg, separated
$\frac{3}{4}$ cup heavy cream
DECORATION
slices of lime
whipped cream

Roughly break up the ginger snaps and process them into fine crumbs. Pour the melted butter through the feed tube and mix for a few seconds. Use the mixture to line the bottom and sides of an 8-in quiche or flan dish. Press the crumbs down firmly and leave to chill.

Make up the juice of the lime to 6 tablespoons with lime concentrate and add enough water to make $\frac{3}{4}$ cup. Pour a little of this on the cornstarch and mix well. Heat the remaining juice. When hot, pour onto the cornstarch mixture, mix well and return to the heat to thicken. Add the grated lime rind and sugar. Allow to cool slightly, then beat in the egg yolk. When the mixture is completely cold, beat the egg white and fold into the mixture with a metal spoon. Lightly whip the cream and fold it into the mixture. Pour into the chilled crumb crust and decorate with slices of lime and whipped cream. SERVES 6 TO 8

Microwave Ovens

Recipes by Carol Bowen

Microwave cooking is fast, economical and clean. Microwaves are electro-magnetic waves of a very short length and high frequency. They are reflected off metals; they pass through materials like pottery, glass, paper, wood and most plastics; and they are absorbed by the moisture molecules – water, fat and sugar – in food. When the food absorbs the energy, the molecules vibrate, causing the food to become hot and to cook.

Contrary to many of the initial fears, the microwave oven is one of the safest appliances in the kitchen. The oven itself, and the containers in which the food is cooked, remain cool, so there is little danger of the user receiving burns and scalds from the microwave oven. The microwaves are retained in the oven cavity and there are several safety devices built into the door which ensure that the energy cannot be switched on when the door is open.

There is an enormous range of microwave ovens available: from small, simple ovens with an on/off switch and one power setting to larger ovens with turntables, several power settings, defrost controls, a temperature probe to indicate the extent to which the food is cooked, and a conventional browning element fitted in the roof of the oven. An average oven would offer a defrost control to enable the cook to thaw food successfully without having to stand over the oven to switch it on and off every few minutes. Variable power settings can be useful for cooking the more delicate foods and slightly tougher cuts of meat, but most dishes can be cooked in an oven with just one, full power, setting.

There is a wide range of dishes and containers which can be used in the microwave oven. Most kitchens have a selection of bowls which are not trimmed with metal and which allow the waves to pass through to cook the food. Glass, paper, certain plastics and wood can be used for microwave cooking, but remember that the food will become hot and so the dish must withstand this heat. Wood absorbs a certain amount of energy, so it is only useful for short time heating, as for warming biscuits. Metals should not be used in the oven – metal-trimmed dishes must be avoided and conventional meat skewers and thermometers must not be used. However, in some cases, small areas of food which are likely to overcook can be shielded with small pieces of cooking foil.

The cooking time is affected by several factors. The quantity of food placed in the oven affects the time required to cook it. Dense foods take longer to cook than light foods. Fish and vegetables cook particularly successfully in the microwave oven. Irregular-shaped cuts or pieces of food should be boned or tied into neat shapes before cooking to ensure an even result. During cooking the dishes may need turning (this is not necessary if the oven has a turntable) and the food may need stirring or rearranging in the dish. If the food is to be covered, use a suitable lid or plastic wrap with a small hole cut in the top to allow the steam to escape.

The main disadvantage of microwave cooking is that the food will not brown. To overcome this, the food can be browned under a broiler or brushed with a colorful seasoning mix before cooking. With a little forethought and the addition of some colorful garnishing ingredients, there is often no need to worry about this disadvantage. There are a few dishes which are not suitable for cooking in a microwave oven: a batter pudding will not remain risen as the oven does not give food a crisp finish; choux pastry does not cook successfully; and the tougher cuts of braising and stewing meat do not have time to become tender.

French Country Pâté

1 tablespoon butter
$\frac{1}{2}$ lb chicken livers
$\frac{3}{4}$ lb boneless rabbit, ground
$\frac{1}{2}$ lb slab bacon, ground
$\frac{1}{2}$ lb boneless lean pork, ground
$\frac{1}{4}$ lb pork fatback, ground
2 cloves garlic, finely chopped
$\frac{1}{4}$ teaspoon ground allspice
salt and pepper
$\frac{1}{2}$ cup brandy
$\frac{1}{2}$ lb sliced bacon
bay leaf

Place the butter in a small bowl and heat it on full power for $\frac{1}{2}$ minute. Add the chicken livers and cook on full power for $1\frac{1}{2}$ minutes. Remove and allow to cool.

Grind the chicken livers and mix with the rabbit, bacon, pork, pork fatback, garlic and allspice. Season generously with salt and pepper and moisten thoroughly with the brandy.

Line a 5-cup terrine with the bacon slices. Spoon the ground meat mixture into the terrine, packing it down well. Place a bay leaf on top. Cover with paper towels and cook on medium power for 6 minutes. Allow to rest for 5 minutes.

Now cook the pâté on medium power for a further 6 minutes. Give the dish a half turn and cook on medium power for a further 4 minutes. Remove and cover with foil. Weight down until cold. Chill for 2 to 4 hours.

To serve, unmold onto a serving dish and cut into thin slices. Accompany with warm toast or Melba Toast (see note, page 14) and a mixed salad. SERVES 6 TO 8

Meatloaf with Pepper Sauce

1 tablespoon oil
1 onion, chopped
$\frac{1}{2}$ lb ground beef
$\frac{1}{2}$ lb ground pork
$\frac{1}{2}$ cup soft brown bread crumbs
1 clove garlic, crushed
1 tablespoon tomato paste
salt and pepper
1 egg, beaten
PEPPER SAUCE
2 tablespoons butter
1 large green pepper, seeded and chopped
1 tablespoon flour
$1\frac{1}{4}$ cups boiling beef broth
1 tablespoon tomato paste
$\frac{1}{2}$ cup sliced button mushrooms
tomato slices or watercress sprigs for garnish

Place the oil in a bowl and cook it on full power for 2 minutes. Add the onion, mixing well, and cook for a further 3 minutes, stirring after 2 minutes. Add the beef, pork, bread crumbs, garlic, tomato paste and seasoning to taste, then mix well. Bind the ingredients together with the beaten egg, then press the mixture into a 5-cup oval dish and cook (on full power) for 5 minutes. Remove from the oven, wrap the dish in foil and leave to stand for 15 minutes. Remove the foil and cook on full power for a further 5 minutes. Re-wrap in foil and leave to stand while preparing the sauce.

Place the butter in a pitcher and cook it on full power for 1 minute to melt. Add the pepper, stir well and continue to cook for 3 minutes. Stir in the flour and cook for a further 1 minute. Gradually add the broth, tomato paste and mushrooms. Cook (on full power) for 2 minutes, stirring after 1 minute. Season to taste and serve with the meatloaf – either poured over it or poured into a warmed sauceboat. Garnish the unmolded meatloaf with tomato slices or watercress sprigs. SERVES 4

Winter Warming Stuffed Cabbage

1 (2-lb) head winter cabbage
$\frac{1}{2}$ cup water
6 tablespoons butter
1 onion, chopped
2 stalks celery, chopped
2 teaspoons ground coriander
$\frac{1}{2}$ lb smoked pork sausage, finely chopped
1 cup soft white bread crumbs
2 tablespoons chopped parsley
2 teaspoons lemon juice
1 egg, beaten
salt and pepper
$\frac{1}{3}$ cup hot chicken broth

Remove the coarse outer leaves from the cabbage. Trim the base and remove some of the thick stems with a potato peeler. Using a sharp knife remove a $\frac{3}{4}$-in slice from the top of the cabbage. Secure the cabbage into a good neat shape by tying string around the middle. Place in a dish with the water. Cover with plastic wrap, snipping two holes in the top to allow the steam to escape, and cook on full power for 15 minutes, giving the dish a half turn halfway through the cooking time. Drain and allow to cool enough to handle.

Meanwhile, place $\frac{1}{4}$ cup of the butter in a bowl and cook on full power for 1 minute. Add the onion, celery and coriander and continue to cook for 3 minutes. Add the sausage, bread crumbs, parsley, lemon juice and egg. Season to taste and blend well.

Using a sharp knife, scoop out and reserve the center of the cabbage, leaving a $\frac{1}{2}$-in shell. Pack the prepared stuffing into the cabbage and place in a shallow dish. Add the broth and cover with plastic wrap, snipping two holes in the top. Cook on full power for 13 to 15 minutes, giving the dish half a turn halfway through the cooking time. Cut into wedges to serve.

Shred the reserved cabbage and place it in a bowl with $\frac{1}{4}$ cup water. Cover and cook on full power for 6 minutes. Drain and toss in the remaining butter. Serve the stuffed cabbage wedges with the buttered cabbage. SERVES 4

Meatballs in Chili Sauce

2 tablespoons oil
1 onion, finely chopped
1 lb lean ground beef
1 cup soft white bread crumbs
1 tablespoon finely chopped parsley
$\frac{1}{2}$ teaspoon dried oregano
salt and pepper
about $\frac{1}{2}$ beaten egg
SAUCE
1 (16-oz) can peeled tomatoes
1 teaspoon chili seasoning
1 onion, chopped
1 green pepper, seeded and chopped
1 teaspoon sugar
3 tablespoons dry red wine
1 tablespoon cornstarch

Heat the oil in a large dish, on full power, for $\frac{1}{2}$ minute. Add the finely chopped onion and cook on full power for a further 3 minutes, until lightly browned.

Meanwhile, mix the beef, bread crumbs, parsley, oregano, seasoning to taste and enough egg to bind the mixture. Divide into eight portions and form into meatballs. Place the meatballs in a single layer on top of the onion. Cook on full power for 5 minutes, turning the meatballs once and giving the dish a half turn halfway through cooking.

Place the tomatoes, chili seasoning, onion, pepper, sugar and wine in a large pitcher and cook on full power for 5 minutes, stirring halfway through the cooking time. Blend the cornstarch with a little water and stir into the sauce. Pour the sauce over the meatballs and return to the microwave. Cook for a further 5 minutes on full power, turning the dish halfway through the cooking time. Serve hot with boiled rice or baked potatoes. SERVES 4

Somerset Pork with Cider Cream

2 tablespoons butter
2 medium-size onions, sliced
1$\frac{1}{2}$ lb pork tenderloin, cubed
$\frac{1}{4}$ lb button mushrooms
1$\frac{1}{4}$ cups hard cider
salt and pepper
2 tablespoons cornstarch
3 tablespoons heavy cream
finely chopped parsley for garnish

Place the butter in a medium-sized casserole dish and cook on full power for 1 minute to melt, then add the onions and continue to cook for 5 minutes. Add the pork cubes and cook for a further 7 minutes, stirring halfway through the cooking time.

Stir in the mushrooms, cider and seasoning to taste, then cook on full power for 8 minutes. Blend the cornstarch with a little water and stir into the pork mixture. Continue to cook for a further 2 minutes, stirring occasionally, remove from the oven and stir in the cream. Sprinkle with chopped parsley and serve immediately, with boiled rice and a green salad. SERVES 4

Jambalaya

1 lb cooked ham, cubed (about 2 cups)
1 green pepper, seeded and chopped
1 small onion, chopped
1 clove garlic, finely chopped
2 tablespoons butter
1 (10$\frac{1}{2}$-oz) can condensed tomato soup
$\frac{1}{4}$ cup hot water
$\frac{1}{4}$ lb peeled and deveined shrimp
bay leaf, crushed
pinch of dried oregano
salt and pepper
1 cup cooked long-grain rice

Place the ham, pepper, onion, garlic and butter in a 7-cup casserole. Cook on full power for 6 to 7 minutes until the onion and pepper are soft.

Stir in the soup, water, shrimp, bay leaf, oregano and seasoning to taste. Cook on full power for 4 minutes. Add the rice, stirring well, and continue to cook for a further 4 to 6 minutes until bubbling hot. SERVES 4

Rabbit Stew with Dumplings

1½ lb boned rabbit *or* 4 large rabbit pieces
2 tablespoons flour
salt and pepper
1 onion, sliced
1 clove garlic, crushed · 2 carrots, sliced
2 medium-size potatoes, cubed
1 (16-oz) can peeled tomatoes, drained
1¼ cups hot chicken broth
bouquet garni
SAGE DUMPLINGS
½ cup self-rising flour
3 tablespoons shredded beef suet
1 tablespoon chopped fresh sage *or*
2 teaspoons dried sage
a little cold water for mixing

Place the meat in a bowl with the flour and a generous sprinkling of seasoning. Toss to coat. Add the onion, garlic, carrots, potatoes, tomatoes, broth and bouquet garni and mix well. Cover and cook the stew on full power for 10 minutes. Give the dish a half turn. Reduce the power to medium and cook for 10 minutes. Give the dish a half turn, stir, re-cover and cook on medium power for a further 20 minutes.

Meanwhile place all the ingredients for the dumplings in a bowl and mix to a soft dough with water. Turn onto a floured surface and form into four dumplings.

Stir the stew and add the dumplings. Cook on medium power for 20 minutes. Allow to stand for 5 minutes and remove the bouquet garni before serving. SERVES 4

207

Speedy Spanish Rice

1 lb ground beef
1½ cups cooked long-grain rice
1 (16-oz) can tomatoes, coarsely
chopped with their juice
1 small onion, chopped
1–2 tablespoons chili powder (according to
taste)
2 teaspoons salt
freshly ground black pepper

Place the beef in a large casserole and cook on full power for 5 to 6 minutes, stirring and breaking up the meat halfway through the cooking time. Drain away any excess fat. Add the remaining ingredients, cover and continue to cook for 8 to 11 minutes, stirring the mixture after 4 minutes.

Leave to stand, covered, for 5 to 10 minutes before serving. SERVES 4 TO 6

Glazed Carrots

1 lb carrots, cut into diagonal slices
2 tablespoons butter
⅓ cup firmly packed brown sugar
1½ teaspoons cornstarch
2 tablespoons cold water

Place the carrots, butter and sugar in a bowl. Cover and cook on full power for 9 to 11 minutes, stirring halfway through the cooking time, until tender.

Mix the cornstarch with the water and stir into the carrots. Cover and cook on full power for 2 to 4 minutes until thickened. Stir before serving. SERVES 3 TO 4

Macaroni Cheese

½ lb quick-cooking macaroni
2½ cups boiling water
salt and pepper
¼ cup butter
2 tablespoons flour
1 teaspoon prepared mustard
2 cups milk
1 cup grated Cheddar or Brick cheese
parsley sprigs for garnish

Place the macaroni in a deep bowl with the water and a pinch of salt. Cover with plastic wrap, snipping two holes in the top to allow the steam to escape. Cook on full power for 8 minutes, stirring halfway through the cooking time, then drain and keep warm.

Place the butter in a large pitcher and cook on full power for 1 minute. Add the flour and mustard, mixing well. Gradually add the milk and season to taste. Cook on full power for 4 minutes, stirring every 1 minute, then add most of the cheese and stir to melt.

Mix the macaroni with the cheese sauce. Place in a serving dish and cook on full power for 2 minutes. Serve hot, topped with the remaining cheese and garnished with parsley. SERVES 4

Braised Celery and Peas

1 bunch celery, trimmed and sliced
1 small onion, peeled and chopped
2 tablespoons butter
5 teaspoons water
½ teaspoon salt
3 cups frozen peas

Place the celery, onion, butter, water and salt in a large dish. Cover and cook on full power for 6 minutes.

Add the peas, cover and cook on full power for 7 to 8 minutes, stirring after 4 minutes. Allow to stand for 2 to 3 minutes, then serve. SERVES 4 TO 6

Blackberry and Apple Crumble

½ lb (1½ cups) fresh or frozen blackberries,
hulled and thawed if necessary
½ lb tart apples, peeled, cored
and sliced
sugar to taste
½ cup butter
1½ cups flour
⅓ cup firmly packed brown sugar
grated rind of ½ lemon

Place the blackberries and apples in a microwave dish and sprinkle with sugar to taste.

Rub the butter into the flour until the mixture resembles fine bread crumbs. Stir in the sugar and lemon rind. Carefully spoon the crumble over the fruit and cook on full power for 11 to 13 minutes, giving the dish a quarter turn every 3 minutes. Place under a hot broiler to brown if liked. Serve hot with cream or custard sauce.
SERVES 4

----------- Variations -----------

Berry Crumble Prepare and cook as above but use red currants, blackberries, raspberries, blueberries or loganberries – or a mixture – instead of the apples and blackberries.

Gooseberry and Orange Crumble Prepare and cook as above but use 1 lb (3 cups) topped and tailed gooseberries with the grated rind of 1 orange instead of the apples and blackberries. Prick gooseberries before cooking.

Rhubarb Crumble Prepare and cook as above but use 1 lb prepared rhubarb, cut into chunks, instead of the apples and blackberries.

Cherry and Lemon Crumble Prepare and cook as above, but use the drained cherries from a 16-oz can with the grated rind of 1 lemon instead of the apples and blackberries.

Plum and Cinnamon Crumble Prepare and cook as above. Omit the apples and blackberries and use 1 lb halved and pitted plums mixed with ½ teaspoon ground cinnamon.

Crunchy Nut Crumble Prepare and cook as above using 1 lb fresh, frozen or canned fruit. Add ¼ cup chopped nuts to the crumble topping.

Oaten Crumble Prepare and cook as above using 1 lb fresh, frozen or canned fruit. Add 3 tablespoons oatmeal to the crumble topping.

Crème Caramel

½ cup water
½ cup sugar
CUSTARD
3 eggs
¼ cup sugar
1 teaspoon vanilla extract
pinch of salt
1½ cups milk

First prepare the caramel by placing the water and sugar in a heatproof pitcher; stir well. Cook on full power for 10 to 12 minutes until golden. Do not allow the syrup to become too brown as it will continue to cook after it is removed from the oven. Pour quickly into a 7-in soufflé dish, then allow to cool and harden.

Beat the eggs with the sugar, vanilla and salt until well blended and the sugar has dissolved. Place the milk in a heatproof glass pitcher and cook on full power for 4 minutes. Gradually add to the egg mixture, blending well. Pour or strain the mixture over the caramel. Cover the soufflé dish and stand it in a shallow dish holding enough hot water to come 1–2 in up the side of the soufflé dish. Cook on a low power for 10 to 13 minutes, giving the dish a quarter turn every 3 minutes, until set. Chill thoroughly.

To serve, invert the crème caramel onto a serving dish.
SERVES 4 TO 4

Pressure Cookers

Recipes by Jane Todd

There are several different types of pressure cooker available, ranging from those which operate at one pressure ($7\frac{1}{2}$ lb) to automatic models with built-in timers. The majority of pressure cookers have three different pressure settings – 5 lb, 10 lb, and 15 lb. Follow the manufacturer's instructions for bringing the cooker to pressure. At the end of the cooking time the pressure can be reduced slowly by leaving the cooker off the heat until it has cooled sufficiently, or by lowering the base of the cooker into cold water. Follow the recipe instructions when reducing the pressure; if the pan is left to cool slowly the food continues to cook during this time.

The pressure cooker is useful for cooking all sorts of dishes: casseroles and stews cook very well, fish dishes are prepared with great haste as are soups, steamed puddings and preserves. The larger cookers offer the advantage of being able to cook vegetables in a steaming container at the same time as the main dish. When the food is placed in the cooker it is important that the cooker is not too full. Moist dishes should not come more than halfway up the side of the pan and solid foods should two-thirds fill the pan. When cooking puddings or other dishes which are covered, make sure that any covering (paper or foil) is secure so that it does not lift the lid of the cooker and block the safety valve.

Store your pressure cooker along with other saucepans, but make sure that the rim of the lid or pan is not damaged as this will prevent the cooker from retaining the pressure. It is important to keep the rubber sealing ring clean for the same reason.

Celery and Mushroom Soup

$\frac{1}{2}$ lb carrots, sliced
$\frac{3}{4}$ lb onions, chopped
1 bunch celery, sliced
$\frac{1}{2}$ lb mushrooms, sliced
$\frac{1}{4}$ lb green beans, sliced
$2\frac{1}{2}$ cups tomato juice
$2\frac{1}{2}$ cups beef broth
salt and pepper
$\frac{1}{2}$–1 tablespoon Worcestershire sauce
bouquet garni
a few mushrooms slices for garnish

Place the prepared vegetables in the pressure cooker (with the trivet removed) and add the tomato juice, broth, seasoning, Worcestershire sauce and bouquet garni, making sure that the cooker is not more than half full. Bring to high pressure and cook for 10 minutes.

Allow the pressure to reduce at room temperature. Discard the bouquet garni and check the seasoning. The soup may be served as it is, pressed through a food mill or processed in a blender. Serve garnished with a few raw mushroom slices. SERVES 4 TO 6

Beef Pot Roast

2 tablespoons drippings
2-lb piece beef pot roast
6 slices bacon
1 onion, chopped
$1\frac{1}{4}$ cups water
$\frac{3}{4}$ cup dark beer
salt and pepper
1 tablespoon vinegar
2 lb potatoes
1 lb leeks
1 lb Brussels sprouts
1 tablespoon cornstarch
2 tablespoons water

Heat the drippings in the open pressure cooker and brown the meat on all sides. Lift out and place the trivet in the bottom of the cooker. Arrange the bacon slices and onion on the trivet, then replace the meat. Add the water, beer, seasoning and vinegar. Bring to high pressure and cook for 20 minutes.

Allow the pressure to reduce at room temperature. Remove the lid and arrange the prepared vegetables in groups around the meat – making sure that the potatoes and leeks are cut quite small so that they will cook in the same time as the sprouts. Replace the lid, return the cooker to the heat and bring to high pressure. Cook for further 4 minutes.

Allow the pressure to reduce at room temperature. Lift out the meat and place it on a serving dish. Surround with the vegetables and keep warm.

Take out the trivet and bacon. Return the open cooker to the heat and thicken the cooking liquid with the cornstarch blended with 2 tablespoons cold water. Check the seasoning and strain the sauce into a sauceboat. SERVES 4 TO 6

English Steak and Kidney Pudding

FILLING
$\frac{3}{4}$ lb chuck steak
$\frac{1}{4}$ lb kidney
seasoned flour
1 onion, chopped
$\frac{1}{4}$ lb mushrooms, sliced
bay leaf
$1\frac{1}{4}$ cups beef broth
SUET PASTRY
2 cups self-rising flour
pinch of salt
pinch of dried mixed herbs
$\frac{1}{2}$ cup shredded beef suet
cold water for mixing

Trim and cut the steak into cubes. Skin, core and slice the kidney. Toss the prepared steak and kidney in a little seasoned flour. Place in the pressure cooker (with the trivet removed) and add the onion, mushrooms, bay leaf and stock, making sure that the cooker is not more than half full. Bring to high pressure and cook for 15 minutes. Allow the pressure to reduce at room temperature, then leave the meat mixture to cool.

Meanwhile, make the suet pastry. Sift the flour and salt into a bowl. Mix in the herbs and suet and add sufficient cold water to form a soft dough. Roll out two thirds of the dough and use to line a 1-quart greased pudding basin or steaming mold.

Remove the bay leaf from the meat and ladle the filling into the lined basin with half the cooking liquid. Keep the rest of the cooking liquid on one side for gravy. Roll out the remaining dough to make a lid and use to cover the pudding, dampening the edges for a secure seal. Cover securely with a piece of foil, making a pleat in the foil to allow room for the suet crust to rise during cooking.

Wash the pressure cooker, place the trivet in the bottom and pour in $1\frac{1}{2}$ quarts boiling water. Stand the basin on the trivet. Put the lid on the cooker, return to the heat and when steam escapes through the vent in the lid, lower the heat and steam (without the pressure weight) for 15 minutes. (This pre-steaming makes the suet pastry light.) Increase the heat, bring to low pressure and cook for 25 minutes.

Allow the pressure to reduce at room temperature. Remove the basin from the cooker, take off the foil and serve from the basin, which may be wrapped in a napkin. Serve with the gravy remaining from cooking the meat. SERVES 4

Steamed Chocolate Pudding

6 tablespoons butter
6 tablespoons sugar
1 large egg
$\frac{3}{4}$ cup self-rising flour
$\frac{1}{4}$ cup cocoa powder
4–6 tablespoons milk
3 tablespoons golden raisins
MOCHA SAUCE
2 (1-oz) squares semisweet chocolate
$\frac{1}{4}$ cup butter
$\frac{3}{4}$ cup hot, strong black coffee

Cream the butter and sugar together until light and fluffy. Beat in the egg. Fold in the sifted flour and cocoa together with the milk to give a soft mixture. Finally, fold in the raisins.

Spoon the mixture into a well-greased 1-quart pudding basin or steaming mold. Smooth the surface and cover with greased foil.

Pour $1\frac{1}{2}$ quarts water into the cooker, place the trivet in the bottom and stand the pudding on the trivet. Simmer in the covered cooker, not brought up to pressure, for 25 minutes, then bring to low pressure and cook for 25 minutes.

Allow the pressure to reduce at room temperature. Take out the pudding, and unmold onto a plate.

To make the sauce, melt the chocolate in the top of a double boiler, then stir in the butter and coffee. SERVES 4 TO 6

Rice Pudding

1 tablespoon butter
2 cups milk
$\frac{1}{2}$ cup evaporated milk
$\frac{1}{3}$ cup round-grain rice
$\frac{1}{4}$ cup sugar
1 small piece cinnamon stick
grated rind of 1 lemon

Melt the butter in the open pressure cooker. Add the milk and evaporated milk and bring to a boil. Add the rice, sugar and cinnamon stick, making sure that the cooker is not more than half full, and bring back to a boil. Adjust the heat so that the milk is simmering. Bring to high pressure on a low heat (this is to prevent the pudding rising in the cooker and blocking the air vent) and cook for 12 minutes.

Allow the pressure to reduce at room temperature, then remove the cinnamon stick. Stir in the grated lemon rind and transfer the pudding to a serving dish.

When cooking rice pudding in a pressure cooker which operates at $7\frac{1}{2}$ lb pressure, allow 20 minutes cooking time. SERVES 4

Honeyed Pears

4 pears
$1\frac{1}{4}$ cups water
$\frac{1}{3}$ cup firmly packed brown sugar
grated rind and juice of 1 lemon
2–3 tablespoons clear honey

Peel the pears, but leave them whole and do not remove the stalks.

Place the trivet in the bottom of the pressure cooker and pour in the water. Stand the pears on the trivet and add the sugar, lemon rind and juice and honey. Bring to high pressure and cook for 4 to 8 minutes, depending on the hardness of the pears.

Allow the pressure to reduce at room temperature. Transfer the pears to a serving dish. Remove the trivet, return the open cooker to the heat and boil the cooking liquid until it becomes syrup. Spoon the syrup over the pears and chill. Serve with a bowl of whipped cream. SERVES 4

Contact Grills

Recipes by Bridget Jones

The contact or sandwich grill is not only a speedy snack-maker but as the recipes in this section show, it is also a versatile worktop cooker. Steaks, chops, hamburgers and sausages can all be cooked in the contact grill. The cooking tray can be used as a container for moist, casserole-type dishes or pastry dishes – quiches and pies for example. In addition to main dishes, rice, vegetables and puddings can also be prepared in the cooking tray.

Those appliances which have a flat side to the cooking plates can be used to make pancakes.

To make the best of your contact grill, keep it out on the work surface ready for use. Wash the cooking plates in hot soapy water and leave them to soak if there are any burnt-on bits. As with other electrical appliances, remember to read and follow the manufacturer's instructions.

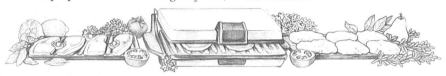

Toasted Sandwiches

——— Savory Fillings ———

BACON AND MUSHROOM
2 slices lean bacon, halved
$\frac{1}{2}$ cup sliced mushrooms

SALAMI AND APPLE
6 slices salami
1 small apple, peeled, cored and sliced

LEMON SARDINE
2 tablespoons butter flavored with grated lemon rind and chopped parsley
1 ($4\frac{1}{2}$-oz) can sardines, drained and mashed

HERBY CHICKEN
2 tablespoons butter flavored with chopped mixed herbs
$\frac{1}{2}$ cup diced cooked chicken
$\frac{1}{4}$ cup diced cream cheese
(suitable for freezing)

SHRIMP AND HAM
2 thin slices cooked ham
$\frac{1}{4}$ lb peeled cooked shrimp
(suitable for freezing)

TURKEY AND CRANBERRY
1 tablespoon cranberry sauce
$\frac{1}{2}$ cup diced cooked turkey

APPLE AND BLUE CHEESE
1 apple, peeled, cored and sliced
$\frac{1}{4}$ lb blue cheese, sliced

GARLIC SAUSAGE AND MUSHROOM CREAM
4 slices garlic sausage
$\frac{1}{2}$ cup chopped button mushrooms
$\frac{1}{4}$ cup diced cream cheese

CURRIED CHICKEN
2 tablespoons peanut butter
$\frac{1}{2}$ cup chopped cooked chicken
1 teaspoon concentrated curry paste
$\frac{1}{4}$ cup diced cream cheese
(suitable for freezing)

COTTAGE CHEESE AND BACON
2 slices lean bacon, halved
$\frac{1}{4}$ cup cottage cheese

CHEESE AND PEAR
$\frac{1}{2}$ cup grated cheese
1 small pear, peeled, cored and sliced

——— Sweet Fillings ———

BANANA AND BROWN SUGAR
1 banana, peeled and sliced
1 tablespoon brown sugar

CREAM CHEESE AND JAM
$\frac{1}{4}$ cup diced cream cheese
1 tablespoon jam

APPLE AND CINNAMON
2 tablespoons butter, creamed with
$\frac{1}{8}$ teaspoon cinnamon
1 apple, peeled, cored and sliced

APPLE AND RAISIN
2 tablespoons butter, creamed with
2 teaspoons honey
3 tablespoons raisins, chopped
1 apple, peeled, cored and sliced

Mozzarella Sardines

2 hamburger buns
$\frac{1}{4}$ lb Mozzarella cheese, sliced
2 (4$\frac{1}{4}$-oz) cans sardines in oiled, drained
salt and pepper
grated rind of 1 lemon
lemon slices and parsley sprigs for garnish

Halve each bun and top each half with the cheese. Arrange the whole sardines on top, season generously and sprinkle with lemon rind. Place in a cooking tray and cook on the hottest setting for 3 to 5 minutes until the cheese has melted. Garnish with lemon slices and sprigs of parsley. SERVES 4

─────────── Variations ───────────

Frankfurter and Pineapple Buns Top each halved bun with the cheese, as above. Substitute $\frac{1}{2}$ lb sliced frankfurters and 4 canned and drained pineapple rings for the sardines and lemon rind. Cook as above and garnish with watercress.

Ham and Tomato Buns Substitute 4 slices of cooked ham and 2 tomatoes for the sardines and lemon rind. Halve the slices of ham, roll up each piece and secure with a wooden toothpick. Quarter the tomatoes and arrange on the buns with the ham. Cook as above. Remove the toothpicks before serving.

Cheese Pâté Fingers

$\frac{1}{4}$ lb blue cheese
$\frac{1}{4}$ lb coarse pâté
4 hot dog buns
lemon wedges for garnish

Cream the cheese with the pâté until thoroughly mixed. Split the buns in half and spread each half with some of the cheese mixture. Place in the cooking tray of the contact grill and cook on the hottest setting for 5 minutes until the rolls and topping are hot but not browned. Garnish with small wedges of lemon and serve with a mixed salad. MAKES 8

─────────── Variations ───────────

Creamed Pâté Fingers Substitute $\frac{1}{2}$ (8-oz) package cream cheese for the blue cheese. Cook as above.

Cheese and Ham Fingers Substitute $\frac{1}{2}$ cup chopped cooked ham for the pâté. Cream the blue cheese with $\frac{1}{4}$ (8-oz) package cheese, then add the ham and cook as above.

St Clement's Spareribs

1 lb country-style spareribs
grated rind and juice of 1 orange and 1 lemon
1 small onion, finely chopped
1 teaspoon wholegrain mustard
1 tablespoon brown sugar
1 clove garlic, crushed
1 tablespoon tomato paste
salt and pepper

Cut between the spareribs and place them in the cooking tray. Mix together the remaining ingredients, season and pour the mixture over the meat. Cook on the hottest setting for 30 minutes until brown. SERVES 2

Eggplant and Leek Risotto

2 tablespoons oil
$\frac{1}{4}$ cup butter
$\frac{1}{2}$ cup long-grain rice
1$\frac{1}{4}$ cups chicken broth
1 small eggplant, diced
1 leek, trimmed and sliced
2 tomatoes, peeled
salt and pepper
CROÛTONS
4 thin slices white bread
$\frac{1}{4}$ cup butter
2 tablespoons chopped parsley

Place the oil, butter and rice in the cooking tray and cook on the hottest setting for 5 minutes. Add the broth, eggplant and leek and cook for a further 15 minutes. Stir in the tomatoes and cook for a further 5 minutes. Taste and adjust the seasoning.

To make the croûtons, remove the crusts from the bread and butter each slice very lightly on both sides. Cook directly between the cooking plates on the hottest setting for 2 to 3 minutes, then cut into small squares or triangles. Mix the croûtons with the parsley and sprinkle over the risotto before serving. SERVES 4

Zucchini Quiche

1 lb zucchini, trimmed, thinly peeled
and sliced
1 tablespoon salt
¾ quantity Pie Pastry (page 87)
1 tablespoon chopped dill
½ cup grated Cheddar cheese
freshly grated nutmeg
3 eggs
1¼ cups milk

Place the zucchini in a strainer, sprinkle with the salt and allow to stand for 20 to 30 minutes. Rinse and pat dry thoroughly with paper towels. Roll out the pastry on a lightly floured board or work surface and use to line the cooking tray from the contact grill. Arrange the zucchini in the pastry case, sprinkle with the dill and cheese and season with nutmeg. Beat the eggs with the milk, pour into the pastry shell and cook on the hottest setting for 20 minutes. Serve hot or cold. SERVES 6

―――――――――― Variations ――――――――――

Asparagus Quiche Use ½ lb cooked, canned or frozen and thawed asparagus instead of the zucchini. Continue as above.

Spinach Quiche Substitute ½ lb cooked, chopped spinach for the zucchini and continue as above.

Sweet and Sour Lamb Chops

2 tablespoons butter
1 green pepper, seeded and sliced
1 onion, sliced
1 large carrot, cut into thin strips
salt and pepper
4 lamb chops
2 tablespoons brown sugar
1 tablespoon wine vinegar
2 tablespoons soy sauce
2 tablespoons tomato paste
¼ cup dry sherry wine

Place the butter in the cooking tray with the prepared vegetables. Season lightly and cook on the hottest setting for 5 minutes. Add the lamb chops and cook for a further 5 minutes. Place the sugar, vinegar, soy sauce, tomato paste and sherry in a screw-topped jar and shake vigorously until well combined.

Pour the sauce over the chops and continue to cook for a further 5 to 8 minutes. Serve immediately, with boiled rice. SERVES 4

Hamburgers

salt and pepper
1 lb ground beef
4 hamburger buns
4 crisp lettuce leaves
1 small onion, sliced into rings
2 tomatoes, sliced
selection of relishes (optional)

Season the beef to taste and shape into 4 burgers. Cook directly between the cooking plates on the hottest setting for 4 to 8 minutes, depending on how well cooked they are required to be.

Split the buns in half and place a lettuce leaf on each base. Arrange the onion rings, tomatoes and choice of relish, if used, on top of the cooked burger before placing it on the bun. Top with the other half of the bun. Serve immediately. Alternatively, sandwich the burger in the bun and serve the salad garnishes separately. SERVES 4

―――――――――― Variations ――――――――――

Blue Cheese Burgers Cream ¼ lb blue cheese with ¼ (8-oz) package cream cheese until smooth. Arrange the cooked burgers on lettuce leaves and top with the cheese cream. Serve immediately.

Provençal Burgers Cook the burgers as above. To make a Provençal sauce, peel and chop 2–3 tomatoes and mix with 1 finely chopped onion and ⅔ cup halved, pitted ripe olives. Season to taste and cook in the cooking tray on the hottest setting for 5 minutes. Arrange the cooked burgers on a serving dish and top with this sauce. Serve with rice or baked potatoes.

Index